TO

L. B. NAMIER

THIS RENEWED TOKEN OF GRATITUDE

AFFECTION AND ESTEEM

PEREGRINE BOOKS

THE HABSBURG MONARCHY

'A very good book indeed, brilliant, acid, and penetrating' – Alan Bullock in the *Spectator*

A J P Taylor is often regarded as the stormy petrel of modern historians. Nevertheless he belongs among the company of those – Trevelyan, Toynbee, Namier, Neale, Runciman, to name a few – who in this century have established Britain's reputation for historical scholarship.

In this volume he recounts the history of the Habsburg monarchy from the end of the Holy Roman Empire in 1806 to the monarchy's dissolution in 1918. 'No other family,' as the author reminds us, 'has endured so long or left so deep a mark upon Europe: the Habsburgs were the greatest dynasty of modern history, and the history of Central Europe revolves round them, not they round it.' And yet, astonishingly enough, this is the only history of that dynasty during this period. It provides an understanding of the problems inherent in the attempt to give peace, stability, and a common loyalty to a heterogeneous population – an understanding which is pertinent to the study of empire in any age.

A J P Taylor was born at Birkdale in Lancashire in 1906 and was educated at Bootham School, York, and Oriel College, Oxford. After eight years as a lecturer in Modern History at Manchester University, he was elected a Fellow of Magdalen College, Oxford in 1938. His output of historical writing has been prolific and many of his books have been published in Penguins. His most recent works are *The Second World War: an Illustrated History* and *My Darling Pussy; the correspondence of Lloyd George and Frances Stevenson*.

The cover shows a detail of 'Einzug Kaiser Franz I in Wien nach der Rückkehr aus Paris, 1814' by Peter Krafft, in the Audienzsaal of the Hofburg, Vienna (photo Erwin Meyer, Vienna)

THE HABSBURG
MONARCHY
1809–1918

—

A HISTORY OF THE AUSTRIAN EMPIRE
AND AUSTRIA-HUNGARY

—

A J P TAYLOR

PENGUIN BOOKS
IN ASSOCIATION WITH
HAMISH HAMILTON

Penguin Books Ltd, Harmondsworth, Middlesex, England
Penguin Books Inc., 7110 Ambassador Road, Baltimore, Maryland 21207, U.S.A.
Penguin Books Australia Ltd, Ringwood, Victoria, Australia
Penguin Books Canada Ltd, 41 Steelcase Road West, Markham, Ontario, Canada
Penguin Books (N.Z.) Ltd, 182–190 Wairau Road, Auckland 10, New Zealand

—

First published by Hamish Hamilton 1948
Published in Peregrine Books 1964
Reprinted 1967, 1970, 1976

—

Copyright © A J P Taylor, 1948

—

Made and printed in Great Britain
by Cox & Wyman Ltd,
London, Fakenham and Reading
Set in Monotype Baskerville

CONTENTS

CONTENTS

MAPS

PREFACE

THIS book is an entirely rewritten version of an earlier work with
the same title, which I published in 1941. It is about half as long
again as its predecessor. Apart from general additions, it treats
Austrian foreign policy with greater detail and relevance. The
Habsburg Monarchy, more than most great powers, was an organization for conducting foreign policy; and its fate was determined
quite as much by foreign affairs as by the behaviour of its peoples.
The creation of the Austrian Empire was dictated by Napoleon; the
establishment of Austria-Hungary by Bismarck; and the Monarchy
fell at the end of a great war, which it had itself helped to bring
about. My attempt to write the history of the Habsburg Monarchy
without discussing Habsburg foreign policy made much of the
original book puzzling; and I hope I have now remedied this defect.

The other principal change is in treatment. Despite efforts to face
reality, the earlier book was still dominated by the 'liberal illusion';
many passages talked of 'lost opportunities' and suggested that the
Habsburg Monarchy might have survived if only this or that statesman or people had been more sensible. It was difficult to escape from
this approach after reading the works of innumerable contemporary
writers of goodwill, who either wrote before the fall of the Monarchy
or still could not believe that it had vanished. These regrets are no
part of the duty of a historian, especially when the story which he
tells makes it clear, time after time, that there were no opportunities
to be lost. The conflict between a super-national dynastic state and
the national principle had to be fought to the finish; and so, too, had
the conflict between the master and subject nations. Inevitably, any
concession came too late and was too little; and equally inevitably
every concession produced more violent discontent. The national
principle, once launched, had to work itself out to its conclusion.
My earlier version had also perhaps a 'national illusion': it tended
to suggest that the national movements were, by the twentieth

century, movements of 'the people'. I have tried here to modify this view and to make it clear that mass-nationalism, where it existed, was very different from the nationalism of the intellectuals.

I have still not found an adequate short title for the Empire with which the book deals. The 'Austrian Empire' existed in full form only from 1804 until 1867; thereafter it became 'Austria-Hungary'. The non-Hungarian half of the Empire did not acquire a name; however I have continued the slipshod contemporary practice of calling it 'Austria' or sometimes 'constitutional Austria', in order to suggest its official description as 'the lands and kingdoms represented in the Reichsrat'. In my earlier book, I translated Reichsrat into Imperial Council; this, though technically correct, gave a derogatory character to an assembly which was at least as much a parliament as the Reichstag; and I have put it back into German. On the other hand, I have broken with the absurd practice of clinging to the German or Italian names of places without a single German or Italian inhabitant; in this book I have restored Zagreb to the Croats and Sadova to the Czechs. Apart from Vienna, an international form, I have broken this rule only with Prague and Trieste; I do not by this imply that Prague is German or Trieste Italian.

The Epilogue does not attempt to summarize the history of the last thirty years; merely to suggest that Habsburg themes continued even after the fall of the Habsburg Monarchy. I first developed its argument in an article on 'National Independence and the "Austrian Idea"' in the *Political Quarterly*.

I am grateful to Mr A. F. Thompson, of Wadham College, for reading my manuscript, and to my colleague, Mr C. E. Stevens, for reading my proofs.

16 November 1947   A J P TAYLOR

CHAPTER ONE

THE DYNASTY

THE Empire of the Habsburgs[1] which was dissolved in 1918 had a unique character, out of time and out of place. Metternich, a European from the Rhineland, felt that the Habsburg Empire did not belong to Europe. 'Asia', he said, 'begins at the Landstrasse' – the road out of Vienna to the east. Francis Joseph was conscious that he belonged to the wrong century. He told Theodore Roosevelt: 'You see in me the last monarch of the old school.' The collection of territories ruled over by the House of Habsburg never found a settled description. Their broad lines were determined in 1526, when Ferdinand, possessing already a variety of titles as ruler of the Alpine-Germanic lands, became King of Bohemia and King of Hungary; yet for almost three hundred years they had no common name. They were 'the lands of the House of Habsburg' or 'the lands of the [Holy Roman] Emperor'. Between 1740 and 1745, when the Imperial title passed out of Habsburg hands, Maria Theresa could only call herself 'Queen of Hungary', yet her empire was certainly not the Hungarian Empire. In 1804 Francis II, the last Holy Roman Emperor, saw his Imperial title threatened by the ambition of Napoleon and invented for himself the title of 'Emperor of Austria'. This, too, was a dynastic name; the Empire was the Empire of the House of Austria, not the Empire of the Austrians. In 1867 the nation of Hungary established its claim to partnership with the Emperor; and the Empire became 'Austria-Hungary'. The non-Hungarian lands remained without a name until the end.

The Habsburg lands were not bound together either by geography or by nationality. They have sometimes been described as the lands of the valley of the Danube. How could this include the Netherlands, the Breisgau, and northern Italy? Or in the nineteenth century, Galicia, Bosnia, the Bukovina, and even Bohemia? The Habsburgs

1. Pronounced: Hapsburgs.

themselves were in origin a German dynasty. They added first a Spanish and later an Italian element, without becoming anchored to a single region or people: they were the last possessors of the shadowy universal monarchy of the Middle Ages and inherited from it a cosmopolitan character. The inhabitants of Vienna, their capital city, were Germans; this was their nearest approach to a national appearance. In other countries dynasties are episodes in the history of the people; in the Habsburg Empire peoples are a complication in the history of the dynasty. The Habsburg lands acquired in time a common culture and, to some extent, a common economic character: these were the creation, not the creators, of the dynasty. No other family has endured so long or left so deep a mark upon Europe: the Habsburgs were the greatest dynasty of modern history, and the history of central Europe revolves round them, not they round it.

The Habsburgs, in their time, discharged many missions. In the sixteenth century they defended Europe from the Turk; in the seventeenth century they promoted the victory of the Counter-Reformation; in the eighteenth century they propagated the ideas of the Enlightenment; in the nineteenth century they acted as a barrier against a Great German national state. All these were casual associations. Their enduring aim was to exist in greatness; ideas, like peoples, were exploited for the greatness of their house. Hence the readiness to experiment, which made Francis Joseph, for example, at the end of his reign the exponent of universal suffrage. They changed ideas, territories, methods, alliances, statesmen, whenever it suited dynastic interests to do so. Only 'the August House' was permanent. The Habsburg lands were a collection of entailed estates, not a state; and the Habsburgs were landlords, not rulers – some were benevolent landlords, some incompetent, some rapacious and grasping, but all intent on extracting the best return from their tenants so as to cut a great figure in Europe. They could compound with anything, except with the demand to be free of landlords; this demand was their ruin.

The Habsburgs began their dynastic career as Archdukes of Austria, the Alpine lands on the south-eastern march of the Holy Roman Empire. In the fifteenth century a Habsburg was elected Emperor, as a harmless nonentity after previous turmoils; and the position became virtually hereditary – only between 1742 and 1745 was there a non-Habsburg Emperor. Still, even the Habsburgs hoped to make the Empire a reality and Germany a united state; they needed more power with which to subdue the German princes. With peculiar mastery they wielded throughout the centuries the weapon of dynastic marriage; and this weapon built the greatness of their House. Charles V, who was elected Emperor in 1519, ruled over the Netherlands, Spain and the Indies, and most of Italy; Ferdinand, his younger brother, took over the Archduchy of Austria and in 1526 became King of Bohemia and King of Hungary. This was a bid for universal monarchy, a monarchy bound by family ties. Its opponents proved too strong: France and the German princes combined against it, and it failed. Ferdinand in 1526 acquired new burdens, not new strength. He owed Bohemia and Hungary to the death of the last Jagellon King in battle against the Turks; and in 1529 the Turks besieged Vienna. Instead of subduing the German princes, the Habsburgs had to be saved by them. Vienna was relieved, and the Turks contented themselves with most of Hungary. The Turkish invasions, it is often said, spoilt the Habsburg plans for dominating Germany; perhaps, rather, they saved the Habsburgs from disaster, and allowed them to linger on until the twentieth century. Had there been no Turkish danger, the Habsburgs would, no doubt, have attempted, like their Hohenstaufen and Luxemburg predecessors, to dominate Germany; they would probably have met the same failure. As it was, the Turks gave the Habsburgs the first of their many 'missions': the Habsburgs did nothing, for more than a hundred years, to liberate the parts of Hungary conquered by the Turks, yet they persuaded others, and even themselves, that they were the defenders of Christianity. Opposites sustain each other, as buttresses support a wall. The Christian churches could survive heresy, but not indifference. The Habsburgs could withstand Turkish attacks; their power declined with Turkish weakness, until finally Habsburg and Ottoman empires fell together.

Habsburg creativeness was exhausted with the failure of Charles V. In 1556, when he abdicated and the Imperial title passed to Ferdinand, began the Habsburg struggle to survive in greatness; the Habsburg monarchy had acquired its lasting character. External enemies had been the danger of the first half of the sixteenth century: disintegration was the danger of the second half of the century. The Estates of the various lands sought to maintain their independence and the privileges of their aristocratic members. Bohemia had already a national religion in the Hussite church; Protestantism spread both in the remnant of Hungary and in the German lands. Even the policy of marriages had its reverse effect; for marriages produce children, and the Habsburgs divided their lands among their offspring until the end of the seventeenth century, new marriages then following to redress the results of the old ones. The idea of the unity of the Habsburg lands questioned the right of the dynasty to dispose of its lands at will; and the Habsburgs strove to keep their dominions apart, not to bring them together. There was never a States General, or general meeting of Estates, as there was in France. Delegates from all the Habsburg lands, except Tyrol, met at Linz[1] in 1614 and proposed a central committee of the Estates; this was to resist the Habsburg ruler rather than the Turk. In other countries the dynasties cooperated with their peoples; the Habsburgs believed that the peoples would cooperate only against the dynasty. They sought an ally against the initiative of their subjects, and this ally they found in the Counter-Reformation.

The alliance of the dynasty and the Jesuits saved the Habsburgs and defeated Protestantism in central Europe; it also gave to 'Austrian' culture the peculiar stamp which it preserved to the end. Austrian Baroque civilization, like the buildings which it created, was grandiose, full of superficial life, yet sterile within: it was theatre, not reality. It lacked integrity and individual character; at its heart was a despairing frivolity. 'Hopeless, but not serious' was the guiding principle which the age of Baroque stamped upon the Habsburg world. Deep feeling found an outlet only in music, the least political of the arts; even here the creative spirit strove to break its bonds, and the air of Vienna was more congenial to Johann Strauss than to Mozart or to Beethoven. The Habsburgs learnt from the Jesuits patience, subtlety, and showmanship; they could not learn from them sincerity and creativeness.

The Germanic lands were won back peacefully by the Counter-Reformation in the latter part of the sixteenth century: Protestantism survived only in a few mountain valleys of Carinthia. The

1. Pronounced: Lintz.

narrow strip of Habsburg Hungary, with its Diet at Bratislava, also succumbed easily. Central Hungary was a Turkish pashalic, wasting to nothing under Turkish exploitation. The Hungarian lands to the east were a dependent principality under Turkish suzerainty; and here Calvinism held out, preserved by the Turks, to thwart the Habsburgs later. The open conflict came in Bohemia. Here the nobility, like the Estates of the Netherlands, called Calvinism and nationalism to the aid of aristocratic privilege. Unlike the Netherlands, Bohemia lacked a rising middle class to transform the defence of privilege into the struggle for new freedoms. The Bohemian nobles invoked the name of Hus and glorified the Czech nation; in fact they never advanced from a refusal to pay taxes. The conflict turned to war in 1618. The Bohemian Diet, alarmed by imperial encroachments, refused to elect the new Habsburg as their King, despite a previous promise. Instead they elected a German Protestant prince, who, it was thought, could count on the army of the Calvinist Union in Germany and of his father-in-law, the King of England. The Habsburg Monarchy seemed in dissolution: the Emperor had neither money nor men, and Bohemian cavalry reached the gates of Vienna. The Bohemian success was short: the nobility would not make sacrifices to defend their privileges, or even their existence; James I, sunk in pacific diplomacy, would not be prompted by the House of Commons into sending an army to Bohemia; the Calvinist Union provided few forces to aid Bohemia, the Catholic League much to aid the Habsburgs. In 1620 historic Bohemia was destroyed at the battle of the White Mountain. Czech[1] Hussite culture was replaced by the cosmopolitan Baroque culture of the Counter-Reformation. The native nobility was expropriated or driven into exile; two thirds of the landed estates changed hands; and adventurers from every country in Europe, the hangers-on of the Habsburgs, set up a new, Imperial aristocracy. The Crown became hereditary in the Habsburg line; the Diet, revived by the

---

1. Pronounced: Check. The absurd spelling, used only in English, is based on the Polish adaptation of Latin characters to Slav sounds; this adaptation is no longer used in any Slav language except Polish. It would be more sensible to write Čechs, as the people do themselves; or to follow the German and French examples and write Checks, an English phonetical spelling. I regret that I lack the courage to do either.

Revised Ordinance of 1627, lost its rights and could only listen to the demands of the Crown for money.

The battle of the White Mountain determined the character of the Habsburg Empire. Previously, Bohemia and Hungary had been similar, semi-independent kingdoms; now Bohemia became a 'hereditary land' like the German lands, and Hungary stood alone. The Czech nation was submerged. Bohemia existed as an administrative unit. Though German was placed on an equality with Czech, Bohemia did not become German: it became 'Austrian', that is cosmopolitan or nondescript. The victory of 1620 was a victory for absolutism, not for centralization. The Habsburgs feared to bring their peoples together, even in subjection; besides, centralizing their states was beyond their administrative capacity. The power which they had assembled to subdue Bohemia was dissipated in a final attempt to reduce Germany to obedience. Old ambitions stirred in dream, and Imperial armies reached the shores of the Baltic. The intervention of France and Sweden defeated these Habsburg projects; and the Peace of Westphalia, which ended the Thirty Years War, embodied the verdict that Germany would not attain unity through the Holy Roman Empire. There was another side to the verdict: the Habsburgs, though thwarted as Emperors, were not condemned to death – they remained great as rulers of their dynastic lands. The House of Austria received European recognition, no longer as holder of the Imperial title, but in virtue of its own strength.

The final element in the constitution of the Habsburg Monarchy was added with the reconquest of Hungary. The Habsburgs were provoked into action by a last outburst of Turkish vigour, which led to the second Turkish siege of Vienna in 1683. When this failed, the Turkish tide ran back rapidly, and Habsburg armies cleared practically all Hungary of the Turks by the end of the seventeenth century. The Habsburgs had another motive for haste. The landowners who made up the Hungarian nation were determined to escape the fate of Bohemia: liberated from the Turks, they rebelled against the Habsburgs and in 1707 deposed their Habsburg king. The battle of the White Mountain was not, however, repeated at their expense; the Habsburg forces were fully engaged in the War of the Spanish Succession and could not be diverted to subduing the Hungarian nobles. Compromise, the first of many between the Habsburgs and Hungary, followed in 1711. By the Peace of Szatmár[1] the Hungarian nobles, led by Alexander Károlyi,[2] deserted their leader, Rákóczi,[3] and recognized the Habsburg ruler as king; he in return recognized the traditional constitution and privileges of Hungary. Hungary thus preserved its feudal Diet, its separate existence, and the privileges of its landed class. Above all, it preserved the *comitat*, the institution unique in Europe, of autonomous local government. Habsburg administration stopped at the Hungarian frontier; Hungary, even in periods of absolutism, was administered by elected committees of the county gentry, and these would never operate measures which ran against their privileges. The pattern of Hungary's future was determined: the Habsburgs were accepted as kings, only so long as they sustained the 'freedom' of the landowners. Alexander Károlyi, the maker of the Peace of Szatmár, saved his class and at the same time founded the greatness of his family; two hundred years later, his descendant proclaimed the end of the Habsburg Monarchy in a last attempt to save great Hungary.

The Peace of Szatmár was confirmed twelve years later in the Pragmatic Sanction, the legal charter of the Habsburg Monarchy. Charles VI, Emperor since 1711, had no male heir. He wished to avoid for his lands the fate of partition which had lately befallen the Spanish Empire – a partition in which Charles had been a competitor. The fundamental law, or Pragmatic Sanction, which he promulgated, settled the succession on his daughter; more, it asserted the indivisibility of the Habsburg lands. The Habsburg Monarchy became a defined Empire, instead of a collection of provinces accidentally ruled by the same prince. To strengthen the Pragmatic Sanction, Charles had it confirmed by the Diets of his states. This was easy in the 'hereditary lands', Bohemia and the German states, where the Diets had lost all force. The Hungarian Diet insisted on a further solemn recognition of Hungary's 'rights, liberties and privileges, immunities, prerogatives, and recognized customs'. Thus the Pragmatic Sanction contained a contradiction, the fundamental contradiction of the Habsburg Empire. For the Habsburgs it was the legal basis of the unity of their Empire; for the Hungarians it was the legal confirmation of their privileges, that is,

1. Pronounced: Sót-mar.   2. Pronounced: Kár-orl-i.   3. Pronounced: Rākôtsi.

of the separate existence of Hungary and so of the disunity of the Empire.

The Pragmatic Sanction did not give Maria Theresa a peaceful succession. In 1740 the survival of the Habsburg Monarchy was in question as it had been in 1618. The King of Prussia demanded Silesia and, by conquering it, changed the balance of German and non-German peoples in the lands of the Bohemian crown; a non-Habsburg, the Elector of Bavaria, was elected Emperor; a French army invaded Bohemia and occupied Prague. Maria Theresa used the weapons of her forebears: patience and obstinacy, a professional army, and a wise policy of alliances. She did not attempt to appeal to the support of her peoples. Her one appeal to patriotism, her dramatic appearance at the Hungarian Diet in 1741, was not a success. The Hungarian nobles indeed declared that they would die for their King, Maria Theresa. They would not, however, pay taxes for her, and their very declaration of loyalty was an assertion that Hungary knew only the King of Hungary and had no concern with the unity of the Habsburg lands. The crisis of 1618 had left the Habsburgs with the belief that the peoples would cooperate only against the dynasty; the crisis of 1740 established the belief that an appeal to the peoples would not help the dynasty but would be exploited by the peoples to extract damaging concessions. When Maria Theresa had overcome her foreign enemies, she went on to create the unity of her Empire.

Charles VI had made the Habsburg lands a legal unit; Maria Theresa translated this unity into practice. When she came to the throne, the provinces were all and the centre nothing; the 'Empire' was merely the court and the army. Maria Theresa gave her Empire the bureaucratic system without which it could not have continued as a Great Power. The Bohemian Chancellery was abolished and a central direction established at Vienna; agents of this central body, independent of the provincial Diets, supervised local administration. The great landlords still exercised 'patrimonial jurisdiction' over their peasants; this survived until 1848. Its value to the lord was financial, rather than political; in fact, the lords often employed the local Imperial authority as their man of law. The *Kreishauptmann*, captain of the circle, was the corner-stone of the Empire which Maria Theresa created, an official halfway between the intendant and the prefect. As in Bourbon France, the provinces remained in existence; as in Napoleonic France, the captain controlled a new, artificial unit, the circle. The territorial magnates lost all real power; to recover it, they became, later, provincial patriots and even, for a little while, liberal.

The Imperial system created by Maria Theresa was strictly Imperial, or even 'Austrian'; it had no defined national character. Still, the members of the Imperial Chancellery in Vienna and most of the captains of circles were Germans: they received a German education and used German as the language of official business among themselves. They would have been surprised to learn that they were discharging a 'German' mission. All the same, once national spirit stirred, the Germanized bureaucracy gave German nationalism its claim to the inheritance of the Habsburgs; and the Habsburgs themselves came to puzzle over the question whether they were a German dynasty.

Hungary escaped the reforms of Maria Theresa, once more protected from subjection by the foreign difficulties of the Habsburgs. Maria Theresa, too, could not afford a battle of the White Mountain. Hungary therefore retained its separate Chancery and its autonomous administration, unchecked by Imperial agents. Maria Theresa meant to sap the privileged position of Hungary by gradual encroachment. She never called the Hungarian Diet after the end of the Seven Years War; she did not keep a separate Hungarian court, and the great Hungarian aristocrats were drawn to the Imperial court at Vienna, where they took on an Austrian, cosmopolitan character. Hungary was treated economically as an Austrian colony in mercantilist fashion. Since the Hungarian landowners paid no taxes, money was extracted from Hungary by heavy taxes on goods imported into Hungary from the other Habsburg dominions; and, to maintain the yield of these taxes, Hungary was prevented from importing from elsewhere or manufacturing goods herself. This system suited the Hungarian aristocrats; the impoverishment of their country was a small price to pay for the maintenance of their privileged position. Every advance in the hereditary lands made Hungary more of an exception politically and socially. Maria Theresa was the true founder of the Austrian Empire; by arresting her reforms at the frontier of Hungary, she was also the founder of Dualism.

Joseph II had watched with impatience the caution and compromise of his mother. When she died in 1780, he set out at once
to carry her work to its logical conclusion and to make his Empire a
centralized egalitarian state. He refused to be crowned King of
Hungary, to recognize the privileges of Hungary, or to summon the
Diet; the *comitats* were abolished and Hungary put under the rule of
German bureaucrats. Joseph II had no doubt as to the character
of his Empire: it was to be a German state. He said: 'I am Emperor
of the German *Reich*; therefore all the other states which I possess are
provinces of it.' Joseph broke, too, the Habsburg connexion with the
Roman Church. Many monasteries were dissolved; Protestants and
Jews were freed of their disabilities; and the Church, deprived of its
privileged position, was put under a state control more rigorous
than that which Napoleon imposed on the French Church in 1801.
Secular thought could at last begin to stir; the embers of Protestantism revived in Bohemia; and, by freeing the Jews, Joseph II called
into existence the most loyal of Austrians. The Jews alone were not
troubled by the conflict between dynastic and national claims: they
were Austrians without reserve.

The agrarian reforms of Joseph II contributed still more decisively
to the future character of the Habsburg lands: everything else
followed from them, even the east-central Europe of the present day.
Abolition of serfdom was among the common stock of the Enlightened Despots; Joseph II almost alone emancipated the serfs
without weakening their connexion with the land. Serfdom strictly
taken (the system, that is, in which the peasants were chattels
attached to the land) existed only in Bohemia and in Hungary; in the
German lands, the peasants were free men, though holding their
land on feudal tenures. Joseph II abolished true serfdom, as did most
of the German princes (though in Prussia even this had to wait until
the time of Stein); but elsewhere in Germany and even in Stein's
reforms, when the peasants were freed from serfdom, the land was
freed from the peasants. The peasants did not receive security of
tenure; only the richer peasants kept their land; the poorer peasants
were 'cleared' from the land and became landless labourers. Joseph
II made this peasant-clearance (*Bauernlegung*) impossible. Maria
Theresa had already carried out a register of all land with a strict
division between noble and peasant holdings – dominical and rusti-

cal land in the legal jargon of the time. Joseph II forbade for ever the acquisition of 'rustic' land by the nobility and gave the bulk of the 'rusticalists' security of tenure. His principal motive was, no doubt, to prevent the increase of 'dominical' land, which paid less taxes and in Hungary none; the effect, none the less, was to preserve the peasantry. Rustic land was still saddled with *Robot*, the labour rent; this survived until 1848. The peasant tenant of 'dominical' land, too, had to wait until then for security of tenure. But the decisive step had been taken. The peasant class attained a security which elsewhere in Europe was won only by the French Revolution. Though the poor peasants still sold their holdings and left the land, especially after 1848, they could sell only to richer peasants, not to the nobility, great or small: ownership shifted within a class, not from one class to another. Therefore, wherever Habsburg rule ran, peasant communities survived[1] and with them the peasant nations. Politically the Habsburg Monarchy remained a despotism; socially it was nearer to revolutionary France than was Prussia or even the states of western Germany. Yet more: in the nineteenth century, once despotism was shaken, French political ideas, too, found a readier response than in Germany – the intellectual leaders in the Habsburg Monarchy had their roots, like the French radicals, in a free peasantry.

Still, the Habsburg Monarchy was far removed from Jacobin France; and for this, too, Joseph II was responsible. His agrarian system also benefited, paradoxically, the great aristocracy, the class which gave to the Habsburg Empire its special flavour. Security of peasant tenure hit the small noble: it prevented the gradual building-up of a noble estate. The great estates were built up already, and they increased at the expense of the small nobility. Similarly every shift to a money economy injured the small noble, who frittered away the small sums that he received; the great nobles received large sums and turned capitalist with them. Except in Hungary there was no important Junker class; and even in Hungary after 1848 the Hungarian 'gentry' followed a different line from the Prussian Junkers. Thus the Habsburg Monarchy preserved in

1. This does not apply to northern Italy, where all land was owned by the lords, and the so-called peasants were, in fact, tenant farmers, as in modern England. This is, no doubt, the principal reason for the industrial development of northern Italy.

strength two classes elsewhere on the decline: great aristocrats, who made the Empire more conservative than the rest of central Europe, and landholding peasants, who made it more radical. Both classes made a balance against the urban capitalist, elsewhere the predominant figure of nineteenth-century liberalism. Joseph II had intended to make his Empire a German state; his agrarian reforms retarded the victory of the social class and economic system which were the standard-bearers of German nationalism. The peasants did not leave the land at the same tumultuous rate as in Germany, to say nothing of England; therefore Austrian industry had to wait longer for the cheap labour provided by a landless proletariat. Backward industry sheltered behind prohibitive tariffs and so cut Austria off from the German Zollverein. It would not do to find here the sole explanation of Habsburg failure to keep up in the race for power. Austrian industrial achievement rested on the handicrafts and skill of Bohemia; and the Habsburg Monarchy lacked the plentiful supply of coal which was the secret of nineteenth-century strength. The two factors worked together; impossible to assess their weight or order. As in France, lack of coal and lack of a landless proletariat combined to produce a single result; and in the nineteenth century, France and the Habsburg Monarchy, the two traditional Great Powers of Europe, were both dwarfed by the chimneys of the Ruhr.

The work of Joseph II was an astonishing achievement of Enlightened philosophy, witness to the force of the Imperial structure. Joseph II interfered with everything great and small; he was the Convention in a single man. This isolation was his weakness. His revolutionary policy did not have the support of a revolutionary class. Napoleon came after a great revolution and could base his support on the French peasants; Joseph II condemned the French Revolution, saying 'I am a King by profession', and so confessed the contradiction that lay at the root of his work. His aim could be completed only by revolution; and revolution would destroy the dynasty. As it was, the nobles defended their privileges, the peasants their superstitions, and Joseph's dominions became a series of Vendées. The strongest resistance, culminating in revolt, came in Hungary, where the claim to traditional rights gave a spurious air of liberalism to the defence of social privileges. Even in Bohemia the imperial nobility, which had been imported by the Habsburgs, cloaked their hostility to social reform in a display of Bohemian patriotism, and in the ante-rooms of the Hofburg the descendants of German, Scottish, or Spanish adventurers ostentatiously exchanged the few words of Czech which they had laboriously learnt from their stable-boys. Bohemian politics of the nineteenth century received their first rehearsal.

Joseph II died in 1790: uncompromising to the last, he insisted that his failure had been complete. Leopold II, his successor, was not so enslaved by theory. He restored the *Robot*, which Joseph II had abolished in 1789; the rest of Joseph's agrarian reforms remained in force. Leopold was ready enough to be crowned King of Bohemia; he would not modify the Revised Ordinance of 1627 nor restore the Bohemian Chancellery. His concessions, like the preceding revolt, were real only in Hungary. The Diet was summoned and the separate privileges of Hungary recognized with new formality; especially the autonomous county administration recovered its full powers. This was the decisive concession. Leopold did not take seriously his promise to call the Diet once every three years; and his successor ignored the promise until 1825. These absolutist periods could arrest the further development of Hungarian separatism; they could not turn the current in the opposite direction so long as all local affairs were out of Imperial control. The *comitats* kept aristocratic Hungary in being; moreover, although bound by law to carry out the agrarian reforms of Joseph II, they handled the landowners gently and so preserved the Hungarian 'gentry' on the land until 1848. Once more a crisis had followed the familiar pattern: the dynasty and privileged Hungary had shrunk from a fight to the death. There had been another compromise, again at the expense of the Hungarian people.

In a wider field, too, events followed the regular pattern. Ever since the time of Charles V, the Habsburg Monarchy had encountered external dangers in the first half of each century, and internal difficulties in the second. Leopold II died prematurely in 1792, leaving the problems of his Empire to his heavy, inexperienced son, Francis II, last Holy Roman Emperor and first Emperor of Austria. These problems were at once overshadowed by the wars against France, which began in 1792 and which lasted, with interruptions, until 1814. Reform and Jacobinism became interchangeable terms. The war brought to the Habsburgs a series of disasters. They were expelled from Italy and from the Rhineland; Vienna was twice occupied by French armies; and in 1806 Napoleon, himself become universal Emperor, compelled Francis to abolish the Holy Roman Empire. Against new forces Francis used old weapons – patience and obstinacy, professional armies and a policy of alliances. The Habsburgs, in the eighteenth century a reforming dynasty, became the champions of conservatism; and the defence of their family position was merged in the general interest of European stability. Once more, and again unintentionally, the Habsburgs found themselves with a mission : to defend Europe against revolution as they had once, supposedly, defended it against the Turks. At the climax of the Napoleonic era even the echo of the Habsburgs' earliest ambition faintly stirred : in the war of 1809 Francis put himself forward as the liberator of Germany and the leader of the German nation. This war ended in catastrophic defeat, and Francis was glad to return to Napoleon's favour by wielding the more familiar Habsburg weapon of marriage. The final war of liberation was not won by popular enthusiasm : it was won by peasant armies, harshly disciplined, and by a grudging cooperation among the great allies just prolonged enough to enable Napoleon to defeat himself by his own energy.

When the war ended in 1814, Francis had already been reigning for over twenty years. He had preserved his dynastic greatness in war, and to preserve this greatness was the most he intended in time of peace. He hated change, popular initiative, or indeed any stirring of life in political affairs. His conservatism stopped short at the privileges of Hungary, which offended his Imperial authority; and he intended to pursue the sapping of Hungary's position which had been arrested under his predecessors. Once peace was restored in Europe, the Habsburg ruler would, it seemed, return to the old struggle against disintegration; the slow and irregular advance of Imperial power against traditional rights and exceptions would be renewed. The nineteenth century added a new theme to the history of the Habsburg Monarchy : the peoples of the Empire began to have their own wishes and ambitions, and these proved in the end incompatible with each other and with the survival of the dynasty.

The Habsburgs still occupied the centre of the stage, but they had to give condescending smiles to the other actors and, finally, to accept promptings from the stage-hands.

CHAPTER TWO

THE PEOPLES[1]

FRANCIS I, told of an Austrian patriot, answered impatiently: 'But is he a patriot for me?' The Emperor was needlessly meticulous. Austria was an Imperial organization, not a country; and to be Austrian was to be free of national feeling – not to possess a nationality. From the battle of the White Mountain until the time of Maria Theresa 'Austria' was embodied in the territorial aristocracy, the 'Magnates'. These, even when German, thought of themselves as Austrians, not as Germans, just as the Prussian nobility regarded themselves solely as Prussians. In Bohemia, home of the greatest estates, they were especially divorced from local feeling; for these great lords were purely Habsburg creations in the period of the Thirty Years War. Even the Hungarian magnates, Esterházys, Károlyis, Andrássys,[2] had little traditional background: their greatness, too, rested on Habsburg grants, made when Hungary was recovered from the Turks and Rákóczi's rebellion was subdued. A native nobility existed only in Galicia and in Italy: the Polish magnates did not owe their greatness to the Habsburgs and never forgot that they were Poles – though they denied this name to their peasants; the Italian nobles were cosmopolitan, but Italy was their world. Apart from Galicia and Italy, the Austrian Empire was a vast collection of Irelands, except that – unlike the Irish landlords, who had at any rate a home of origin in England – the Austrian nobility had no home other than the Imperial court.

1. The allusions in this chapter will be made clearer by reference to the details of national structure in each province, given in the Appendix.

2. Pronounced: Ónd-rāshy.

The Austrian nobility lived in a closed circle: the great lords knew only their own class, married only within their own class, and used the cosmopolitan language of the court – at first French or Italian, later German. Széchényi,[1] 'the greatest Hungarian', kept his private diary in German; and even in the twentieth century Michael Károlyi, the last great Hungarian aristocrat, spoke French and German better than Hungarian. This class provided the high army officers, the diplomats, and the few great ministers of state; they dispensed justice in their feudal courts and, before the centralizing work of Maria Theresa and Joseph II, carried on the administration of the Empire. The Monarchy enabled the aristocrats to exploit their peasants, and in return the aristocrats sustained the Monarchy. The reforming work of the Monarchy threatened the aristocratic position. Centralization threatened their independence; agrarian reform challenged their economic privilege; and the growth of an Imperial bureaucracy destroyed their monopoly of local administration. As a result the aristocracy, in the nineteenth century, had to defend their traditional privileges against the Monarchy, although these were the creation of the Monarchy. Like the Irish garrison, these landowners, alien in spirit and often in origin, took on liberal and even national airs. Yet they never forgot that their existence was bound up with that of the Monarchy: though they played at resistance, they always returned to court, and, time and again, disappointed their liberal or national associates. The great landowners, despite their occasional Frondes, remained to the end the hard core of the Habsburg Monarchy.

Still, from the moment that Maria Theresa established a central Chancellery at Vienna, there was another class that could claim to be essentially 'Austrian' – the bureaucracy, the men who worked the Imperial organization. This class, too, had no single national or even class origin. Some were great aristocrats, some Hungarian, some, like Kolovrat, even Czech. Most were Germans from urban communities; though they possessed titles, they belonged, in the Austrian phrase, to the 'second society'. The bureaucrats had no sympathy either with local patriotism or with aristocratic privilege; their ideal was a uniform Empire, run on Enlightened principles. Like Joseph II, their supreme example, they were not nationalist

1. Pronounced: Sáy-tchain-y.

fanatics; but they never supposed that the Empire could be anything other than a German state. German, inevitably, was the language of the central administration; equally therefore it became the language of local administration, once this was brought under central control. The Imperial bureaucrats had a cultural, as well as a centralizing, task: they were to spread Enlightenment. This, too, meant the extension of German. No other language of culture existed: there were no works of literature, of philosophy, even of agronomy, except in German; no men of learning except at the German universities; no source of culture on which to draw except Germany. In exactly the same way Macaulay, not a man of illiberal or nationalist spirit, supposed that the cultural level of India was to be raised by Indians reading the works of Shakespeare and studying the doctrines of the Glorious Revolution.

The tie which made the bureaucracy German was more than culture. The bureaucrats, often by origin, always by employment, were towndwellers; and the towns of the Habsburg Monarchy were all German in character. The Habsburg Monarchy was overwhelmingly agrarian. The few historic towns which had once sprung from the country had had their history interrupted: Czech Prague by the Habsburgs, Hungarian Budapest by the Turks. What remained were trading-posts, some deliberately settled by the Habsburgs, some gradually developed by enterprising merchants, all German in speech and culture. Prague, Budapest, Zagreb, Brno,[1] Bratislava were as German as Linz or Innsbruck,[2] so much so that they had German names: Prague (for Praha), Ofen, Agram, Brünn, Pressburg.[3] In Prague in 1815 there were 50,000 Germans and only 15,000 Czechs; even in 1848 respectable people spoke only German in the streets, and to ask the way in Czech would provoke an offensive reply. In Budapest the Hungarians were little more than a third of the population as late as 1848; in the eighteen-twenties there were two German daily newspapers and no Hungarian; and the Budapest town council transacted its business in German until the eighteeneighties. Yet Prague and Budapest were the capital cities of nations in full revival. The smaller towns remained German far longer, some, such as Brno, until the twentieth century. Here again the only

1. Pronounced: Brr-no.   2. Pronounced: Innspruck.

3. Bratislava had also a Hungarian name, Pozsóny (Páwz-shōny).

exceptions were northern Italy and Galicia, acquired too late to
follow the Habsburg pattern. In Cracow and Lvov Poles predominated; and the traders were Jews, not Germans. Italy had
been the birthplace in modern Europe both of trade and of urban
life: the Italian towns needed no Germans to create them.

The German character of the towns had little or nothing to do with
race. Some towndwellers were Habsburg imports from Germany;
many were migrants from the countryside. German was a class-
name. It meant essentially a trader – shopkeeper, merchant, handi-
craft-worker, or moneylender. From this it extended to anyone who
practised urban arts – writers, schoolteachers, clerks, lawyers. The
enterprising son of a peasant, Czech, Rumanian, or Serb, who
entered a town, learnt a German art and spoke German to his
fellow shopkeepers; his children despised their father's peasant
dialect, and his grandchildren, safely arrived in state jobs, forgot that
they had ever been anything but Germans and towndwellers. Thus
the towns were at once islands of German culture and of Imperial
loyalty. It would have made no sense for these traders to care for the
provincial liberties which were exclusively the privileges of the
landed nobility. The conflict between the centralizing monarchy
and the provinces was thus also a conflict between the urban middle
classes and the territorial aristocracy; and this, in its turn, appeared
as a conflict between German domination and national diversity.
Of course, the German middle classes, too, had their conflict with
the Monarchy. Though they supported the Empire, they wanted an
Empire based on 'liberal' principles, as they came to be called in the
nineteenth century. They resented the influence of the great aristocracy at court; wanted a say in policy as well as in administration;
and disliked the spendthrift, muddled finances of the Habsburgs.
Still, these complaints did not challenge the existence of the Empire;
they were disputes only as to the speed with which it should go along
the path of centralization and reform. The German bureaucrats and
capitalists were and remained Imperial.

This class was, however, only the *pays légal* of the Germans, and in
the course of the nineteenth century fell out of step with their fellow-
nationals. National problems dominated the last century of Habsburg history; and the first of these problems in point of time was the
nationalism of the Germans. This did not at the outset challenge the

existence of the dynasty; it sought only to change the character of
the Empire, perhaps merely to develop it. In so far as the old Empire
had a national character, that character had been German. The
Holy Roman Emperor was universally, though loosely, called
'German Emperor'; and the Empire had been known since the
fifteenth century as the 'Holy Roman Empire of the German
Nation'. Between 1806 and 1815 no Germany existed; after 1815 the
German subjects of the Habsburgs were once more members of the
'German Confederation'. Moreover, the culture of the Empire was
everywhere German, apart from the cosmopolitan culture of the
court; the universities were German; it was plausible to argue later
that German was the Austrian 'language of state'. Even representative government, the classical liberal demand, would strengthen the
German position. The Germans, though only one third of the
population, paid two thirds of the direct taxes; and an individual
German paid in taxes twice as much as a Czech or an Italian, nearly
five times as much as a Pole, and seven times as much as a Croat or
Serb. Therefore a restricted suffrage based on taxation, which was
the universal liberal programme, would return a parliament predominantly German in character. The Germans found themselves
in a dilemma only when nationalism developed into the demand for
a unitary national state. Some took the extreme course of advocating
the overthrow of the Habsburgs in favour of national Germany;
others the course, equally extreme, of proposing the merging into
national Germany of all the Habsburg lands, including even
Hungary. Most, however, supposed that Germany would follow the
boundary of the German Confederation; this included the Czechs
and Slovenes, but not Hungary. This hope was defeated in 1866:
the Germans of Austria were excluded from national Germany, and
the conflict of loyalties began. But now the Germans could not turn
so easily against the Habsburgs. The other nationalities of the
Empire had begun to voice their claims, claims directed against the
Germans rather than against the Emperor. The break-up of the
Habsburg Empire might bring to the Germans something they
desired – inclusion in the German national state. It might instead
bring something much worse – the loss of their privileged position in
lands that were traditionally theirs. Thus the Germans remained to
the end torn in their loyalties: certainly not unreservedly 'Austrian'

like the great landowners and the great capitalists, but at the same time hoping that the Empire might still be transformed into an Empire 'for them'.

The Habsburg Monarchy of the early nineteenth century rested, then, on two supports – the great aristocracy and the German upper middle class. It was harassed, but not threatened in its existence, by a wider German feeling, vaguely liberal and national. This balance was challenged by two other forces, which demanded a change of character and sometimes the end of the Monarchy: the traditional nationalism of the smaller nobility in Hungary and Croatia, and the innovating nationalism of the peasant peoples. The unique political history of Hungary had produced a social result, remarkable in Europe, unique in the Habsburg Monarchy: the lesser landowners had survived. In Bohemia and the German lands there was nothing between the great aristocrat and the peasant. In Hungary, out of a population of ten millions, half a million were 'nobles'. These half millions were the 'Hungarian nation'. Like German, Hungarian or Magyar[1] was a class term: it meant an owner of land exempt from the land-tax, one who attended the county assemblies and took part in the elections to the Diet.[2] The holdings of these squires ranged from large estates, almost on the scale of those of the magnates, to smallholdings, inferior to those of many peasants. About a third of the nobility had estates which gave some leisure and profit; and these families were the champions of 'thousand-year-old Hungary'. The phrase glossed over the century and three quarters of Turkish domination; it presented Hungary as of unique antiquity and assumed that Hungary was incorporated in the privileges of the landowners. In the nineteenth century the traditional patriotism took on the guise of modern nationalism, and the conservative defence of traditional rights was transformed into the assertion of liberal principles. The reality remained the same: the claim by the nobility to their privileged position. This lesser nobility had never

1. Pronounced: Módjor. Magyar is merely the Hungarian for a Hungarian. There is no word in Hungarian to distinguish between a citizen of the Hungarian state and one who speaks the Hungarian language. In western countries, Hungarian and Magyar are used to make this distinction. The practice is useful, though historically misleading.

2. The Hungarian Diet had thus a larger electorate than the unreformed British House of Commons.

done more than acquiesce in Habsburg rule; their privileges were all bars to Imperial encroachment, in administration, in law-making, or in taxation. In the past they had repeatedly been deserted by the magnates, who had made their fortunes sometimes by mediating between Habsburg ruler and Hungarian Diet, more often by acting as Habsburg agents. The central event in the history of Hungary in the nineteenth century was the compromise between the magnates and the lesser nobility; this was the essential prelude to the compromise between Hungary and the Habsburgs, which preserved the antiquated social order in Hungary until the twentieth century.

A lesser nobility existed also in Croatia, itself a dependent kingdom of the Hungarian crown. This nobility, too, was without national character; or rather its nationalism, too, defended the privileges of a class. There had been no hostility between Hungarian and Croat noble. Indeed Croat privileges owed their survival to the association with Hungary; in isolation the Croat nobles would have shared the fate of the Czechs. In 1790, at the height of the struggle against Joseph II, the Croat Diet transferred the granting of taxes to the Hungarian Diet, as a stronger body more capable of resistance; and at the same time they put the Croat county authorities under the Hungarian lieutenancy at Budapest, instead of under the Governor of Croatia, an Imperial agent. Even in the nineteenth century, the Croat nobility thought closer links with Hungary its safest course. In 1827 the Croat Diet resolved that Magyar should be taught in Croat schools; and in 1830 demanded it of all Croatian officials. Only when Magyar, instead of Latin, was demanded of themselves did the Croat nobles begin to change course and to sense the conflict between their national and their class interests. Magyar nationalism pushed the Croat nobles into the arms of the Habsburgs. As well, two other factors made the Croats different from the Hungarian nobles. Firstly, there were no Croat magnates. The great landowners in Croatia were Hungarian magnates, indifferent to Croat privileges; therefore the Croat nobility could hardly have risked a conflict with the Empire. In any case, the second difference made such a conflict much less likely. The Hungarian gentry lived aloof and remote in their counties; few of them entered royal service; they tended to regard the Habsburg King as a foreigner, often as an enemy. Croatia had never been overrun by the Turks and, as the frontier kingdom, had taken an active part in the struggle against them. The Croat gentry had a tradition of military service, and for generation after generation supplied a large proportion of the regimental officers to the Habsburg army. They had a loyalty to the dynasty, the Hungarians only a calculating bargain with it. Besides, the Croat nobility were much less adroit; after all, regimental officers in every country are narrow and blundering politicians. These Croat nobles were fated to be deceived by everyone in turn – by their Hungarian fellow gentry, by their King, finally even by the Croat people.

Not only in Croatia, but throughout the Empire, the revolutionary happening of the nineteenth century was the intrusion into politics of the people, 'the masses'. Democratic claims were not unique to the Habsburg Monarchy; what was unique was the presentation of these claims in national form. The traditional, or, as they came to be called, the 'historic' nations were class nations: the Hungarian gentry, the Germans traders. Neither had assimilated the peoples from whom the Hungarians drew their rents, and the Germans their profits; there was no Austrian amalgam, and as a result every widening of the political society increased the national complexity of the Empire. The peasant masses asserted their existence; this was the cardinal fact in both national and social history. This generalization simplifies, and distorts, the actual process. In the first phase, which reached its climax in 1848, the peasant masses hardly stirred; at most they put out new shoots of intellectual life. The nations who reappeared on the stage of history in 1848 were the creations of writers and still existed only in imagination; they were nations in which there were more writers than readers. These writers were the outcome of the agrarian system which Maria Theresa and Joseph II had made: they were the sons of well-to-do peasants, an Austrian version of the class that had produced the Jacobins in France. The Jacobins completed French national unity; in central Europe the intellectuals disrupted the unity of the Empire. They were neither great landowners nor traders; therefore they could not become either 'Austrian' or German. A middle class, the lesser nobility, existed only in Hungary; and in Hungary the intellectuals, even if Slovak or Rumanian by origin, could become 'Magyar' like the gentry. Elsewhere, the intellectuals had to create their own nationality, the dormant nationality of their peasant fathers.

The early national movements were created and led by writers, principally by poets and historians; and their politics were those of literature rather than of life. The national leaders spoke as though they had the support of a conscious, organized people; yet they knew that the nation was still only in their books. One of the Czech pioneers remarked at a meeting with his fellow writers in Prague: 'If the ceiling were to fall on us now, that would be the end of the national revival.' Living in the closed world of imagination, these early leaders fought over again historical battles decided centuries ago. They did not know when to compromise and when to resist; especially they did not know what to resist with. They did not understand that politics is a conflict of forces; they supposed that it was a conflict of arguments. They mobilized rights, not supporters. The Jacobins had used the Rights of Man to inspire revolutionary armies; in the Habsburg Monarchy the national leaders thought that rights alone were enough, and an accumulation of rights irresistible. They laboured over the legality of their claims as assiduously as Charles VI had sought European confirmation for the Pragmatic Sanction. Every nation claimed to be the heir of one of the ancient kingdoms on the ruins of which the Habsburg Monarchy had been built; and those nations which could not discover a kingdom claimed at least a province. The German nationalists claimed the inheritance of the Holy Roman Empire; the Hungarians claimed all 'the lands of St Stephen' as a Magyar national state; the Czechs followed with the claim to all 'the lands of St Wenceslaus'; the Croats demanded the 'Triune Kingdom', once ruled by the King of Croatia. Historic and national claims were mixed together; this was the classic legerdemain of nineteenth-century Austrian politics. The majority in each province insisted that the historic unit must become a national unit; the minority demanded a redrawing of the province on national lines. Thus, the German majority in Styria asserted against the Slovenes there the provincial unity which the Czech majority asserted against the Germans in Bohemia.

The national leaders fought with intellectual weapons, and for intellectual prizes. They founded national academies and demanded national universities. The Germans sought to maintain their monopoly of state employment, the others to break into it. The national struggle was a struggle for jobs in the bureaucracy. The masses were evoked as a shadowy presence off-stage, reinforcements that were not expected to appear. In the second half of the nineteenth century the masses no longer accepted this humble role. After 1848, the towns began to grow at an ever-increasing rate. The abolition of the *Robot* during the revolution broke the last legal tie which held the peasant to the soil; and, more profoundly, the traditional way of life, which was an even greater tie than the *Robot*, was eaten away by the implacable acid of the revolutionary ideas which had spread from France. Rural life cannot survive the impact of rationalism. The peasant flood poured into the towns and submerged the German 'islands'; the towns at last took on the nationality of the countryside. Moreover this growth of the towns was both cause and effect of industrialism; and, here again, the class conflicts which sprang from this took on national form. The old-established capitalists and the skilled artisans were Germans; the new, thrusting capitalists and the unskilled workers Czechs or Slovenes. Thus the second phase of the national movements, though still urban, was on a wider scale: mass passions were aroused, which the intellectual leaders could no longer moderate or control, and the nationalities began to fight for wealth and power, not for academic principle.

Finally, in the twentieth century, there followed a third phase, which was not complete when the Habsburg Monarchy tumbled in ruins. Nationalism is an intellectual concept, impossible without literacy. The man who cannot read and write speaks a 'dialect'; this becomes the 'national language' only on the printed page. The national movement sprang from the peasants; it could not embrace them so long as they were illiterate, capable only of describing themselves as 'the men from here'. With the growth of the towns, nationalism ran back towards its source. Mass literacy, product of the towns and of the industrial system, spread to the countryside, and created peasant nationalism. This nationalism, too, echoed class conflicts and ambitions: it hated the great estates, but disliked also the life of the towns and even urban nationalism with its richer intellectual flavour. The professors were shouldered aside; and the last national leaders in the Habsburg Monarchy were priests, enemies of the French revolutionary ideas from which the national movements had sprung. The nationalist intellectuals had appealed to the masses; the masses answered by repudiating intellectual values.

This broad pattern of national development conceals great variations in time and space. The Habsburg Monarchy sprawled across Europe from Switzerland to Turkey and spanned the centuries. The deepest division was, no doubt, between the master races and the submerged peoples: Magyars, Germans, Poles, and Italians on the one side, the Slav nations (other than the Poles) and the Rumanians on the other. But the master races also quarrelled among themselves, even though threatened by a common danger: the Italians fought for liberation from the Germans, and 'Magyarization' did not spare the Germans in Hungary. Nor were the submerged peoples brought to a single character by common subjection. The Czechs, with their flourishing intellectual life and expanding capitalist industry, became a middle-class nation; the Croats, with their lesser nobility and thread of historic continuity, retained an aristocratic air; both were distinct from the 'peasant nations'. Again, the nations in whom a Protestant tradition lingered – the Czechs and the Magyars – had more independence of spirit than the Roman Catholic peoples, Croats or Slovenes, for whom the Habsburgs still possessed a religious sanction; and both Protestant and Roman Catholic nations were more at home in the Habsburg Monarchy than the Orthodox nations, Serbs and Rumanians, for whom the Empire was at best an alien convenience.

The dynasty still overshadowed the national ambitions and disputes; and the conflicting nations sought to capture the dynasty, not to overthrow it. Only the Italians, in the early nineteenth century, and the Serbs, in the early twentieth, asked to be quit of the Habsburg Empire; and the Empire was shaken to its foundations by the one, and broke to pieces on the other. With all other peoples the Habsburgs could manoeuvre. In the first half of the nineteenth century the dynasty appeared threatened by the two great historic nationalities, the Germans and the Magyars; to defend itself, it revived the policy of Joseph II and called on the submerged peoples. This was the core of 1848, turning-point of Habsburg fortunes. The dynasty could not escape from its own historical legacy: it could not abandon the outlook of the Counter-Reformation or ally itself with peasants against their lords. Dynastic power, and Magyar and German

Germans	
Magyars	
Czechs	
Slovaks	
Croats	
Serbs	
Slovenes	
Italians	
Rumanians	
Poles	
Little Russians	

GERMANY

BOHEMIA

MORA

LOWER

UPPER

AUSTRIA

Vier

Danube

SWITZER^LD

VORARL-
BERG

TYROL

SALZBURG

CARINTHIA

STYRIA

H

Drav

GORZ

CARNIOLA

Save

Trieste

ISTRIA

Rijeka

CROATIA

ADRIATIC

ITALY

DALM

B

RUSSIA

GALICIA

UKRAINE

BUKOWINA

Tisza

Danube

Buda-Pest

HUNGARY

TRANSYLVANIA

Maros

RUMANIA

SLAVONIA

SERBIA

CZERNAGORA

NATIONALITIES
of the
HABSBURG
MONARCHY

J.F. Horrabin

privileges, were each in their way denials of democracy; and the Habsburgs dared not employ democracy against the Magyars and the Germans for fear that it might rebound against themselves. In face of the threat from the submerged peoples the old combatants made up their quarrels; this was the compromise of 1867. From this compromise the dynasty failed to escape; and the dynasty, Germans, and Magyars were involved in a common ruin.

CHAPTER THREE

OLD ABSOLUTISM: THE AUSTRIA
OF METTERNICH, 1809–35

IN 1804 the lands of the House of Habsburg at last acquired a name: they became the 'Austrian Empire'. This threatened to be a death-bed baptism. In 1805 the Habsburg dream of universal monarchy gave a last murmur, and Francis aspired to defend old Europe against Napoleon. Austerlitz[1] shattered the dream, destroyed the relics of the Holy Roman Empire, and left Francis as, at best, a second-class Emperor. Austria emerged at any rate as an independent country and strove for an independent policy. The result was the war of 1809, the attempt to discover a new mainspring of action in leading the liberation of Germany. This war almost destroyed the Austrian Empire. Napoleon appealed for a Hungarian revolt and even sketched plans for a separate Kingdom of Bohemia. What saved Austria was not the strength of her armies nor the loyalty of her peoples, but the jealousy of her Imperial neighbours: Alexander of Russia and Napoleon could not agree on terms of partition and were content with frontier gains – Alexander carried off eastern Galicia, and Napoleon turned the South Slav lands into the French province of Illyria. The events of 1809 set the pattern of Austrian policy for forty years, or even for the century of the Empire's existence. Austria had become a European necessity. In harsher terms,

1. The battle is too famous to be given its correct name of Slavkov.

the Great Powers were agreed that the fragments surviving from the Habsburg bid for universal monarchy were more harmless in Habsburg hands than in those of some new aspirant to world empire. The nature of the Austrian Empire was clearly shown in the contrast between Austria and Prussia. Both were restored to the ranks of the Great Powers on the defeat of Napoleon; but Prussia carried herself there by harsh reforms, Austria by pliant diplomacy and ingenious treaties.

This Austria was personified in Metternich, who became Foreign Minister in 1809 and who represented Austria to Europe for thirty-nine years. For him, as for Europe, Austria was a diplomatic term. He was a German from the Rhineland, western European in up-bringing and outlook, a belated rationalist of the Enlightenment, delighting to construct abstract systems of politics and convinced of his infallibility. Metternich's diplomatic skill carried Austria through the dangerous years between 1809 and 1813, and made Austria the centre of the European order which followed the downfall of Napoleon: the Congress of Vienna was the symbol of his achievement. For, since Austria was a European necessity, Europe was an Austrian necessity. Austria could not follow a policy of isolation, or even of independence; she had always to be justifying her existence, to be fulfilling a mission, to be constructing systems of alliance. Metternich's foreign policy sprang from the hard experiences with which he had entered his office: he dreaded action, sought always to postpone decisions and cared only for repose. Europe, too, in the generation after Napoleon, desired repose; and thus Metternich was in tune with European sentiment. His misfortune was to outlive the war-weary generation and to survive into a Europe which demanded more positive ideals.

Metternich, like the other European statesmen of 1815, supposed that any new threat to the European order would come again from France; and his foreign policy was designed to exorcise the ghost of Napoleon. Napoleon's empire had rested on French supremacy in Italy and in western Germany; these were now grouped under Austrian protection. Francis did not resume the title of Holy Roman Emperor, and this renunciation later acquired a symbolic importance. In 1815 the change seemed more nominal than real. The old title had been a sham, felt as such even by the Habsburgs;

the German Confederation, created in 1815, was a closer union than the decayed Empire, and Austria, as the presiding Power, had still the principal say in German affairs. Austria did not renounce the headship of Germany in 1815. Rather the reverse: she asserted her German character and, though she accepted Prussia as a second Great Power in Germany, this partnership was one in which Prussia did the work and Austria enjoyed the distinction. Austria and Prussia had both been too shaken by the Napoleonic Wars to indulge in rivalry; common fear of Napoleon had brought them together, and common fear of France and, still more, of French ideas kept them together for a generation after Leipzig and Waterloo. In theory, Austria and Prussia were combined in the defence of Germany; in practice Austria left the main task to Prussia and discovered, too late, the penalty of her adroitness.

The peculiar Austrian mission, *chef d'œuvre* of Metternich's diplomacy, was the security of Italy. This task originated in accident – the routine stroke of eighteenth-century diplomacy by which, in 1797, Austria acquired Venetia in compensation for the Austrian Netherlands. Venetia and Lombardy (an Austrian possession since the war of the Spanish Succession) were both lost to Napoleon and became the Kingdom of Italy; in 1814 they returned to the Habsburg Empire and were given a separate existence as the Kingdom of Lombardy-Venetia, no longer outlying provinces, but essential to Austria's existence. Austrian foreign policy was centred on the Italian question for more than forty years – even in 1866 Italian considerations lost for Austria the war against Prussia. The Italian 'mission' was to be Austria's justification in the eyes of Europe. Even the troubles which it involved had their advantage: it drew European attention to Austria, as an interesting ailment draws attention to a man otherwise undistinguished. The Italian question moderated Austrian difficulties in more than one diplomatic crisis: England wanted to preserve Italy from France, Russia to preserve it from England – therefore both handled Austria more gently elsewhere. And there were deeper motives for the Austrian persistence in Italy. Lombardy-Venetia was the last link with the idea of universal empire. It made the Austrian Empire a Mediterranean power and a part of western Europe, saved the Habsburgs from being purely German princes.

Most of all, the 'Austrian idea' was at stake in Italy. The Habsburg Empire rested on tradition, on dynastic rights, and on international treaties; the 'rule of law' was essential to it. The national principle which Napoleon had launched in Italy denied the rule of law and challenged the basis of Habsburg existence. With other opponents the Habsburgs could compromise; they might strike a bargain even with German nationalism, as the Greater German projects implied for half a century; only Italian nationalism was implacable. The Italian radicals did not seek concessions from the Habsburgs, did not seek to 'capture' the dynasty, or to secure a special position within the Empire; they did not even seek historic respectability by invoking 'the iron crown of Lombardy'. The Italian movement, small and without material strength, represented an idea totally subversive of the Habsburg Monarchy, and therefore Metternich and his system were in perpetual conflict with it. The greater part of the Austrian army was concentrated in northern Italy; Italy was the main topic of Metternich's diplomacy; and the destinies of the rest of the Empire were determined by Italian events both in 1848 and in 1859. Radetzky's victories caused the failure of the revolutions of 1848; Magenta and Solferino brought down absolutism in 1859. Like the conflict with Serbia a century later, the clash between the Habsburg Empire and Italian nationalism was symbolic, a clash of two worlds.

Metternich's foreign policy rested on the assumption that western affairs were primary: French aggression, he supposed, was the main threat to the Vienna settlement, and the security of Germany and Italy his main problem. The assumption was wrong: France had passed her zenith and would never again seek to dominate Europe. The threat to Austria's existence, which finally destroyed her, came from Russia, not from France, and the deepest Austrian problem was the Eastern Question. In the eighteenth century the Eastern Question had been a simple competition between Russia and Austria in acquiring Turkish territory. This solution was no longer possible. The latest Russian acquisition, in 1812, had brought Russia to the bank of the Danube; any new gain would carry her across it. But the Danube was Austria's only economic link with the outer world in the days before railways and her most important link even after their coming; she could not let control of the mouth of the

Danube pass to Russia without ceasing to be an independent Power. Further partition was ruled out; this fact, only slowly realized by Austrian diplomats and never realized by Russian, dominated the Eastern Question between 1812 and 1914. Turkey, too, had become a European necessity; Austria and Turkey, both dependent on the rule of law rather than on their own strength, were bound together. Gentz, the political writer who supplied Metternich with ideas, wrote in 1815: 'The end of the Turkish monarchy could be survived by the Austrian for but a short time.'

To keep the peace between Russia and Austria and yet to prevent any further Russian advance in the Near East was Metternich's greatest diplomatic achievement, all the greater for his rating it less highly than his struggle against 'the revolution'. Still, the two hung together, and perhaps Metternich knew what he was doing when he exaggerated the peril from France and from radical nationalism. For this was the means by which Russia's attention was distracted from the Danube and from Constantinople. Monarchical solidarity and the conservative cause lured first Alexander I and then Nicholas I from the rewards which, as a result of defeating Napoleon, Russia seemed strong enough to secure. Alexander, the more open to general ideas but also the more liberal, supposed after 1815 that the Turkish Empire was already in his hands. The Italian revolts of 1821 brought him back to his European responsibilities; and the Congress of Verona, called in 1822 to discuss the Greek question, could be fobbed off instead with intervention against the liberals in Spain. Alexander's attention was distracted from the Near East; and this was for Metternich worth the ensuing quarrel with England. The sleight-of-hand had to be performed anew after 1825 with Nicholas I, more stubborn though more conservative than his brother. Nicholas indeed deserted the conservative cause and, in 1829, Russian armies crossed the Danube on the march to Constantinople. This was the greatest crisis of Metternich's diplomacy. He was led into projecting an Anglo-Austrian alliance against Russia and so into contemplating a Balkan war on the pattern of 1878. His system was saved by the revolutions of 1830; in France, in Italy, and, especially, in Poland. These seemed to justify his conservative fears and to make the ambitions of Nicholas the more at fault. Besides, the task of conquering Turkey proved beyond Russia's strength and diplomatic skill: even the Russian statesmen decided that Turkey was a necessity for the time being. In 1833 Nicholas met Metternich at Mnichovo Hradište,[1] coming 'as a pupil to a master'. The conservative alliance between Russia and Austria was restored on a double foundation: resistance to the revolution in Europe, and no tampering with Turkey.

The agreement of Mnichovo Hradište was the guarantee of Austria's security, at once the object for which Metternich had been striving for twenty years and the basis of his future policy. Russia and Austria agreed on a negative policy in the Near East; and the price for this Russian concession was only that Austria should continue to exist. No doubt the Tsar's monarchical convictions were reinforced by the thought of the general opposition which a Russian advance in the Near East would encounter; still, the convictions were real, a victory of Metternich's diplomatic skill. The conservative friendship between Austria and Russia was the foundation of Metternich's policy and of Metternich's Austria. Prussia made a willing third in the conservative alliance; French turbulence was checked; and England could parade liberal principles without endangering the settlement of Europe. Yet Metternich's success concealed Austria's weakness. Austria was preserved to suit the convenience of others, not by her own strength. A Great Power becomes a European necessity only when it is in decline; the truly great do not need to justify their existence.

Habsburg creativeness had had a last explosion with Joseph II. Francis, battered in youth by his uncle Joseph and in manhood by his son-in-law Napoleon, had been hammered into obstinate negation. His only quality was a stubbornness in resisting foreign enemies and domestic change. Mediocre in character and intelligence, he would have made a tolerable Tsar, ruler of a ramshackle empire where most things ran on without direction from above. But Austria was not Russia: it was a centralized state, with a more developed and extensive bureaucracy than any other in Europe. Thanks to Maria Theresa and Joseph II, the Emperor of Austria could really govern: he could make his will felt throughout the Empire. Francis had no will and left the bureaucrats without direction or policy. The defects of this system are not so startling to the modern observer as they were

1. Pronounced: Mnihovo Hradishte. German name: Münchengrätz.

to contemporaries, with their smaller experience of bureaucratic rule. The Austrian bureaucracy was fairly honest, quite hard-working, and generally high-minded; it probably did more good than harm. It was also slow, manufactured mountains of paper, regarded the creation of new bureaucratic posts as its principal object, forgot that it dealt with human beings; these qualities are now familiar to the inhabitant of any civilized state. Still, Austrian bureaucracy was perhaps more than usually lacking in policy; and the defect was the more obvious since most of the Austrian bureaucrats were able and clear-sighted. Hartig, one of Metternich's closest colleagues, expressed the general view: 'Administration has taken the place of government.'

Organs of government existed, but Francis could not be persuaded to use them. He abolished, revived, and again abolished the Council of State, which had conceived the reforms of Maria Theresa; he established instead a Conference of Ministers, but failed to summon it. Some bureaucrats still carried on the reforming work of Joseph II; others regarded resistance to 'Jacobinism' as their sole duty. Some continued the sapping of provincial and aristocratic privileges which had been begun by Maria Theresa; others regarded the provinces and the nobility as the buttresses of the Empire. Some still thought, as Joseph II had done, that the Empire should be based on rationalist philosophy; others wished to call on the police services of the Roman Church. The greatest bureaucratic zeal went into the struggle against 'dangerous thoughts'. The Empire of Francis I was the classic example of the police state. There was an official, lifeless press; correspondence, even the correspondence of the Imperial family, was controlled; a passport was needed to travel from one province to another or from a town into the country. Yet, like the rest of the system, the censorship was a nuisance rather than a tyranny. Though foreign books and papers were forbidden, the educated classes knew what was astir in the world, and, long before 1848, there was a clear radical programme, not on paper, but in men's minds.

The bureaucratic machine was most successful in a sphere where it was most out of touch with contemporary feeling. Austria was the last surviving example of a planned mercantilist economy; in this, more than in anything else, it challenged liberal doctrine. Hungary, with its separate tariff and its separate system of taxation, lay outside this economy and remained almost exclusively agricultural until after 1848; in the rest of the Empire industrial development was still promoted from above. Old Austria, before its death, left two legacies to central Europe, neither of which could have been produced by *laissez faire*: the Austrian railway system and the port of Trieste.[1] Austria was ahead of Prussia in railway development and began, in the Semmering line, the first railway in Europe through mountainous country. Trieste, a project inconceivable before the age of railways, was deliberately built up by Imperial initiative to give central Europe an outlet to the Mediterranean and so to escape dependence on the Danube. Even in Lombardy-Venetia, Austrian rule brought economic benefits. Taxes and military service were lighter than previously under Napoleon or than they were afterwards in national Italy; and, as well, Austrian officials were honest — a unique experience for the Italians. Still, these achievements counted for nothing in the balance of politics. Austrian rule often benefited the peasant masses, but these were dumb; it offended the liberal sentiment of the educated middle classes, and these determined the political atmosphere of the time.

Many of the bureaucrats desired to win wider favour, though without weakening their system; Metternich was the most fertile, though not the most energetic, of these reformers. In 1821 he was given the title of Chancellor, as reward for his successful diplomacy; and this position gave him some claim to act as general adviser to the Emperor. Besides, he was quick, superficially clever, and with great experience of the world; and, though himself incapable of constructing a general system of politics, had in his assistant Gentz the ablest political writer of the age. Francis disliked change when it was proposed by Metternich as much as when it was proposed by anyone else; and none of Metternich's projects was applied. Metternich lacked that driving force to translate ideas into action which is the mark of the great statesman; and Habsburg circumstances were such that, if he had possessed it, he would only have driven himself out of public life. He was a professor in politics; and his schemes, intellectually adroit, guessed at all the devices by which later professors hoped to solve, that is to evade, the 'Austrian problem'. That problem

1. This is the Italian version. Correct name: Trst.

was, in essence, simple: the Habsburg Monarchy and nationalism were incompatible, no real peace was possible between them.

Metternich saw this more clearly than many of his successors, certainly more clearly than the well-meaning theorists of the early twentieth century who attributed the failure of the Habsburg Monarchy to some imagined 'lost opportunity'. Metternich explored too, all the remedies, and despaired of them. He tried repression and associated his name for ever with the horrors of the Spielberg. This repression was half-hearted: it could not have been other without the Monarchy losing the civilized character which it genuinely possessed. Metternich practised also the method of the 'Austrian mission': economic amelioration which would make the masses grateful for Habsburg rule. The mission was genuine, the result disastrous; every advance in prosperity increased the national problem, at first of the Germans, later of the other peoples. An economic programme, to achieve its effect, would have had to appeal to the masses, not to offer middle-class prosperity; the Habsburgs would have had to become Communists, as Metternich was accused of being in Galicia in 1846 and as Bach was accused after 1848. Perhaps this is what Metternich meant by wishing that he had been born a century later. As it was, he was forced back on constitutional concessions, or rather deceptions: these were to appease discontent without lessening the Emperor's power. In the words of his biographer, they offered to a hungry man pictures of still life. Francis Joseph had, later, the same aim; hence Metternich's suggestions anticipated all the constitutional developments of Austria in the second half of the nineteenth century. The composition and very name of the central Parliament; the composition of the provincial Diets; and the relations between Parliament and Diets were all first sketched in Metternich's useless memoranda, which lay disregarded in a drawer of the Emperor's desk. Metternich was the ablest man who ever applied himself to the 'Austrian problem'; the practical effect of his actions was least. Understanding best the Habsburg Monarchy, he despaired of it soonest.

Austria was suffering from a centralized system of government which lacked direction. Metternich's proposals offered two distinct, indeed rival, remedies: to give the centralized system direction and to make it less centralized. Metternich had seen a centralized system working successfully in the Napoleonic Empire, and in all his schemes sought to capture the secret of Napoleon's success. This secret was simple: to have a man of genius as Emperor. This was not a secret which could be commended to Francis nor even admitted by Metternich; and therefore a false solution had to be found in Napoleon's Council of State which supposedly laid down the broad principles of Imperial government. Metternich urged a Reichsrat, or Imperial Council, on Francis for more than twenty years. The Reichsrat, Metternich explained, was not to encroach on the Emperor's power, but to formalize it: it was to be 'the expression of the legislative power of the monarch'. His real intention was revealed when he described it as 'restraining the ruler from outbursts of momentary impulse'. Francis preferred to have no restraint and disregarded the scheme; no man relinquishes power without being forced to do so. Still, the name of Reichsrat had been put into circulation; and it was as the Reichsrat that the Austrian Parliament met until 1918. Metternich had puzzled, too, over the composition of his projected Council. He recognized that it would not improve the bureaucratic system, if it were merely composed of bureaucrats; and he proposed to bring in new blood. Some of this was merely old blood: retired bureaucrats were to criticize their successors. Some was Imperial blood: the archdukes were to contribute their wisdom, a suggestion particularly unwelcome to Francis, who disliked all his relatives except the half-witted. The real innovation in Metternich's scheme was the proposal that the provincial Diets should send delegates to the Reichsrat, which would thus become, though in strictly advisory capacity, an Estates General of the Empire. Here too Metternich's influence survived: the Reichsrat was elected by the Diets from 1861 until 1873 and on a class system of 'estates' until 1907.

Still, the Austrian Parliament would have developed even without these echoes of Metternich's project. His influence had a more special significance in the other part of his proposals – the revival of provincial autonomy. Respect for the provinces was the kernel of the conservatism which Metternich learnt from Gentz, and this romantic anti-Jacobinism revived the decaying provinces to the confusion of later times. Monarchy and conservatism were not historic allies, in the Habsburg Empire least of all. The Habsburg rulers had been the destroyers of historical institutions since the battle of the White

Mountain; and Joseph II had given the existing Empire a Jacobinical pattern. Traditional institutions survived in those countries where monarchy failed, in England and the United Provinces; not in countries where monarchy succeeded. The great storm of the French Revolution forced old enemies together: aristocracies, who had been ceaselessly in revolt against their kings, developed grotesque loyalty; kings grew romantic over the traditions which they had done their best to destroy. In France Charles X lost his throne by attempting to restore to the Church and to the nobility the privileges of which they had been deprived by his ancestors; in Prussia Frederick William IV tried to revive the provincial patriotism which had been the weakness of Prussia; and even in England the epigones of Pitt defended the abuses which Pitt had hoped to reform. Everywhere monarchy was treated as a sentiment rather than as a force; and kings hoped to save themselves from Jacobinism by a 'historical' camouflage. They collected traditions as geologists collect fossils, and tried to make out that these fossils were alive.

The greatest enthusiasm for these historical fossils came not from those who had grown up among them, but from strangers, converts simulating respect for alien traditions. Historical awe for the Austrian provinces and their Diets was the invention of Metternich, a Rhinelander, and of Gentz, a Prussian. The Diets in fact possessed neither power nor significance: they were showy assemblies of the artificial Habsburg nobility, solemnly 'examining' – without power of rejection – the laws and proposed taxes that were put before them. Metternich did not propose to give the Diets any power or to make them more representative: he merely wished the historical charades to be played more widely and more often. The Diets were therefore called more regularly and revived in the provinces where they had lapsed; they remained decorative. Yet this political antiquarianism made a deep mark in Austria's history. The moribund provinces became the old bottles into which the new wine of nationalism was poured. Metternich thought that by reviving the provinces he was preparing a 'historical' federalism which would strengthen the Empire; actually the provinces became battlegrounds of national ambition and a decisive bar against cooperation between the nationalities. Manufactured traditions were the ruin of Austria; and Metternich was the founder of this trade.

His adventurous, speculative spirit, intellectually convinced of conservatism yet without genuine background, led Metternich along another line of experiment, in contradiction with his policy towards revival of the provinces, though springing from it. Delving in provincial antiquities, Metternich made an unexpected discovery: many of the provinces were not originally German in character. Historical revivalism would thus have the further advantage of weakening the danger from German nationalism. Metternich patronized the Czech literary revival, with its strong historical bent. This could be reconciled with the historic unit of Bohemia. More surprisingly, he welcomed the unhistorical movement for a single South Slav language, an intellectual conception which had its origin in Napoleonic Illyria and was in implication as revolutionary as the idea of national Italy. The main attraction of 'Illyrian' was its providing weapons against Hungarian demands, weapons of which the Habsburgs could never have too many. And, no doubt, Metternich, a western German, ignorant of Slav affairs, supposed the Illyrian language could be entangled with Croat history, as the Czech revival overlapped with historic Bohemia. In any case, these literary activities were not meant to have any practical political outcome; they were 'cultural nationalism', a substitute for freedom much favoured by absolute rulers. All the same Metternich, by promoting Illyrianism and subsidizing the poet Gaj[1] who popularized it, was unconsciously acting against the decaying historic provinces and in favour of national reconstruction. Indeed, Metternich, without realizing what he was doing, actually proposed to divide the Empire on national lines. One of his abortive reforms was a proposal to divide the centralized Chancellery into four departments: Austria, Italy, Illyria, and Bohemia-Moravia-Galicia. The first three of these were national groupings, since 'Austria' means the Germanic lands; and even the fourth was meant to be national, since it followed the Illyrian analogy and associated Czechs and Poles as 'Western Slavs'. With the existing Hungarian and Transylvanian Chancelleries, there would thus have been six national units, each using its own language. Except on the one point of Galicia, Metternich in these schemes anticipated all future plans for reconstructing the Habsburg Monarchy; and like the future plans, his,

1. Pronounced: Guy.

too, were futile, never put into operation. The destinies of central Europe, in Metternich's time and since, were made by the conflict of classes and institutions, not by clever ideas.

The difference between paper schemes and real politics, between simulated conservatism and the genuine article, was shown in Hungary, the only province with a living history. Francis regarded Hungary with traditional Habsburg distrust. Much as he had disliked his uncle Joseph II, he disliked Hungarian resistance to Joseph II still more; and he, too, meant to end Hungary's privileges. This had been impossible during the French wars. The Diet had had to be called in order to secure grants of men and money; and in 1809 Francis had had to pose as a Hungarian patriot in order to counter Napoleon's appeal for a Hungarian revolt. In 1811 Francis sought to equate Hungarian and Imperial currency by depreciating Hungarian currency to the Vienna level; the Diet rejected his demand, and he dissolved it in anger, resolving never to call another. The constitutional provision to summon the Diet every three years was again broken; but, unlike Joseph II, Francis did not also abolish the autonomous administration of the county meetings. To govern Hungary with middle-class German officials demanded a reforming enthusiasm abhorrent to Francis. Deadlock followed. The county committees evaded the orders which they received from the Hungarian Chancellery in Vienna and refused to levy taxes or soldiers without an act of the Diet; they impeded the royal commissioners who were sent in sporadically to undertake the collection of money and levying of men, and in 1823 – peak of resistance – the county of Bács[1] actually dismissed all its officials in order to make the work of the commissioners impossible. Metternich had always regretted this conflict with the 'historic' element; and, vain of his diplomatic skill, he assured Francis that he could manage the Hungarian Diet. It was summoned in 1825, a victory of Hungarian separatism over Habsburg centralism.

Metternich supposed that the Hungarian nobility would be content with a Diet on the level of the other artificial Diets, a historical farce with Metternich playing the chief role. The promoters of the Imperial cause in Hungary were the Germans, urban traders originally introduced into Hungary by the Monarchy of deliberate

1. Pronounced: Bātch.

purpose. These might have been won to Metternich's side by a programme of fiscal and franchise reform: ending the nobles' exemption from taxation and increasing the representation of the towns. But this would have been 'liberalism' and, as well, an association with German nationalism: Metternich preferred to patronize historic Hungary, as he patronized historic Bohemia. The great aristocracy in Hungary, too, saw the menace of liberalism and of nationalism; but instead of seeking Habsburg protection, they found safety by putting themselves at the head of the national movement and so won the support both of the lesser nobility and of the German town-dwellers. The pioneer of this change was Széchényi, a great landowner, who had penetrated the secret of Whig success in England; in a gesture which founded modern Hungary, he offered a year's income from his estates to found a Hungarian Academy. The great aristocracy became patriotic; and, at the same time, patriotism became national. The first demands for the 'national' tongue, Magyar, instead of Latin were made in 1825; they were made still more insistently in the Diet of 1830. Hungary had previously been distinguished from the rest of the Empire only by her antiquated privileges; henceforward she appeared as a distinct national state.

The Hungarian Diets of 1825 and 1830 belied Metternich's cleverness and weakened his influence with the Emperor. Metternich was shaken, too, by the increasing confusion of the Austrian finances. He had been engaged to promote peace. Instead, he contemplated war with Russia in 1829 and had to call for mobilization in 1830, during the alarm which followed the July Revolution in France; these were expensive steps. Success in finance was the making of Metternich's rival, Kolovrat, a Bohemian aristocrat who had been called to the central government in 1826. Kolovrat had none of Metternich's highflying conservatism; he was a bureaucrat in the tradition of Joseph II, jealous of the provinces and contemptuous of tradition. His main motive was personal – dislike of the 'foreigner' Metternich and of his expenditure of Austrian strength in European schemes. Playing at opposition to Metternich, he posed sometimes as a liberal, sometimes as a Bohemian patriot. Of great private wealth, he constantly used the weapon of threatened resignation to get his way; and Metternich, chained to office by his need for money, was helpless against him. In 1831 Kolovrat balanced

Austria's accounts, a unique event in the reign of Francis; henceforth he was secure in the Emperor's favour. Francis had no personal liking for Kolovrat and he got on well with Metternich; but Kolovrat enabled him to disregard Metternich's criticism of the system of government. Domestic affairs, and especially the appointment of officials, became the sphere of Kolovrat; Metternich was confined to the direction of foreign policy.

In 1832 Metternich once more tried his political skill in Hungary. He recognized now that the Diet could not be satisfied with decorative functions and hoped to divert it by a programme of practical reform, modernizing the confusion of Hungarian law. The Hungarian nobility, trained for generations in county meetings, understood the realities of politics and resisted this programme of reform from above. The lower house was kept from open defiance of royal authority only by the exertions of the magnates, and no reforms were accomplished. Against this failure, Metternich could set foreign success: the agreement with Russia in 1833. His standing with Francis began once more to rise; and at the beginning of 1835, Francis promised to create the Imperial Council which Metternich had so often advocated. This promise, too, was not fulfilled. Francis died in February 1835. On his deathbed he put his signature to two political testaments to his son, which Metternich had drafted long before. One laid on Ferdinand the duty of freeing the Church from the control which Joseph II had imposed upon it;[1] the other enjoined him not to alter anything in the bases of the state, to consult Archduke Lewis (the youngest brother of Francis) in all internal affairs, and, above all, to rely on Metternich, 'my most loyal servant and friend'. Kolovrat was not mentioned. It seemed that Metternich was at last free of his rival and could carry out the programme of

---

1. This injunction illustrates the confusion in Francis's conservatism. The Church reforms of Joseph II were 'enlightened'; therefore Francis disliked them. On the other hand they existed; therefore he could not bring himself to alter them. Contemporary conservative doctrine taught the alliance of Altar and Throne; Habsburg tradition was to keep the Church under strict control. As a result, Francis spent his reign resolving to undo the work of Joseph II, and did not act on his resolves; just as he promised to carry out the reforms proposed by Metternich, and left the schemes in a drawer. Final gesture of confusion, he ordered his son to execute the tasks which he had lacked the resolution to perform, yet knew that Ferdinand was too feeble-minded even to transact ordinary business.

constructive conservatism which he had long advocated. Returning to the Chancellery, he announced the death of Francis to his physician with the words: 'Ferdinand is Emperor.' The doctor, simpleton or sycophant, replied: 'And you are Richelieu.'

CHAPTER FOUR

PRE-MARCH

WITH the death of Francis began the interregnum of 'pre-March', the strange period of waiting which everyone was conscious would end in the 'deluge'. The new Emperor Ferdinand was an imbecile, epileptic and rickety; his character was expressed in his only sensible remark, 'I'm the Emperor and I want dumplings!'[1] Metternich had foreseen the evils of an Empire without an Emperor, yet he had strengthened Francis's unwillingness to change the succession. There was no attractive alternative: Francis Charles, the younger brother, though not actually half-witted, was almost as ill-fitted to rule, and besides, Metternich argued, to alter the succession would shake the principle of hereditary monarchy. Metternich's real motive was more practical, a true diplomat's trick: with an Emperor incapable of governing, Metternich would become the real ruler of the Habsburg Monarchy and at last carry out his programme of conservative reform. Yet he lacked the self-confidence of Richelieu or Bismarck and, even now, had to shelter behind an archduke; he supposed that he had made himself safe by choosing Archduke Lewis, the most insignificant of Francis's brothers. The House of Habsburg had two able members, Archduke Charles, a great military organizer, and Archduke John, a convinced liberal; but both had sought reform by criticizing Metternich and therefore they remained excluded from power.

The nomination of Lewis was the stroke of a diplomat, not of a statesman; for if Metternich were really to reform the Monarchy he

1. Strictly he demanded noodles. But for a noodle to ask for noodles would be in English an intolerable pun.

needed the support of a strong, resolute man, not of a nonentity. Metternich did not understand the realities of the political situation: he genuinely supposed that the only defect was in the character of the Emperor and allowed neither for the dead-weight of bureaucracy nor for the jealousy of the true-born Austrians against his clever 'foreign' schemes. In fact, the success of Metternich's intrigue made Kolovrat the leader of a patriotic Austrian resistance in court circles. At first Kolovrat ignored the way in which he had been passed over. The conflict broke out in 1836. Metternich had already perceived the danger to Austria's German position in the Zollverein, which had been founded under Prussian leadership in 1834, and he intended to change the Austrian tariff, so as to make Austrian inclusion in the Zollverein possible. As a beginning he proposed in 1836 a reduction in the sugar duties, a blow against the great estates, which had already discovered the profitable crop of sugar-beet. Kolovrat protested and, withdrawing to his Bohemian estate, threatened to resign. This was Metternich's opportunity. He proposed to Lewis the creation of a Reichsrat, or sham-parliament, and a Conference of Ministers, or sham-cabinet, both under the chairmanship of Metternich – constitutional bodies without representative character, a true conservative's dream. Lewis, glad enough to be free of responsibility, agreed.

These were paper schemes, without solid backing from any class or party; made by one court intrigue, they could be undone by another. The defeat of Metternich was initiated, with deserved symbolism, by Archduke John, the liberal Habsburg. During the Napoleonic Wars John had wanted Austria to lead German national resistance, and he had patronized the Tyrolese revolt against the Bavarian rule imposed by Napoleon; these activities had endangered Metternich's diplomacy of delay and had brought the disapproval of Francis. John, who had completed his liberalism by marrying a postmaster's daughter, had been exiled from court for a generation. He knew Metternich only as a reactionary and as a friend of the obscurantist Church, and supposed that Metternich's coup marked the victory of his reactionary policy. He came to court for the first time in twenty-five years and urged on Lewis the disastrous effects of adopting Metternich's plans; coached by the aristocrats who feared for their sugar-beet profits, he praised Kolovrat as a successful financier and as a liberal spirit. Metternich had no force behind him;

his only weapon was argument, but three hours and a half of argument failed to shake John's opposition. Lewis, badgered and bewildered, withdrew his approval; scrapped the Reichsrat; and decided that he himself would preside at the Conference of Ministers, which became again a formality as it had been in the reign of Francis. Kolovrat returned in triumph to his bureaucratic desk.

Metternich's diplomacy, successful in negations, had failed in constructing. Nothing had changed; or rather things changed for the worse. The Imperial power was put in commission: a 'pre-conference' of Lewis, Metternich, and Kolovrat decided on the business which should be passed on to the ministers. This pre-conference did the work of the ministers over again, as Francis had done, and with even greater delay. Kolovrat and Metternich hated each other, and Lewis hated activity of any kind. There was therefore always a majority against action; the stoppage was complete. Not only had administration taken the place of government; even the administration was not working.

Metternich had failed to reform the central government; his attempts to revive provincial sentiment had more results in 'pre-March', though not the results which he intended. Oddly enough, Metternich and Kolovrat bid against each other for provincial favour, especially in Bohemia: Kolovrat, though a 'Josephine' centralist, disliked the Germans and paraded Bohemian patriotism; Metternich, though a German, disliked centralization. Traditional provincial ceremonies were revived. Ferdinand had been crowned King of Hungary in 1830, during his father's lifetime; he was crowned King of Bohemia in 1836 and received the iron crown of Lombardy in 1838 – futile masquerade of Austrian Italy. Metternich wished to invent a new pseudo-historical rigmarole and to have Ferdinand crowned Emperor of Austria in the presence of delegates from the provincial Diets; this was a manufacture of tradition too artificial even for pre-March Austria.

Still provincial sentiment was astir, even in the German provinces. The Diets were the only means through which the general discontent with the decay and lethargy of the central government could be voiced; they became organs of liberalism, just as the French Parlements, assemblies of the privileged legal class, acquired a false air of liberalism before the great Revolution. In 1840 Andrian, a member

of the Tyrol Diet, published *Austria and her Future*, a book which re-
flected and aroused the opinion of the educated administrative class;
in it he argued that the Empire was nothing and the provinces all.
Even the Diet of Lower Austria, which met in Vienna and was
mainly composed of bureaucrats in the central government, asserted
provincial rights as a gesture against the dead hand of the pre-
conference. This was an absurdity. Provincial rights could have a
superficial attraction for the landowning nobility, who hoped thus
to rule their lands without interference from Vienna. It was suicidal
for German bureaucrats to preach provincial rights, for this was to
attack the organization which carried German culture, and so employment for German officials, to the farthest bounds of the Empire.
It was possible to talk of provincial rights in Prague, in Ljubljana,[1]
or even in Innsbruck; it was a contradiction to talk of them in
Vienna. The German bureaucracy certainly needed a wider support;
this support it could find in the German middle class, not in the
dissatisfied provincial nobility, and in fact the provincial enthusiasts
in the Lower Austrian Diet became the leaders of liberal centralism
twenty years later.

The awakening of the Diets counted for more where they could be
associated with national sentiment. In Bohemia the Diet, exclusively
composed of great landowners, played at Czech patriotism. In 1840
it claimed the right to reject, as well as to 'examine', proposals put
before it; in 1846 it demanded the restoration of its rights as they had
existed before the battle of the White Mountain and the Revised
Ordinance of 1627. The heirs of the aliens who had been brought
into Bohemia by Habsburg absolutism were thus demanding the
rights of the Czechs whom they had supplanted; so the English
owners of Irish land posed in the eighteenth century as the defenders
of Irish independence. These Bohemian aristocrats understood nothing of Czech nationalism. Jealous of the privileges of their Hungarian cousins, they supposed that, by a historical claptrap, they,
too, could escape the Imperial official and the Imperial tax-collector.
The national intellectuals were also spurred on by the Hungarian
example. Lacking other allies, they associated with the great nobles
of the Diet. Palacký,[2] the most influential of the Czech revivalists,

1. Pronounced: Lyublyana. German name: Laibach.
2. Pronounced: Palatsky.

had grown up in Hungary and imagined that the Bohemian, like the Hungarian, nobility could acquire a national character; besides, Palacký learnt in Hungary an awe for titles and a lack of confidence, unusual in a Czech. The Imperial government, too, though it rejected the Diet's 'constitutional' demands, was ready to play the Bohemian card against Hungary: the Bohemian play-acting was used to make Hungary ridiculous. More seriously, the government was already thinking of the Slavs as possible allies, against Hungary rather than against the Germans. This had been a strand in Habsburg policy since the days of Leopold II, who had used the threat of a Serb rising to bring Hungary to a compromise, and who founded a Chair of Czech at Prague University in 1791, after listening to a lecture by Dobrovský, first Czech pioneer, on the solidarity of the Slav peoples. Now, in the forties, the Bohemian nobility, with their German names and cosmopolitan upbringing, were encouraged to write pamphlets in favour of Czech culture and even to defend the claims of the Slovaks in Hungary.

The great event of pre-March was the victory of intransigent Magyar nationalism in Hungary, or, to put it in personal terms, the defeat of Széchényi by Kossuth.[1] Széchényi had propagated national spirit, in order to persuade the nobility to renounce their exemption from taxation; the symbol of his policy was the bridge across the Danube at Budapest, built by the taxes levied on noble land. Certainly Széchényi wished Hungary to become a modern national state, but he wished it to become so by natural growth, and without hostility to the Imperial government. He had little sympathy with the crude lesser nobility, buried in their counties; his ideal was Whig, an alliance of great aristocrats and urban middle class against the stupid Tory country squires. Széchényi inspired Metternich's Hungarian programme in the pre-March period – administrative and economic reform for the benefit of the towns. The chairmen of the county meetings were to be made government officials; the towns were to be given equal representation with the counties in the Diet; the Hungarian tariff wall was to go; and Hungary was to be included in the Austrian railway system. These reforms would have ruined the lesser nobility; and they needed a strong assertive middle class to carry them out. Facts were against it. There were 600,000

1. Pronounced: Kawsh-shoot.

nobles, with their families; the total population of the towns – and many of these were inflated villages – was 575,000. The programme of Széchényi and Metternich was clever, but unreal.

All the same it might have made gradual headway, had it not been for the appearance of Kossuth, the saviour of the gentry. Lewis Kossuth had an active political life only for ten years; yet he left a deeper mark on central Europe than any other single man. Though a petty noble by birth, he owned no land; he was a journalist, with nothing to lose by violent courses. He was a 'convert' to Magyarism, of Slovak origin, with a Slovak mother who could never speak Magyar; his Slav background gave him a cocksureness alien to the Hungarian caution and sense of reality. A Slav without land, he wished to be accepted as a Hungarian gentleman; and his great stroke was to insist that Magyar nationalism, not the ownership of land, was the true dividing line. He, too, studied the politics of western Europe; indeed he imported the term 'gentry' as a description of the ignorant lesser nobility – and of himself. Where Széchényi learnt Whiggism, Kossuth learnt nationalism; and he captured the gentry by assuring them that they, and not the towns, were the heart of the Magyar nation. The backward country squire, hating all foreign ways and living in a dream-world of medieval law, learnt to his delight that his worst prejudices were praiseworthy and that he had preserved Hungary. Always in revolt against the leadership of the great nobility, the gentry could now compel the great nobility to follow them. Kossuth's superb gifts of writing and oratory were directed to the one object of arousing national passion; confident in his own abilities, he recognized neither the force of historical tradition nor the obstacle of material facts, regarded every concession by others as a sign of weakness, and outbid his competitors by increasing radical demands. His journalism dominated Hungary of the forties; and in 1847, though not qualified by holding land, he was elected to the Diet. This truly symbolized Magyar evolution from class to nation. Kossuth became the popular hero of Hungary and, in time, of radicalism throughout Europe, though he had nothing in common with the serious, conscientious radicalism of his contemporaries; he was rather the first dictator to rise to power by prostituting idealism to the service of national passion.

Hungary was a Magyar national state; this simple dogma carried

Kossuth to success. Kossuth used this weapon even in the sphere of economics and defeated Metternich's criticism of the Hungarian tariff barrier by advocating 'national economics'; the doctrine which List offered to the German middle classes was used by Kossuth to win the Germans of Hungary away from the Imperial government and over to his side. Still, the Germans were the least of Magyar problems; they were town-dwellers, and, except for the Saxons in Transylvania, without roots in the countryside. But great areas of Hungary were without any Magyar population, other than absentee landowners; and the Magyars were a minority in the state which they claimed as theirs. This was the key to Hungarian politics for the next hundred years: the Magyars pursued a pseudo-liberal policy, but could carry it out only by illiberal methods. They could maintain their national position only by establishing an artificial monopoly of all public life and by preventing the cultural awakening of the other peoples in Hungary. This policy had been, in origin, without conscious purpose; it had sprung from the inevitable abandonment of Latin. Kossuth turned it into a weapon of national dominance. In 1840 Magyar was declared the only language for official use. The Diet of 1844 marked Kossuth's full victory: it abolished Latin entirely, and established Magyar as the exclusive language for the laws, for all government business, and, above all, for public education. The language law of 1844 was a double stroke in favour of the gentry. It protected them from the intrusion of Imperial officials, who would use German; and it barred the way against intellectuals sprung from the peasant people. Hungary could not remain for ever economically isolated from the world; and once this isolation broke down, the gentry estates would decay. Kossuth gave the gentry a new means of existence: a monopoly of state employment.

Kossuth's doctrine did not stop at the 'lesser Hungary'; national Hungary claimed to be the heir of St Stephen, as the French revolutionaries were the heirs of St Louis, and claimed all the 'lands of the Crown of St Stephen'. This demand threatened the autonomy of Transylvania and Croatia. Transylvania was the easier victim. Its Diet, with more than usual feudal complication, gave equal representation to the Magyars, Széklers[1] (a Magyar offshoot), and Saxon

1. Pronounced: Sayk-lers.

Germans; the Rumanians, who were the majority of the population, had no franchise. Only the Saxons tried to maintain an independent position, and even they were overawed by Kossuth's demagogic campaign: class pride barred them from turning to the voteless Rumanian majority. By 1848 Magyar frenzy dominated Transylvania.

Croatia was a more difficult affair. Here was a Diet as old as the Hungarian, with its own rigmarole of feudal law, and with a dim tradition of the Croat Crown. Even the language law of 1844 admitted Croat exceptions and allowed Croat deputies to the Hungarian Diet to continue to use Latin for six years; then they must use Magyar. The Croat nobility had always made common cause with Hungary against Habsburg encroachment, and they were bewildered by the new Magyar policy. Against Magyar, they defended, not Croat, but Latin. They did not grasp the national issue and knew nothing of the 'Illyrian' revival, which was Croatia's only line of safety. The Croat nobles who were opposed to Magyar demands actually met Gaj, the pioneer of Illyrian, for the first time in 1833 at Bratislava, seat of the Hungarian Diet; both they and he were ignorant of each other's existence in Zagreb. Still the Croat language was heard in the Croat Diet before the end of the thirties; and in 1847 the Croat Diet, in its last Latin resolution, made the 'Croatian–Slavonian language' the national tongue. Thus Kossuth's Hungary and national Croatia were in head-on conflict.

The Imperial government had been helpless witnesses of Kossuth's success. Metternich, with his usual acute perception, had early seen the danger of Kossuth's activities and had tried the only weapons known to an eighteenth-century rationalist politician – arguments, imprisonment, and bribes. All had been half-hearted and, like everything else in the Empire, ineffectual. The Imperial government had declared its determination to protect the cultural rights of the nationalities in Hungary; faced with the unruly Diet of 1844, it lost its nerve and acquiesced in the Magyar language law, contenting itself with the grudging recognition of German as the language of correspondence with the Imperial authorities. This was the sole concession to an Empire which had existed for three hundred years and which had freed Hungary from the Turks. Yet Metternich knew that Estates-liberalism, even in Hungary, was a movement of landowners; the Habsburg politicians had not forgotten the weapon of Joseph II, the appeal to the peasantry. Themselves landowners and conservatives, they hesitated to use it. The weapon was forced into their hand by events in Galicia. In 1846 the Polish patriots – landowners and intellectuals – broke into national revolt, a premature fragment of the revolutions of 1848. The Austrian authorities, panic-stricken at the arrival of the revolution which they had long prophesied and with inadequate regular forces, called on the peasants to rise against their masters. The result was a Jacquerie. The Poles, ashamed of this revelation of the narrow class-nature of their nationalism, later claimed that the peasants were 'Ruthenes', Little Russians; in fact both national and peasant risings took place in purely Polish districts, and the peasants were Poles without national consciousness. The Galician revolt was suppressed with scythe and flail; and with it shook the agrarian structure of the Austrian Monarchy. During the revolt the Imperial authorities had had to promise abolition of *Robot*, the labour-rent; after the revolt they dared not again enforce it. Thus, beneath the aristocratic fronde of the Diets and the national fanaticism of Kossuth, the peasant masses were astir; and whoever could present himself as their liberator from the *Robot* would win their favour. The stage was set for 1848.

In the international field, too, the framework of the future was being prepared. Russian backing was the only security in which Metternich had any real faith; like so many others before and since, his scepticism stopped at the Russian frontier. The Austro-Russian agreement of 1833 held without strain during the new crisis in the Near East between 1839 and 1841. Indeed this was for Metternich the perfect Near Eastern crisis, since the disturbing element was France, not Russia; and the storm-centre was on the Rhine, as well as in the Levant. This confirmed his doctrine that a crisis in the Near East would open the door to the revolution in Europe; and certainly had it not been for the implicit revolutionary threat from France, the Tsar Nicholas would not have followed a policy so impeccably conservative, loyally cooperating with Austria and England to maintain the integrity of the Turkish Empire. All the same, the evidence of Turkey's weakness was not lost on Nicholas, while the recollection of Russian weakness in 1829 was fading fast. All through the forties Russia was edging ever more openly away from the policy of the *status quo* in the Near East and harking back to the schemes of partition which had almost caused a breach between Austria and Russia in 1829. Metternich had to look around for new allies. He could not count on support from Prussia, indifferent to Near Eastern matters; and England was kept aloof by a mixture of liberal sentimentalism and well-founded doubt as to Austria's strength. France remained; and Metternich, in his last years, began to hope for alliance with the conservative elements in France to maintain the *status quo* first in Italy, and later in the Near East. The abortive Franco-Austrian cooperation which proved so disastrous to Austria during the Crimean War was, in origin, Metternich's combination. But this alliance could not work without a stable conservative government in France; this was provided later by Napoleon III, it was beyond Guizot's skill in 1847.

Thus doubts of French stability forced Metternich back to dependence, however unsatisfactory, on Russia. For thirty years Russia had promised support against 'the revolution'. In 1847 the revolutionary peril was unmistakable, and Metternich no longer needed to exaggerate it. The revolt in Galicia had been only the first murmur of the Polish storm; Lombardy was in open revolt, with the Austrian soldiers confined to barracks for fear of insults in the streets; Hungary, under Kossuth's leadership, had broken away from the control of Vienna; and even in Vienna liberal clubs met under the eyes of the police. The revolutionary danger was universal; for this very reason Russia would not act against it. Two Tsars, Alexander and Nicholas, had accepted the doctrine that Austria was a European necessity; they meant necessary as an ally, not as a liability. Were Russia to intervene against the revolution, she would bring down on herself the hostility of all four 'master nations', Poles, Magyars, Germans, and Italians; and behind these four lay the shadow of a new Napoleon. For Russia to save Metternich was to invite a second 1812. Instead Russia abandoned her alliance with a *status quo* Power and, as in 1939, contracted out of European affairs, buying time with the sacrifice of principle. This bargain proved profitable for Russia. It was the ruin of Metternich. He, who had never acted alone, was now alone against the revolution; without foreign allies or support at home. His rivals at court, and even the members of the Imperial family, laid all the fault on him and encouraged the belief that with his fall all would be well. Instead Metternich brought down old Austria with him in his fall; the Austrian problem emerged; and a hundred years of European conflict have not restored to central Europe the stability which was destroyed on 13 March 1848.

CHAPTER FIVE

RADICAL OUTBREAK:
THE REVOLUTIONS OF 1848

IN 1848 the doctrine of the Rights of Man broke into the Habsburg Empire. The dynastic idea was challenged, and, once challenged, could never recover the unconscious security of the past. The 'Austrian idea' became an idea like any other, competing for intellectual backing; and the dynasty survived not on its own strength, but by manoeuvring the forces of rival nations and classes. The year 1848 marked the transition from an unconscious way of life to the conscious search for one; and, despite the victory of the Habsburg army, the intellect remained the deciding consideration in Austrian politics.

The revolution took place in an Empire overwhelmingly rural in character, and its only irresistible force was the will of the peasants to be rid of the *Robot* and of other feudal dues. This elemental upheaval had little connexion with the radical programme of the town intellectuals, yet was not altogether divorced from it. The peasants, too, were men, despite Magyar proverbs to the contrary; they sensed, at any rate, the national lines which divided them from their lords, particularly when these were reinforced by religious distinctions, and therefore in the early days of the revolution accepted the radicals as their leaders. Hence the seemingly adult nature of the national programmes, anticipating the political demands of the twentieth century. Curiously enough, the peasant revolt against the *Robot* made their lords revolutionary as well, or at least unreliable supporters of

Imperial authority. The Hungarian lesser gentry, threatened in their very existence, became a truly revolutionary class; this gave the Hungarian revolution, and thereafter Hungarian history, its unique character. Even the great lords were shaken in their loyalty once the implicit bargain between them and the Habsburgs was broken: the Emperor had not kept the peasants down, and the magnates had to seek other allies. Their Fronde became, if not serious, at any rate more persistent: at first obstinately reactionary, later experimenting with nationalism.

Peasant discontent, though universal, was unconscious: it had to be exploded by a spark from the towns. In 1848 a revolution occurs wherever there is a town with more than 100,000 inhabitants. Thus there were two serious revolutions in Austrian Italy, in Milan and Venice. There were only three such Austrian towns north of the Alps – Vienna, Budapest, and Prague. Of these only Vienna, with over 400,000 inhabitants, was a town on the modern scale and with a modern character. It had almost doubled its population since 1815, mainly by immigrants from the countryside; and this raw poverty-stricken mass had an inadequate industrial employment. Contrary to common belief, the revolutions of 1848 were not caused by the Industrial Revolution, but by its absence. Towns increased faster than the industries which provided employment and goods; and, as a consequence, their growth led to a declining standard of urban life. Industrial development, as the later history of the nineteenth century showed, is the remedy for social discontent, not its cause; and Vienna was never so revolutionary as when it was least industrialized. In Vienna a 'proletariat' of landless labourers existed, but not yet the capitalists to employ them; this was the pattern of 1848. The proletariat provided a revolutionary army, more concentrated than the universal peasantry; it, too, lacked its own leaders and found them – sure sign of economic and political backwardness – in the students of the university. Here, too, Vienna was unique: there was no other university of full stature in the Austrian Empire. The university students were the field officers of the revolution; they had not the maturity to provide responsible leadership and certainly did not find it in their professors. Besides, except for the medical students they were all bureaucrats in the making; and sooner or later felt the pull of real life.

Neither Prague nor Budapest had the revolutionary character of Vienna. Both were small in comparison, Prague just over 100,000, Budapest just under it. Neither was yet growing at the modern rate – both had had over 60,000 inhabitants in 1815. The old-established inhabitants therefore still predominated, and these were Germans – two thirds of the population in Budapest, and almost as large a proportion in Prague. On the other hand, the university students in Budapest were mostly Magyars; the Czech students a struggling minority. The Hungarian revolution was captured by the Hungarian gentry, and the students played a subordinate part in it; the Prague revolution remained in the hands of the students and, lacking real force, experienced the first defeat of 1848. In fact Prague, despite its size, stood on the same level as the little towns of a few thousand inhabitants which gave their names to the programmes of 1848. In these an enlightened Czech schoolteacher, an Orthodox Serb priest, or a Lutheran Slovak pastor stamped nations out of the ground. So the Slovak nation appeared in misleading maturity at Liptovský Sv. Mikuláš[1] on 10 May 1848; the Serb nation at Karlovci[2] on 13 May; and the Rumanian nation at Blaj[3] on 15 May.

The Austrian revolutions, like the German, were touched off by the Paris revolution of 24 February; this example fired the intellectuals to emulation. In Budapest a group of radical students, unhampered by the Diet which still met at Bratislava, made themselves masters of the streets with a revolutionary programme before the end of February: they demanded a democratic constitution with universal suffrage, abolition of the *Robot* without compensation, and equal rights for the nationalities. This programme, though it incidentally challenged the dynasty, challenged the gentry more directly – economically by attacking the *Robot*, politically by attacking their franchise; it was indeed this sort of programme which, in other countries, drove the property-owning liberals over to the side of 'order'. Kossuth, alone in Europe, persuaded his followers to outbid the radicals instead of seeking dynastic protection against them; he silenced the democratic clamour against the gentry by raising national clamour against both the Habsburgs and the nationalities. Unless the gentry took the lead, the radical intellectuals would

1. Pronounced: Mikoolash. 2. Pronounced: Karlovsti. 3. Pronounced: Blahzh.

capture the peasantry; with this argument Kossuth carried the 'March laws' through the Diet at Bratislava.

The March laws, which created modern Hungary, had three aspects: constitutional, liberal, and national. Their deepest object was to preserve the gentry; this object was concealed, but the most successful. Personal union was substituted for the Pragmatic Sanction: the Hungarian Chancellery at Vienna was abolished; a Palatine, or Viceroy, at Budapest was to exercise all the prerogatives of the King-Emperor without reference to Vienna; a Hungarian minister was to be attached to the Imperial court as a sort of High Commissioner; there was to be a separate Hungarian army, budget, and foreign policy. In short, Hungary acquired dominion status. Instead of the feudal Diet at Bratislava, there was to be a Parliament at Budapest, elected on a uniform, though restricted suffrage, and with a constitutional ministry responsible to it; the nobility lost their exemption from taxation, and the towns received representation in Parliament. Magyar speech was an essential qualification for election and this Magyar national state was to include all 'the lands of the Crown of St Stephen'. Transylvania and Croatia were both incorporated in the unitary Hungarian state – their Diets and Governors abolished. The two Diets were to meet for the last time, to confirm their abolition – as events turned out with very different consequences. These dazzling achievements of national liberation and mastery cloaked two essential departures from the radical proposals: though *Robot* was abolished, compensation was to be paid by the state; and, through the restricted property qualification, the gentry retained their hold on the county franchise and administration. The nobility who were totally without land retained their rights only during their lifetime; all the greater was the victory of the middle gentry, the core of 'historic Hungary'.

Events in Hungary, as so often, stimulated imitation in Bohemia. On 11 March, the radical intellectuals of Prague, too, formulated their programme; the Bohemian Diet, lacking a Kossuth or a gentry, stood aside and did not attempt to compete. The meeting of 11 March, in the concert hall of a café (the Wenceslaus-Baths), was attended by Czechs and Germans, both politically inexperienced. Its original demands were for the usual liberal 'freedoms' – freedom of discussion, suppression of the censorship, and the like. At the last moment a Czech intellectual, Brauner, added from his sick-bed demands more relevant to Bohemian conditions: abolition of the *Robot*; equality of Czech and German in schools and in the administration; Silesia, Moravia, and Bohemia – the 'lands of the Crown of St Wenceslaus' – to have a common central chancellery and a parliament for general affairs, meeting alternately at Prague and Brno. Thus casually a sick man's impulse launched the national question in Bohemia and its overlap with historic claims. Yet these two topics were to dominate Bohemia's destinies, and so the destinies of all central Europe, from that evening of 11 March 1848, until they received final settlement in 1945 with the expulsion of the Germans from all the historic lands of St Wenceslaus.

Last, since most serious, was the revolution in Vienna. Here was the remaining power of the dynasty; and the revolution was a struggle for power, not a collapse. Political society in Vienna, more cosmopolitan, and more experienced in the problems of government, was too mature to follow a crude radical programme. Revolution in a mature people, as the constitution of both second and third republic in France shows, strives to avoid a revolutionary outcome; and Vienna was halfway to maturity. The Imperial government sought to bargain and to manoeuvre with the revolution, as it had bargained and manoeuvred with so many other enemies. On 12 March, Metternich made his last act of state: he proposed to call delegates from the provincial Diets to an Estates General, an attempt to rally the nobility in defence of their privileges and the Emperor's. This programme was antiquated: the nobility had not the strength to resist the revolution and, besides, seeing the *Robot* crumbling, laid the blame on the Imperial government. Instead of leading the nobility, Metternich was jettisoned to win its support, and that of the prosperous middle class as well. The leader of this 'imperial and royal' revolution was the Archduchess Sophia, wife of the Emperor's brother Francis Charles and mother of Francis Joseph; behind her were all those jealous of Metternich and, especially, a narrow, ultramontane group for whom Metternich was too enlightened and reforming. The Diet of Lower Austria, on which Metternich relied, was to be used as a means of pressure against him.

The Vienna revolution of 13 March began as a court conspiracy; it soon showed the folly of invoking the masses to take part in a court game. Vienna opinion was already stirred by the radical Hungarian agitation at Bratislava, only forty miles away; and on 3 March Kossuth himself came openly to Vienna to incite the crowds. The Diet of Lower Austria met on 13 March and, as planned, demanded Metternich's resignation. Quite against plan, this demand was taken up by the streets; and a true revolution took place. Street-fighting was avoided only by the government's collapse of nerve; had it tried to resist, the central fabric of the Habsburg Monarchy would have been destroyed. Metternich resigned; and old Austria fell with him. In Vienna power passed from the existing authorities to a student committee, itself the only protection against proletarian 'excesses'. A final blow followed to Metternich's system. On 18 March Lombardy, assured by the news of Metternich's fall that revolution was safe, revolted and called on the King of Sardinia for aid; this, in turn, led to a rising in Venice, and the establishment of a Venetian republic. Austria's Italian mission was ended, and her army challenged even at its centre of concentration.

The fall of Metternich exhausted the programme of the 'imperial' revolution. A responsible Prime Minister was created; it was not said to whom he was responsible, and the first Prime Minister was Kolovrat, at last – for a few days – Metternich's supplanter. The new Foreign Minister was merely Ficquelmont, whom Metternich had long designated as his successor. A general meeting of the Estates, 'with increased representation for the middle classes', was promised on 15 March for some undefined future time; and a 'central committee of the Estates' met in Vienna from 10 April to 17 April. These futile shufflings could not still the agitation in Vienna: every day there were new riots and new demands, followed by further jettisoning of individuals and new concessions. Kolovrat vanished from the scene within a few days; Ficquelmont survived until 5 May, when he was driven from office by a student demonstration; then, throughout May, responsibility rested with Pillersdorf, an elderly bureaucrat, who had acquired in pre-March an undeserved reputation as a liberal. Without policy, the Imperial family strove merely to keep afloat; as earlier in the crisis of the Napoleonic Wars or later in the last crisis of 1918, it would recognize anybody or anything, if only it could secure recognition in return. A fresh revolt on 25 April led to the publication of a parliamentary constitution for the whole Empire, hastily drafted on the Belgian model. This did not satisfy the Vienna radicals, who wanted to make their own constitution. On 15 May, after more demonstrations, the constitution of 25 April was withdrawn, and a Constituent Assembly, elected by universal suffrage, promised. Two days later, on 17 May, the Imperial court fled from Vienna to Innsbruck. This breach with the revolution thrust the moderate liberals back into the arms of the radicals, and on 26 May the Vienna revolution reached its greatest success: a Committee of Public Safety was set up, partly to direct the revolution, more to supervise the activities of the remaining ministers.

As to the Germans of Vienna, so to the other master races, the court made indiscriminate concessions. In Italy, Radetzky, the commander-in-chief, was instructed not to resist the revolts or the Sardinian invasion which followed; a minister was sent to establish home rule in Lombardy; and when this failed, the Austrian government proposed, in mid May, to cede Lombardy to Sardinia and to grant autonomy to Venetia. This offer, too, was rejected: the Italians demanded the surrender by Austria of all her Italian territory, and England, to whom Austria appealed, would not mediate unless Venetia, or at least some part of it, was included in the offer of independence. Habsburg Italy could not be saved by negotiations; Radetzky, ignoring the orders from Vienna, prepared to recover it by force, and the Imperial government, ignoring in its turn his disobedience, displayed in the sending of reinforcements an isolated practical activity. Approval of Radetzky did not stop at the government; the Italian claims to Trieste and in Tyrol stirred Austrian patriotism even in the most radical, and revolutionary students left the barricades which they had erected against the Imperial forces in order to serve in the Imperial army in Italy.

There was no such conflict between the radicals of Vienna and Hungary. Archduke Stephen, Palatine of Hungary, surrendered to the revolution without waiting for the King-Emperor's approval and transferred his power to a responsible government, headed by a radical magnate, Batthyány;[1] Kossuth became Minister of Finance and the maker of policy. The court murmured disapproval, but acquiesced; and on 11 April the 'March laws' were constitutionally confirmed by Ferdinand. The revolution in Hungary was thus

1. Pronounced: Báwt-ya-ni.

legalized; the Empire of the Habsburgs was split in two, and Hungary, hitherto a Habsburg province, though a privileged one, became a separate state. The court, no doubt, meant to retract its concessions; and many even of the Hungarian politicians thought that victory had been pressed too hard. Deák,[1] one of the liberal gentry, thus explained his support of Kossuth's programme: 'There is no reasoning with a drunken man, and the Diet is at present drunk.' In the summer of 1848, Deák, in fact, withdrew from political activity, convinced that Kossuth's extremism was leading Hungary to ruin and that a compromise would have to be made with the Habsburgs. Still, when the time for this compromise came, it had to be made on the basis of the March laws, not on the basis of the Pragmatic Sanction. Hungary, not the dynasty, could appear to make concessions. The terms could be modified; after 11 April 1848, the existence of Hungary could not be questioned.

These concessions, though indiscriminate, followed a pattern: except for the twinge of German provincial feeling in regard to Tyrol, court and revolutionaries alike accepted the remodelling of the Habsburg Empire in accordance with the wishes of the 'master nations'. The Vienna liberals assumed that the Empire was a German state which would play the chief part in a new liberal Germany, and they pressed as strongly for elections to the German national assembly in Frankfurt as for a Constituent Assembly in Austria. The abortive constitution of 25 April, which mentioned the provinces only as agencies for bringing local grievances to the attention of the central government, was a crude expression of this German view. It was revealed even more strikingly in the proposals of the 'central committee of the Estates', which sat from 10 April to 17 April preparing for the Estates General which never met. The Committee was attended only by members from the Diets of the German provinces – high bureaucrats of Vienna and enlightened German nobles who had led the agitation against Metternich; in short, the most moderate and experienced Austrian Germans of their day. These Germans recognized the claims of the other historic nations: Hungary, they proposed, should be united to the Empire only by a personal tie; Lombardy-Venetia should be surrendered to an Italian national state; Galicia should be given autonomy, in

1. Pronounced: Dee-āk.

anticipation of the restoration of Poland. The remainder of the Empire was to be a unitary German state, a member of the German Confederation, and held together by German culture. This programme assumed the twilight of the dynasty, and the Germans of the official class retreated from it as the dynasty recovered. Still, they had revealed an outlook common to all the Germans of the Monarchy; were the dynasty to fail, they would go with Greater German nationalism, not into a federation with the non-historic peoples. The only difference between the various groups of Germans was in timing: the radicals turned against the dynasty in 1848, the bulk of the Germans believed that there was still some life in it.

There was exact correspondence between German and Hungarian radicalism. Kossuth overrated Magyar strength; still, even he realized that the Magyars could hold their own only in association with German nationalism, and he offered the Germans patronage and alliance. Two Hungarian emissaries were sent to the German National Assembly at Frankfurt: they asked the Germans not to agree to the creation of Slav states in the Austrian Empire, and gave Germany a Hungarian guarantee of the integrity of the German Confederation against Czech or Slovene separatism. Vain and cocksure, Kossuth and the Hungarian radicals supposed that Greater German nationalism could be directed against the dynasty and the Slav peoples, and would yet stop short at the frontier of Hungary. Kossuth would have liked, too, to support the claims of the Italians and the Poles. Circumstances enforced a diplomatic caution. Even Kossuth had the sense not to provoke a Russian intervention deliberately and therefore, at first, kept quiet about Galicia. Moreover, national Hungary was running straight into war with the Croats and hoped to play off the Imperial government against them. It gave grudging support for the war in Italy, 'on condition that the Austrian government cooperated in subduing Croatia and, at the end of the war, conceded all the justified national demands of the Italians'. The Imperial government, in fact, would be allowed to survive only if it became the instrument of the master nations.

This was not the programme of the dynasty. In the first weeks of collapse, while conceding everything to the Germans and the Magyars, it contradicted this pattern by concessions to the Czechs and the Croats. These had at first no design, sprang from sheer weakness; by the beginning of May, the court realized that it had stumbled on a new diplomatic weapon, and the flight to Innsbruck freed its hands. Innsbruck, centre of provincial, not of national feeling, was neutral ground, from which the court could balance between master and subject peoples. Already, in March, the court had granted Croatia a position totally at variance with the Hungarian 'March laws'. Hungary had declared Croatia abolished; the Croat Diet answered by ending the connexion with Hungary. Both acts were approved by the King-Emperor. Moreover, before placing Croatia under the Budapest government, the Emperor appointed a Croat patriot, Jellačić,[1] as governor of Croatia. It took three months of protests for the Hungarian government to secure his dismissal on 10 June; and even then he enjoyed secret Imperial approval. His restoration to office, never in doubt, was an open declaration of war with Hungary on 4 September. Jellačić was a landowner and an Imperial officer, distinguished from the petty Croat nobility only by ability and force of character. His own inclination was to a conservative programme of dynastic loyalty and Croat 'historic' rights; but in the whirlwind of 1848 he rejected no allies and took up, as well, the national programme of a single South Slav state within the Habsburg Empire. Gaj, spokesman of Illyrianism, and Jellačić, the Habsburg general, worked together, a strange partnership. The gentry of the Croat Diet declared: 'We are one people with the Serbs.' Jellačić spoke of the Serbs as 'our brothers in race and blood'; and he welcomed the Serb national rising, which proclaimed a separate Serb Voivodina at Karlovci on 13 May. In fact, Jellačić behaved exactly as the German upper-middle class behaved: out of Imperial favour, he was a South Slav nationalist; restored to favour, he shook off the national principle and returned to 'historic' claims.

In Transylvania, the court had to acquiesce in Magyar victory, though with regret. The Rumanian national meeting at Blaj on 15 May had demanded that the question of union with Hungary should not be considered until the Rumanians had representation in the Diet. This claim was disregarded, and the Diet, meeting on the old franchise at Cluj,[2] voted itself out of existence on 30 May. A Rumanian deputation to the court at Innsbruck was faced with this

1. Pronounced: Yellachich.   2. Pronounced: Kloozh.

act of union and told it must negotiate with the Hungarian government.

The contradictions of Imperial policy reached their height in Bohemia. The first Bohemian petition of 11 March was made impossibly moderate by the collapse of authority in Vienna; the Prague intellectuals were no longer content with an autonomous Bohemian administration and the individual 'freedoms'. They, too, wanted their March laws. The second meeting at Prague on 29 March was purely Czech: spurred on by the Hungarian example, it demanded the unity and independence of 'the lands of St Wenceslaus' – Bohemia, Moravia, and Silesia – with a single parliament and a government responsible to it. The analogy with Hungary was formally complete; the reality sharply different. The Hungarians were revolutionizing a historic constitution; the handful of Czechs appealed to a tradition which ended in 1620. Hungary had never lost control of its own local administration through the county meetings; Bohemia had been governed by Imperial agents since the time of Maria Theresa and was an integral part of the unitary state which Maria Theresa and Joseph II had created. Even the Czechs acknowledged this; for, while Hungary admitted only personal union, they were ready to accept an Estates General of the Austrian Empire for the transaction of common affairs, once they were granted an independent ministry.

There was an even more decisive difference between Hungary and Bohemia. The Magyars, though a minority of the population of Hungary, included all the propertied and educated inhabitants, with the exception of the German bourgeoisie, and even these were being rapidly 'Magyarized'. The Magyar national state was achieved in the 'lands of St Stephen' at the expense of Croats, Slovaks, Serbs, and Rumanians – the Croats a remote border people, the rest without political voice. In contrast, the Czechs, though a majority in Bohemia, were themselves only reawakening from cultural unconsciousness and were challenging the Germans, a fully conscious historic people; not content with this cultural struggle in Bohemia, the Czechs of Prague were demanding Silesia and Moravia as well. Silesia was predominantly German; and though the Czechs were in a majority in Moravia, they lacked a cultural centre and therefore remained politically under German leadership. Silesia and Moravia could be brought under Prague only by force; and the Czechs possessed none. The Magyars won the frontiers of St Stephen by their own force against Imperial will; the Czechs proposed that Imperial force should be used to gain them the frontiers of St Wenceslaus. This demand was too much for the Imperial government even at its weakest. The Imperial reply of 8 April granted the equality of Czech and German as official languages and promised to set up a responsible government at Prague; it left the union of Bohemia, Silesia, and Moravia, to be considered by the forthcoming Imperial parliament.

The Germans of Bohemia were only a small part of the Czechs' problem. The Czechs lived under the shadow of German nationalism and, alone of all the Slav peoples, had the Germans as only rivals. National Germany, too, claimed a legacy of history – the legacy of the Holy Roman Empire, in which Bohemia had been included; and all German nationalists assumed that Bohemia would be part of the new German national state. Only two Austrians attended the pre-parliament at Frankfurt; and the committee of fifty, which this created to prepare for a German National Assembly, wished to increase its Austrian membership. Of the six representative Austrians invited by the committee to join it, one was Palacký; and his letter of refusal of 11 April first announced the claims of the Czech nation to existence. Much of his letter was taken up with historical wrangling, as barren as the historical arguments of the Germans. Its essence, however, lay in the sentence: 'I am a Bohemian of Slav race.' Therefore he could not participate in the affairs of national Germany. Still, he did not demand an independent Czech national state and he repudiated the idea of a Russian universal monarchy, already dreamt of by some Pan-Slav mystics. Palacký found a third solution, neither Russian nor German: the Austrian Empire should be transformed into a federation of peoples, where all nationalities should live freely under the protection of the Habsburg power. This was the programme of Austroslavism; and from the moment that it was launched by Palacký, it became the decisive question in Habsburg, and even in European, destinies. To provide a central Europe neither Russian nor German was the last, and least genuine, of the Habsburg 'missions'.

Austroslavism was a programme of timidity made by a man who

was wholeheartedly the servant of his people and yet lacked faith in their strength: the dynasty was asked to give the Slav peoples the freedom that they were too weak to take for themselves. So anxious was Palacký not to provoke German indignation that on 8 May he refused to become Imperial Minister of Education; his appointment 'would be interpreted as a declaration in favour of the Slavs'. Yet the dynasty would enter a Slav alliance only if the Slavs had force to offer: the Emperor was not a well-meaning professor who could devote himself to an idealistic 'mission'. And once the Slavs had force to offer, they would not support the dynasty, but demand freedom for themselves. This was the flaw of Austroslavism: the dynasty would accept an alliance only when the Slav peoples no longer needed it.

In 1848, from first to last, the dynasty never took seriously the idea of working with the subject peoples; it welcomed them as an element to be played off against Magyars and Germans, without caring for their ultimate destiny. As the breach between the court and Vienna widened, court favour towards the Czechs increased. On 29 May, Leo Thun, the Governor of Bohemia, answered the establishment of the Committee of Public Safety in Vienna by refusing to take orders from the Vienna government and by setting up a sort of provisional government of Czechs and German moderates in Prague. The government in Vienna condemned this separatism; the court at Innsbruck made welcome a Bohemian delegation and agreed that the Bohemian Diet should meet before the opening of the Imperial constituent assembly. If this Diet had met, Bohemia would have refused to send members to the Vienna parliament and would have negotiated with it as an equal body on the Hungarian analogy.

Bohemian hopes were wrecked, oddly enough, by the outcome of what had been in origin a work of Austroslavism, the Slav Congress at Prague. Palacký and his friends had wished to organize a counterblast to the German national assembly at Frankfurt; besides they needed to consult on practical steps to save the Austrian Empire. The only other Austrian Slavs directly menaced by the Germans were the Slovenes, whose national feeling had hardly begun to stir. The Slovene members of the Carinthian and Styrian Diets, for instance, voted in 1848 with the Germans in favour of the two provinces as historic units and against a programme of national reconstruction, although this would have liberated them from the Germans and joined them to the Slovenes of Carniola. The Congress needed a wider basis. Besides, though the Czechs wished to avoid conflict with the Magyars, they could not repudiate the Slovaks, whose few cultural leaders had found refuge at Prague; and once the Slovaks were admitted, the Croats followed. The Poles of Galicia, too, had to come in as Austrian Slavs, though their outlook was that of a master-race; in fact, the Galician Poles attended the Congress primarily to see that it took no resolution in favour of the Little Russians, the Polish subjects in eastern Galicia. The Poles who were menaced by the Germans lay outside the Austrian Empire, in Posnania; to invite them would contradict the Austroslav principle from which Palacký set out. Finally it was decided, as a compromise, to limit the Congress to Austrian Slavs, but to welcome other Slavs as guests. Of these guests the strangest was Bakunin, sole and self-nominated representative of the greatest branch of the Slav race. The compromise was, in any case, evaded by the Poles: the Congress divided into national amalgams, Polish–Little Russian, Czechoslovak, and South Slav, each free to determine its own membership, and the Polish group at once admitted the Prussian Poles.

The Slav Congress, which met on 2 June, was thus a mixture of Austroslavism and Slav nationalisms, spread over with a vague Slav solidarity. It produced two contradictory programmes: a revolutionary manifesto to the peoples of Europe, and a conservative address to the Habsburg Emperor. The manifesto, mainly the work of the Poles, concentrated its attack on the partitions of Poland and asked the Germans, Magyars, and Turks to treat their Slav subjects better – the Poles were loyal to their fellow master-nations. The address to the Emperor set out in detail the demands of the Slav provinces and peoples in the Habsburg Monarchy and, especially, protested against any union with Germany; this national equality under the Habsburgs was to include even the Little Russians of Hungary, a demand unwelcome to the Poles. The Congress intended to plan further cooperation between the Austrian Slavs; this plan was ended by the riots in Prague on 12 June.

The Whitsuntide riots were the turning-point of the revolutions of 1848, and so of the fortunes of central Europe. Yet they had no purpose and little significance. The Congress, perhaps, increased the political excitement in Prague; and the Prague radicals, both Czech and German, were, no doubt, anxious to imitate the success of the revolution in Vienna. Still, the radical demonstrations on 12 June were no different from half a dozen earlier demonstrations. The difference lay in the reaction of Windischgrätz,[1] the Imperial general in Prague, who had been denied his chance as dictator in Vienna in March, and now accepted the challenge of the Prague streets. The street-fighting in Prague was the first serious battle against the revolution; and in this battle the revolution was defeated. The defeated party were radicals, not exclusively Czechs, but all those who supposed that the old order had collapsed and that Europe could be remodelled on radical lines. The victory of Windischgrätz certainly defeated the programme of Bohemian autonomy: elections to the Diet were postponed, and the delegation to Innsbruck learnt, on its return, that its journey had been fruitless. Yet the Czech moderates, and they were the majority, welcomed the defeat of the Prague radicals. They continued to set their hopes in Austroslavism, all the more when Bohemian radicalism had shown its feebleness; now, however, they had to seek the success of their programme at the central parliament in Vienna, instead of at Prague. Thus, the Czech leaders were eager to attend the Constituent Assembly which they had intended to boycott and, in their fear of Frankfurt and German nationalism, supported the centralized Austrian state which had been in large part a German creation.

The victory of Windischgrätz, tolerated by the Czechs, was welcomed even more openly by the Germans. The Frankfurt Assembly was already irritated by the refusal of most Bohemian constituencies to elect deputies to Frankfurt; the Prague riots aroused alarm of a Czech 'blood-bath', and the Assembly considered sending Prussian or Saxon troops to assist in putting down the revolt. Giskra, later mayor of Brno and a liberal minister in Austria, paid tribute to Windischgrätz and added: 'As a Moravian German I demand that the Czech movement shall be completely suppressed and annihilated for the future.' Thus the Germans, too, supposed that the dynastic forces were doing their work and equally welcomed the meeting of the Constituent Assembly. In fact, the Constituent Assembly was regretted only by Windischgrätz, the victor of Prague; and there

1. Pronounced: Vin-dish-greats.

was from the outset an underlying falsity in a parliament which met under his protection. The radicals had been defeated at Prague; the dynasty was not strong enough to repeat the victory of Prague elsewhere. Hence the only liberal episode in Habsburg history, which lasted from July 1848 until March 1849.

CHAPTER SIX

LIBERAL EPISODE: THE CONSTITUENT ASSEMBLY, JULY 1848–MARCH 1849

THE Constituent Assembly which met in Vienna in July 1848 was the only full Reichstag, or imperial parliament, in the history of the Austrian Empire. It represented a double compromise: the liberals accepted the Empire and the dynasty; the dynasty accepted liberalism. The compromise sprang from weakness and fear, not from conviction. The Czechs feared German nationalism; the moderate Germans feared the disruption of the Empire by German radicalism or its capture by the Slavs; all middle-class liberals feared the vague social aspirations of the 'proletariat'. The dynasty, on its side, needed backing against Hungary and for the war in Italy.

The meeting of the Constituent Assembly enabled the dynasty to repair the breach between Vienna and itself. Archduke John came to Vienna to open the Assembly; and when he was elected Regent of Germany in August, the Emperor and the Imperial family returned to Vienna in his stead. A government was appointed more resolute, though still liberal. The Foreign Minister, Wessenberg, its real head, though of the Metternich school – he had been Metternich's colleague at the Congress of Vienna in 1814 – was a man of liberal mind and had always advocated a 'western' orientation in Austrian foreign policy: he had wished to rely on England instead of on Russia and had been dismissed from the foreign service in 1834 for working too closely with England in the Belgian question. Now he hoped to win English support for a liberal settlement of the Italian question; then the Habsburgs, freed from dependence on Russia, could follow a liberal policy also in Hungary and Galicia. The strong man in the new ministry was Alexander Bach, ablest of the Vienna radicals in pre-March. Bach had been driven into radicalism by his impatience with pre-March inefficiency; his real desire was for a united Austrian Empire run on modern principles. Though a German and a radical, he was an Austrian patriot, not a German nationalist. Believing in uniformity and in power, he stood comparison with the Jacobin dictators who created modern France; except that, lacking the support of a resolute middle class, this Austrian Jacobin had to base himself on the Habsburg dynasty. Besides, the Habsburg army did not follow the pattern of the French armies of the *ancien régime*. Instead of disintegrating, Radetzky's army in Italy defeated the Italians at Custoza[1] on 25 July and recovered all Lombardy early in August. Still, the Austrian government was vaguely bound to a conference on Italian affairs which it had promised to England and France; and so long as there was a prospect of self-government in Lombardy-Venetia this, too, was an element in the liberal episode.

The Constituent Assembly represented only the lesser Austria. Lombardy was under martial law; Venetia still a republic, as a concession to the 'sister republic' France; Hungary had acquired independence by the March laws. As elsewhere in Europe, universal suffrage put the radicals in a minority. Vienna and the German towns returned radicals; these were seconded only by the 'Poles in frock-coats', that is, of the upper and middle class. Rural German districts, distrusting the town intellectuals, returned peasants. The Czech peasants, however, trusted their intellectuals, and the Little Russians trusted their Uniat priests; as paradoxical result, the most solidly peasant areas did not return peasant deputies. Thus Upper Austria returned 13 peasants out of 16 deputies; Bohemia and Moravia 16 peasants out of 138 deputies. One of the few Germans to straddle between town and country was Hans Kudlich, a radical student, but the son of a peasant; and Kudlich raised the agrarian question which dominated the Constituent Assembly until the Act of Emancipation was passed on 7 September.

This act, the greatest achievement of the revolutions of 1848,

1. Pronounced: Custotza.

completed the work of Joseph II. It abolished, without compensation, the hereditary rights of the landlords in jurisdiction and administration; it abolished *Robot*, the labour service, partly at the expense of the state, partly at the expense of the tenant;[1] and it gave the peasant tenant of 'dominical' land security of tenure. The act of 7 September determined the character of the Habsburg Monarchy for the rest of its existence. Once *Robot* was ended, the landowners had no interest in keeping a large peasant population tied to the soil: the smaller peasants sold their holdings to wealthier peasants and moved into the towns. A labour force was placed at the service of developing capitalism; at the same time, these peasant migrants swamped the established German town dwellers and captured the towns for the nationality of the surrounding countryside. Moreover, with emancipation, the class struggle between aristocracy and peasantry ceased; and the peasants turned, in national consciousness, against each other. Kudlich himself illustrated this; for, after his one historic moment, he became an ordinary German radical and in 1872, returning from exile in the United States, preached German national union in Silesia against Czech encroachments. In the words of Eisenmann: 'The struggle of nationalities became a war of the masses, instead of a duel between privileged persons.' Even the class struggle reinforced the national conflicts: the employers of labour in the towns were mostly Germans, the workers Czech, Slovene, or Polish immigrants.

The poor peasant was driven into the towns; the rich peasant gained – bought the land of the poor peasant and won security of tenure even on the lord's land. As a result peasant parties became ever more conservative in their social outlook; on the other hand, since these wealthy peasants could pay for the education of their children, the peasant parties became increasingly nationalistic. The great aristocrats thought themselves ruined: they denounced the Act of Emancipation and the Imperial government which carried it

1. In the similar Hungarian law passed in March, all compensation was paid by the state. In Galicia, the governor, to keep the Polish peasants loyal and divided from their lords, had already promised abolition of *Robot* at the expense of the state. When, later, Galicia became autonomous, the Polish landlords who controlled it objected to paying compensation to themselves; and the Empire had to pay the bill. Thus, the German and Czech peasants paid for the emancipation of the peasants in Galicia.

out as 'Communistic'. The opposite proved true. The great estates, freed from the inefficient *Robot*, could be conducted more economically. The steam ploughs of Hungary, striking feature of the late nineteenth century, were the result of peasant emancipation. Moreover, with the lump sum received in compensation, the magnates could enter capitalistic enterprise. According to Denis, the Bohemian magnates in 1880 owned 500 out of 800 breweries, 80 out of 120 sugar factories, and 300 out of 400 distilleries. The Hungarian magnates owned as well saw-mills, paper-factories, coal-mines, hotels, and spas, all originating from the compensation for *Robot*. In the twentieth century great estates predominated in the Habsburg Monarchy more than ever before; this was the result of the emancipation of 1848. The small gentry were truly ruined: they could not run their estates without *Robot*, and the compensation was too little to set them up as capitalists. This class was, however, unimportant outside Hungary; the ruin of the Hungarian gentry had profound political consequences.

The Imperial government also gained from emancipation. Abolition of the hereditary jurisdictions left the Imperial officials in sole control of local administration and thus completed the dependence on Vienna. Moreover the emancipation was carried out by Imperial officials and was accepted by the peasants as the gift of the Emperor, not as the act of the Constituent Assembly. Until September 1848, the peasantry were in an aggressive revolutionary spirit throughout the Empire; once sure of emancipation, they lost interest in politics and watched with indifference the victory of absolutism. Bach had expected this result from the start, and he had acquiesced in Kudlich's proposals, only insisting that the cost of emancipation should be shared between the tenant and the state. Still, the Imperial ministers were not so much taking a long view as living from hand to mouth. They were distracted men, trying to run a creaking Imperial machine in the midst of a revolution; and finance was their most practical preoccupation.

Finance also opened the way for the breach with Hungary and the decisive consequences that followed. By the 'March laws' Kossuth had achieved his full programme: Hungary had only personal union with the rest of the Empire. This destruction of Imperial unity was not merely shocking to every Austrian, even to a radical like Bach;

the entire burden of the national debt at once fell on the Austria that remained. The moderate Magyars, such as Deák, who recognized that Hungary needed an association with the other Habsburg lands, were willing to compromise on this critical question of finance; they were defeated by Kossuth's chauvinist eloquence and withdrew from public affairs. Kossuth thus seemed isloated, in dispute both with the liberal Austrian government and with the liberals in Hungary. The court circle, grouped round the Archduchess Sophia, was emboldened to proceed against him and, on 4 September, without informing the Austrian ministers, restored Jellačić as Governor of Croatia. On 11 September Jellačić crossed the Drave and began the invasion of Hungary. Against this union of dynasty and Croats Kossuth tried to play off the union of Magyars and Germans, and appealed to the Vienna parliament to mediate between Hungary and the dynasty. Like all his radical contemporaries, he did not understand the nature of Austria and supposed that the Constituent Assembly at Vienna was a German parliament of nationalist outlook.

The question whether to receive the Hungarian delegation was debated in the Assembly from 17 September to 19 September; this was the first public discussion in history of the 'Austrian question', and it stated the themes of future development. The radical Germans, who wanted the hereditary lands to become an integral part of national Germany, accepted Kossuth's programme of personal union; and so did the 'Poles in frockcoats', aspiring to a similar independence in Galicia. The more moderate Germans wished to belong to Germany, but wished also to preserve the Imperial unity which made it grander to be an Austrian than to be a Bavarian or a Saxon: they wished, that is, to have in Austria all the advantages of being German and yet to have in Germany all the advantages of being Austrian. They accepted Bach's argument that the constitutional privileges of Hungary had been tolerable only so long as the rest of the Empire was under absolute rule; now Hungary must accept the Imperial parliament along with the other common institutions of finance, army, and foreign policy. The Czechs did not favour this centralist position: their ambition was federalist and they hoped for a parliament at Prague ranking equally with the parliament at Budapest. Still they could not support Kossuth; for this implied accepting the Magyar national state and so abandoning their fellow Slavs, the Serbs and the Croats, and above all their brothers, the Slovaks. Besides, though they disliked centralist rule from Vienna, they feared the German nationalism of Frankfurt still more; and so maintained a strong Empire, though hoping to temper its force against themselves. The majority against Hungary was swelled by the Slovenes, also anxious to avoid German nationalist domination, and by the Little Russians, who were voting implicitly against a Polish domination of Galicia. Austroslavism and Great Austrianism combined against the claims of the master-nations.

The Habsburg Empire had won a parliamentary majority; it had still to win a war. Imperial troops were sent to the assistance of Jellačić; and this provoked in Vienna the rising of 6 October, the most radical revolution in the year of revolutions. The October revolution aimed at destroying the Austrian Empire and substituting a national Germany and a national Hungary; its object, in fact, was to reduce Vienna to a provincial town. This was not a programme to appeal to the middle-class liberals, who were conscious of the benefits of being citizens of a great Imperial capital; and they were the more repelled by the support which the Vienna masses gave to this programme as an outlet for their social discontent. The October revolution was doomed unless it received support from national Germany or national Hungary, the two causes for which it was fighting. National Germany had no force to offer. The Frankfurt parliament, itself terrified of radicalism, was already sheltering under the protection of Prussian troops; its only support was the resolution of 27 October that German and non-German lands could be united only by personal union, a programme that was at the very moment being shot to pieces with the Vienna barricades. National Hungary used the breathing-space to set up a Committee of Public Safety under Kossuth's leadership. A Hungarian army advanced gingerly towards Vienna and then timidly withdrew.

On the outbreak of the revolution the court fled to Olomouc[1] in Moravia; it was followed by the majority of members of the Constituent Assembly. In Vienna there remained a rump of German radicals and Poles in frock-coats. Even now the dynasty kept in touch with both sides, an insurance against a radical victory. Messenhauer,

---

1. Pronounced: Ol-o-muts. German name: Olmütz.

who directed the defence of Vienna, was confirmed in his position by the ministry; and the official *Vienna Gazette* published side by side the proclamations of Messenhauer and of Windischgrätz, the Imperial commander-in-chief. Kraus, the Minister of Finance, remained with the rump in Vienna and actually paid from Imperial funds two emissaries who were sent to Kossuth with a request for help. These precautions were unnecessary; Vienna remained isolated. Kudlich, who had introduced the Act of Emancipation, tried to exploit his reputation by raising the peasants of Lower and Upper Austria. Without success. The armies of Windischgrätz and Jellačić reduced Vienna and defeated the radical programme in Europe. The first act of the government, after its victory, was to reject the Frankfurt resolution of 27 October and to appoint Windischgrätz as commander against Hungary. At the same time it abandoned any serious intention of winning English support by concessions in Italy and prepared there for a renewal of the war. Thus national Germany, national Hungary, and national Italy were all three ruined by the defeat of the October revolution.

A forceful Imperial policy demanded forceful ministers and a forceful Emperor. On 21 November the elderly Wessenberg gave place to Felix Schwarzenberg,[1] brother-in-law of Windischgrätz and adviser of Radetzky. On 2 December Ferdinand abdicated in favour of his nephew Francis Joseph. Ferdinand vanished from the stage of history, reappearing only in 1866 to comment on the Prussian occupation of Prague: 'Even I could have done as well as this.' Schwarzenberg, the new Prime Minister, was a man of violence: violent in his personal life, violent in his policy. He held the belief, not uncommon among men of dry intellectual power, that force was everything and ideas nothing. He had served with Radetzky in Italy and, taking the war of 1848 as a serious affair, had a faith in the Austrian army, unusual for an Austrian statesman; one of the first victims, in fact, of the great Italian illusion, which contributed a note of farcical light relief to a hundred years of European politics. Schwarzenberg, though a member of one of Austria's greatest families, had no respect for tradition or for the aristocracy, and condemned a scheme for a hereditary House of Lords with the remark that there were not twelve noblemen in Austria fit to sit in it. Though himself without

1. Pronounced: Shvartzenberg.

ideas, he was quick to pick them up from others, at least in outline, and chose able colleagues regardless of their antecedents. Count Stadion, who became Minister of the Interior, was an aristocrat, loyal but resolutely liberal, who had tried out his liberal policy with success as governor of Galicia; Bach, the Minister of Justice, was an untitled lawyer who had stood on the radical side of the barricades as late as 26 May; Baron Bruck, the Minister of Commerce, was a German trader from the Rhineland, who had founded the greatness of Trieste and conceived the vision of Mitteleuropa, an economic union of all central Europe under Austrian-German leadership. These men, differing widely in origin and outlook, were united in putting power first. Schwarzenberg added the same note in foreign policy. Metternich had depended on Russia, Wessenberg on England; both these were associations of principle – conservative with Russia, liberal with England. Schwarzenberg intended to escape these moral alternatives by cooperating with Louis Napoleon, the adventurer similarly unprincipled who had just become President of the French Republic. The alliance of Habsburg and Bonaparte did not startle him. His government was a government of Jacobins; and their object was to transform Francis Joseph, heir of the Habsburgs, into a Napoleon, child of the revolution.

The Emperor who was cast for this strange role was a boy of eighteen, conscientious and ignorant of the world. Like Schwarzenberg he distrusted ideas: Schwarzenberg was too clever to have principles, Francis Joseph too blinkered to understand them. The dynastic idea dominated him to the exclusion of all other. As Archduke he had been plain Francis; the additional name evoked Joseph II, the 'People's Emperor'. Francis Joseph had nothing of Joseph II except the name; for him the dynastic idea meant the maintenance of dynastic power and nothing more. Like Francis I, he would have made a dutiful bureaucrat: in the German phrase he had *Sitzfleisch*, a tough behind. It was a perpetual puzzle to him that he could not make his Empire work merely by sitting at his desk and signing documents for eight hours a day. Still, he had a certain flexibility of policy, though not of mind. His whole life was dominated by the experiences of 1848, when the Empire seemed tumbling in ruins; this memory gave his actions an urgency and impatience foreign to his nature. Schwarzenberg was dominated by the political theory

that the basis of government was force, not ideas; Francis Joseph
was as sceptical of this theory as of any other, and in this scepticism
carried through, or tolerated, changes of system which more than
once altered the ideological basis of his Empire. About two things
he never wavered: he was determined to maintain the strength of his
army and to assert the prestige of the Monarchy abroad. Long and
bitter experience taught him that these aims could be secured only by
concessions in domestic affairs; experience never taught him that
these were wrong aims or that the peoples must be won for the
Empire, instead of being cajoled into enduring it. He inherited from
his ancestors, and especially from Joseph II, a great capital of goodwill; he expended this capital in maintaining dynastic power and so
left the Empire without a reason for existence in the minds of its
peoples. Francis Joseph rejected ideas; yet dynastic right was itself an
idea, and an archaic one at that. The revolutions of 1848 had broken
the natural 'unconscious' course of Austrian history; and Francis
Joseph, 'the last monarch of the old order', was a revived institution,
as 'made' as any other. Lacking faith in his peoples, he felt no responsibility towards them and made concessions from fear, not from
conviction. As a result, he became the principal artificer of the collapse of the Habsburg Empire.

The reign of Francis Joseph opened, strangely enough, with a
Constituent Assembly accidentally surviving; and until Hungary
was subdued it was worth keeping the support of the moderate
Czechs and Germans who were untainted by the June riots in
Prague or the October revolution in Vienna. The Constituent
Assembly, deprived of any say in government, was removed to
Kroměříž[1] in Moravia to continue its constitutional labours. Both
Czechs and Germans had shed their radical wings: the Czechs were
Austroslavs, the Germans loyal Austrians. The question whether the
Empire should survive had been answered by events; the Consti-
tuent Assembly had only to consider how the Emperor could be
reconciled with individual and national liberty. Moreover, after the
events of October, the dynasty had asserted its independent force; it
could not be 'captured' by either Czechs or Germans, and both
sides therefore were driven into agreement and compromise. There
was still a profound difference of outlook: the Germans wished to

1. Pronounced: Krom-ersh-izh.

maintain the centralized state, created by Maria Theresa and Joseph II; the Czechs wished to recover the provincial rights of Bohemia. On the other hand, the Germans were ready to impose limitations on the central Power now that it had been so obviously recovered by the dynasty; and the Czechs were ready to sustain the central Power which protected them from the German national state of Frankfurt. The Czechs dropped their federalist ideas and acquiesced in the unitary state; the Germans acquiesced in a large measure of provincial autonomy.

Palacký, with rare intellectual honesty, would have liked to devise new provinces, each with a single national character. This was rejected by the other Czechs who would not give up 'historic' Bohemia, despite its German minority; and the Germans, though claiming their national rights in Bohemia, would not surrender the Slovene districts of Carinthia and Styria. Besides, the Germans, anxious for the centralized state, wished to prevent any identification of provinces and nations. Thus even at Kroměříž both Czechs, for the sake of Bohemia, and Germans, for the sake of the Empire, opposed the transformation of Austria into an association of national communities; and they continued to agree on this opposition, though on nothing else, until the downfall of the Habsburg Empire. The constitution of Kroměříž made one concession to national minorities within the provinces: it devised subordinate 'circles', with local Diets and local autonomy. For the men of Kroměříž supposed that national ambitions would be satisfied with schools and local government in the national tongue; they had no vision of a nation wishing to decide its own destinies. Like the German Constituent Assembly at Frankfurt, they had no understanding of power, the central problem of politics; they assumed that power would remain with the dynasty, as indeed it had. Thus the Kroměříž constitution made no attempt to solve the problem of how different nations could combine to establish a common government; it was concerned only with the problem of how different nations could live at peace under the government of the Habsburgs. In essence, it confessed that without the dynasty the Empire could not exist and so condemned, in anticipation, all the later schemes to substitute for the Habsburg Monarchy a 'Danubian Confederation'. The peoples would not work together except under Habsburg orders.

Still, even to agree to live at peace under the Habsburgs was an achievement, never repeated in the history of the Habsburg Monarchy. This unique fact led later observers to overrate the significance of the Kroměříž constitution. Czechs and Germans had cooperated to find a solution; and the solution depended for its success on their cooperation's continuing. It was not likely to do so once the temptation to 'capture the dynasty' was renewed. Mayer, who drafted the Kroměříž constitution, became within a year or two Bach's most trusted agent in forcing the Empire into a rigid mould of centralized absolutism based on German supremacy; Lasser, Mayer's chief supporter at Kroměříž, worked with Schmerling to maintain this German centralization with the thin cover of a sham, German, parliament and was the principal author of the system of 'electoral geometry', by which the Germans secured an artificial majority in the Austrian parliament. The Czechs had to wait longer for their chance of 'capturing' the dynasty. Instead they sought the alliance of the 'feudal' nobility of Bohemia against their German colleagues of Kroměříž; and in 1879 Rieger, Palacký's son-in-law and principal Czech spokesman at Kroměříž, entered into partnership with the Imperial government to end the hegemony of the German liberals. Besides, even the temporary agreement at Kroměříž was due to the defeat of the Czech and German radicals by the Habsburg army; sooner or later this radicalism was bound to revive. The Kroměříž constitution, far from representing an agreement of the Austrian peoples, was made by deputies remote from the peoples, cautious educated men, who hoped to secure their bureaucratic or academic future and supposed that this would satisfy the national aspirations of the masses.

Yet while the Assembly carried on its constitutional discussions at Kroměříž, the real force of nationalism was being shown in Hungary, where Serbs, Slovaks, and Rumanians on the one side, Magyars on the other were slaughtering each other in the most fierce racial war of modern times. The Kroměříž parliament agreed on the need for a strong Austrian Empire; this could not be attained without a settlement of the Hungarian question and yet Kroměříž averted its eyes from Hungary. Only Palacký proposed, half-heartedly, a partition of Hungary into national states. The Czechs shrank from a proposal which implied also the partition of 'historic' Bohemia;

yet would not endorse Magyar claims, which implied abandoning the Slovaks. The Germans would not go against a fellow master-nation on behalf of subject Slav peoples, yet would not endorse claims which threatened Greater Austria. Both Czechs and Germans had to pretend that the Hungarian problem did not exist and thus prepared the way for a dynastic settlement with Hungary over their heads. The silence of Kroměříž in regard to Hungary made the Assembly useless, too, to the Schwarzenberg government, which wanted assistance against Hungary, not a model liberal constitution. Schwarzenberg and his colleagues were now ready to act against Hungary; and as a preliminary assertion of Imperial power, the Kroměříž assembly was dissolved on 4 March 1849, its constitutional draft uncompleted.

Still, Schwarzenberg, Stadion, and Bach wished to show that they, too, were revolutionaries of a sort. Though they had been brought to office by Windischgrätz, they had no sympathy with his outlook or with that of his aristocratic friends. These 'old conservatives' – disciples of Metternich, reinforced by the Hungarian magnates who had broken with Kossuth – proposed only to undo the work of 1848 and to restore the Hungarian Diet as it had existed before the March laws; this was the policy of alliance between Emperor and nobility, futile in Metternich's time, made still more futile by the agrarian revolution. Schwarzenberg and his colleagues had no intention of returning to pre-March; they disliked its muddle and feebleness quite as much as the liberalism which followed it. By March 1849, Windischgrätz had lost political influence, and his protests were disregarded. Stadion hastily drafted a constitution as a counterblast to the work of Kroměříž. This constitution treated the entire Empire, including Hungary and Lombardy-Venetia, as a unitary centralized state. There was to be a single Imperial parliament, elected by direct suffrage, with a responsible government under a Prime Minister; Hungary was divided into new provinces, according to nationality; and these provinces, along with the rest of the provinces, were reduced to mere administrative areas. The Stadion constitution 'solved' the Austrian problem by abolishing it; this assortment of lands with widely differing traditions and with peoples at every stage of development was assumed to be as free from traditions and as nationally uniform as the France of Napoleon. The effort of Joseph

II was renewed, and under much less favourable conditions; the attempt could succeed only if Schwarzenberg and his ministers maintained the Jacobinism of their opening.

The Stadion constitution was issued by decree on 4 March 1849, at the moment when the Kroměřiž parliament was dissolved. It would come into operation, it was declared, as soon as 'the provisional emergency' was ended. Meanwhile the cabinet was responsible only to a non-existent parliament and to an inexperienced young Emperor. They ruled as dictators, reconquering Hungary and Italy for the Habsburgs, and issuing laws of revolutionary consequence as 'provisional decrees'. Liberal pretence had been dropped; and absolutism of a new kind began.

CHAPTER SEVEN

NEW ABSOLUTISM: THE SYSTEM OF SCHWARZENBERG AND BACH, 1849–59

THE dissolution of the Kroměřiž assembly marked the beginning of open attack on the master-nations. Talk of concession in Italy was abandoned; Sardinia was provoked into renewing the war, and Radetzky won a decisive victory at Novara on 26 March; the republic of Venetia was reduced in a leisurely aftermath in July. The thin link with national Germany was also broken: on 5 April the Austrian deputies were ordered to withdraw from the Frankfurt Assembly. Hungary was a harder task. Kossuth had achieved a startling recovery since the dark days of September 1848. Then Great Hungary had seemed in dissolution: there was a Slovak national rising in the north, a Serb national rising in the Voivodina, combined Rumanian and German resistance in Transylvania, and a Croat invasion across the Drave. Kossuth had been urged to compromise even by his radical followers. He did not waver. Instead of seeking to conciliate the nations of Hungary, he whipped up Magyar frenzy and actually welcomed the national conflicts as an opportunity to exterminate the non-Magyar peoples. He alone prevented the compromises which were being offered to the nationalities by the other ministers, and flung in the faces of these awakening peoples phrases which still burnt after a century. He said to the Serbs: 'the sword shall decide between us', and drafted plans for 'rooting them out'. He described Croatia as 'not enough for a single meal', called the Rumanians 'the soul of the conspiracy against Hungary'.

This appeal to national passion was successful. The Magyar soldiers were persuaded that they could save their state only by murdering those citizens who did not speak their tongue. Jellačić was driven back; the Slovak territory and most of the Voivodina subdued; the Rumanians sought, with little effect, the help of the Russian troops who had been occupying the Danubian principalities since the beginning of the revolutions. Greater success followed. In the winter of 1848 Windischgrätz advanced into Hungary and occupied Budapest; then he was outmanoeuvred by the Polish generals who were in command of the Hungarian army and, early in April 1849, compelled to withdraw. At the very moment when the Habsburgs broke with national Italy and national Germany, national Hungary broke with the Habsburgs: on 14 April, the Hungarian parliament at Debreczen,[1] much depleted by moderate withdrawals, deposed the Habsburgs and elected Kossuth as Governor. Thus Kossuth's doctrine that Hungary could be a great state without either an association with the Habsburgs or the cooperation of the non-Magyar peoples was carried to its logical conclusion. Yet the victory of Kossuth was not due to the superior virtue of the Magyars nor even to the chauvinist enthusiasm which he aroused; the victory was won by the Hungarian army, which was itself a fragment of Habsburg power.

The Habsburgs could, no doubt, have defeated Kossuth in time with their own army, the acquiescence of the Hungarian magnates, and the support of the non-Magyar nations. This programme was interrupted by an urgent offer of Russian help. The tsar disliked the success of the Polish generals in the Hungarian army and feared the example which Hungary set to Poland. Besides he had a motive of deeper calculation. Russian policy in the Near East, after twenty

1. Pronounced: Debretsen.

years of quiet, was once more moving towards action; and the occupation of the Danubian principalities, ostensibly to protect them from revolution, had been the first step in a new march to Constantinople. The tsar was anxious that the Habsburg Empire should not emerge from its crisis without a debt of gratitude towards Russia; on the other hand he shrank from revealing precise Russian ambitions for fear that Austria would draw back. As so often before and since, Russia pursued a will-o'-the-wisp and hoped that the Great Power whom she had helped to success would then voluntarily present Russia with the prize which she had not dared to demand.[1] As well, the tsar took seriously the conservative principles which he had learnt from Metternich; he did not grasp that they meant nothing to Schwarzenberg or that, even if they had, they could never extend to seeing Constantinople and the mouth of the Danube in Russian hands.

The tsar's line suited Schwarzenberg's book. He was ready to accept Russian help in Hungary or, later, in Germany and yet determined from the first not to acknowledge the unwritten debt. In May 1849, a Russian army entered Hungary, and in August the Hungarian army capitulated to the tsar at Világos.[2] Kossuth fled to Turkey and spent forty years in exile maintaining an empty dignity as Governor; the dream of a great independent Hungary was ended. Yet Habsburg success was as illusory as the success of Kossuth had been. It had been achieved with Russian help and depended on the continuance of Russian friendship. Moreover, it was purely a military conquest, not a political victory. The Czech and German moderates had welcomed the defeat of Czech and German radicalism; no one in Hungary welcomed the defeat of Kossuth. The magnates who sheltered round Windischgrätz and the liberals who looked to Deák agreed with Kossuth's aim of a great

1. This was the blunder made by Alexander I when he tolerated Napoleon's defeat of Austria in 1809 and subsequently when he assisted in the defeat of Napoleon in 1814. It was repeated by Alexander II when he made possible Bismarck's victories over Austria and France, and by Stalin in 1939. Curiously enough the Russians are taken in only by German (Austrian) good faith. With the Western Powers they try for more precise agreements, as in 1915 and in 1944; these too prove barren.

2. Pronounced: Víll-ā-gosh.

Magyar Hungary; they differed from him only in believing that they could attain this aim, the nobles by intrigues at court, and Deák by legalistic opposition. The execution of Batthyány and of thirteen Hungarian generals created martyrs and a legend which could not be extinguished by a few years of absolute rule. Moreover the magnates, though genuine patriots, had deserted Kossuth in good time; there were no widespread confiscations and therefore no new Imperial nobility, such as had followed the conquest of Bohemia in 1620. As Eisenmann says: 'To take Világos for the White Mountain was to be mistaken by more than two hundred years.'

Still, for the time being, Világos removed the last obstacle to the great experiment in centralized absolutism. Stadion went out of his mind in the summer of 1849; Schwarzenberg was immersed in foreign affairs; Bach, Stadion's successor as Minister of the Interior, was thus left as virtual dictator and used his power to revolutionary purpose. All historic claims and privileges were swept away. Hungary, it was argued, had forfeited her constitution by deposing Francis Joseph; and where Hungary was destroyed, no other state or province was likely to survive; even Croatia, which had been loyal from start to finish, lost her Diet and local self-government and her territorial integrity. The Austrian Empire became, for the first and last time, a fully unitary state. There was a single system of administration, carried out by German officials on orders from Vienna; a single code of laws; a single system of taxation. In June 1850, an 'emergency decree' casually abolished the tariff barrier between Hungary and the rest of the Empire; from that moment there was also a single commercial system. The 'Bach system' worked only for ten years, until 1859; yet its effects could never be undone. Before 1848 the frontier between Hungary and the rest of the Empire had divided two societies; after 1867 it divided two parliaments. Henceforth, until the end of the Monarchy, the Hungarian citizen smoked the same cigars and cigarettes, was regulated by the same police, and filled up the same bureaucratic forms as a citizen elsewhere in the Monarchy; in fact much that is regarded even now as characteristically Hungarian was introduced into Hungary by Bach and his agents. Old Hungary, with its autonomous counties, was genuinely without bureaucracy; county autonomy after 1867 meant only that the Austrian bureaucratic system was operated by Hungarian bureaucrats. This was the legacy of the 'Bach hussars'.

The Bach system was carried out by Germans, though not by German nationalists. This was the spirit, too, of Schwarzenberg's foreign policy: a mechanical echo of Greater German radicalism, without either radical or nationalist enthusiasm. Schwarzenberg was won by Bruck for the 'Empire of seventy millions', a union of all German and Austrian lands under Habsburg leadership; his intention was to force the entire Habsburg Empire into a revived German Confederation and, still more, into the German customs union. This was a programme challenging to Russia and to France, destructive of Prussia and the German princes; it could be accomplished only by revolutionary demagogy, not by the Habsburg army, and Schwarzenberg's ambition revealed, in fact, the triviality of his intellectual cleverness. It was easy to defeat the Prussian schemes for a North German union under Prussian leadership. The Austrian army had been victorious in Italy and in Hungary; and the tsar again supported what he mistakenly supposed to be the conservative side. In December 1850, by the agreement of Olomouc, Prussia abandoned her plans and accepted the revival of the German Confederation. This was Schwarzenberg's last success. At a conference in Dresden early in 1851 the German princes ruled out his attempt to include all the Habsburg lands in the German Confederation and in the customs union; and the tsar, at last taking alarm, supported their opposition. Deadlock followed. Schwarzenberg, by his policy of force and prestige, had committed Austria to a struggle for the headship of Germany; and yet, by his internal policy, estranged German sentiment.

The defeat of Prussia removed the last excuse for preserving the Stadion constitution in theoretical existence. The Schwarzenberg cabinet, though revolutionary in outlook, had no revolutionary support; and once the dangers deriving from 1848 had been overcome, Francis Joseph fell under the more congenial influence of conservative magnates and generals. These hankered after the 'historic' institutions of pre-March; and, since they could not recover their Diets and patrimonial jurisdictions, sought at least to restore the 'historic' powers of the Emperor. Ministerial despotism seemed to them revolutionary; and they advocated instead return to the pre-

March system in which the ministers had been merely administrators, and the Emperor the sole legislative and coordinating authority. Yet the men who wished to return to a system which had shown its rottenness in 1848 had been themselves its bitterest critics; and the memoirs of Kübeck,[1] now the leader of this group at court, are our principal source for the incompetence of the pre-March regime. Kübeck was jealous of Bach as Metternich had been jealous of Kolovrat; he urged Imperial absolutism and yet knew that the Empire could not be conducted by a single man, especially by one young and commonplace. Kübeck therefore fell back on the threadbare proposal, which Metternich had hawked round the court of Francis for so many years, of a 'substitute parliament' or Imperial Council which should advise the Emperor without infringing his absolute power; and, more fortunate than Metternich, actually had his scheme accepted by the Emperor. Francis Joseph was delighted with the advice of the elder statesmen of the Empire that he should rule the Empire himself, instead of leaving it in the hands of Bach, a revolutionary lawyer; and, inspired by the *coup d'état* of Louis Napoleon on 2 December 1851, was anxious to have his own *coup d'état* before the end of the year. The Stadion constitution was therefore officially abolished, and Kübeck's plan, hastily botched together, substituted as the Patent of 31 December 1851: Austria was to be governed by the Emperor alone, with a nominated Reichsrat, or Imperial Council – naturally with Kübeck as president – advising him on legislation.

Kübeck's success made little difference to affairs. Francis Joseph, hitherto theoretically a constitutional monarch, became theoretically absolute; in practice he continued to leave things to the ministers who had ruled Austria for the last three years. Schwarzenberg had casually acquiesced in the Kübeck Patent, confident that, whatever its provisions, he could maintain his supreme position as Prime Minister. Francis Joseph so little understood the spirit of the Kübeck Patent that, when Schwarzenberg died suddenly in April 1852, he proposed to make Bach Prime Minister. Kübeck and Metternich, now returned from exile, persuaded him that absolutism and a Prime Minister were incompatible. As a result Schwarzenberg was the only Prime Minister of the Austrian Empire, apart from the

1. Pronounced: Kewbeck.

casual figures of the revolutionary year, in all its long history. Bach remained Minister of the Interior; Francis Joseph became, and all his life remained, Prime Minister of the Empire, deciding policy and acting on the advice of ministers, who differed profoundly from each other. The destruction of ministerial rule did not help the Imperial Council; Francis Joseph, with simple common sense, saw that a legislative body, even though composed of his nominees, was as incompatible with absolutism as a cabinet of ministers, and never consulted it on any important point. The Imperial Council served only to demonstrate the futility of Metternich's pre-March schemes, and Kübeck soon retired from his empty dignity as president. The military and landed aristocracy, frivolous and irresponsible, thus destroyed the cabinet, which had at any rate a single policy and a collective will; they put nothing in its place and revived the worst evil of the old regime – the ministers dared do nothing without orders from above. The work of Kübeck in 1851 ensured the survival of the method of government described by Bismarck: 'The Emperor of Austria has many ministers; but when he wants something done, he has to do it himself.'

The Kübeck Patent, though trivial in action, was a symbol that the hope of liberalism from above was ended. Schmerling,[1] who had defended the Austrian cause in the Frankfurt parliament and then succeeded Bach as Minister of Justice, had already left the government; he was soon followed by Bruck. Bach fought longest against the inevitable. He had promoted a temporary absolutism in order to transform the Empire into a unit without provincial or national separatism; and not until late in 1852 did he give up the hope of crowning his work with a centralized liberal constitution. He made his final decision only after Schwarzenberg's death: he prized administrative efficiency more than liberal principle and became a supporter of absolute monarchy in order to preserve the 'Bach system'. By an ironical, but deserved, stroke of fate, it fell to the Jacobin minister, Bach, to undo the Church reforms of Joseph II, which had survived even the conservatism of Metternich and pre-March. By the Concordat of 1855 the Roman Catholic Church was given a freedom from state interference and a control over education which it had not enjoyed since the worst days of the Counter-Refor-

1. Pronounced: Shmairling.

mation. Like the revived Monarchy, the revived Church was artificial, a deliberate attempt to defeat the modern spirit with weapons taken from a seventeenth-century museum; and the alliance of Crown, Church, and army, once natural, was now a product of abstract reason, as intellectual as the liberalism which it opposed.

The new absolutism was without promise; this was its worse feature. Before 1848 men had been acutely aware of the evils of the system; yet they had believed in the possibility of a solution, acceptable to, if not promoted by, the Emperor. Now any solution had been ruled out: the Habsburgs had preferred force to conciliation. Certainly there were no longer privileged nations or languages. All were equal, but all were equally discontented; for all had tasted the reality, or the promise, of national freedom in 1848. Even the Germans, who benefited from the German character of the central administration and from the elevation of the prestige of Vienna, were not satisfied. As the most educated nation, they desired a constitution; as the wealthiest nation, they resented the financial burdens imposed by the demands of the army. Unbalanced budgets were the weakest point of the new absolutism. Armies of repression had to be paid for; and even the efficiency of the Bach officials could not bring in enough to meet the rising expenditure. The eighteen-fifties were everywhere in Europe a period of great capital investment; in the Habsburg Monarchy barracks took the place of factories and railways, and Austria now lost the economic lead over Prussia which she had hitherto possessed. Even the economic achievements of the old regime were sacrificed. The state railways, planned by Kübeck in pre-March, were handed over to a company of foreign capitalists. French capitalists took over the railways of Lombardy; this was an ominous reflection on the boasted military strength of the Austrian Empire. The German capitalists of Vienna lost all remaining faith in the Bach system with the economic crisis of 1857; this shook neo-absolutism as gravely as the crisis of 1847 had shaken the regime of pre-March. Still, Bach and his administrative machine were tougher than Metternich and the muddle of the pre-conference. The Metternich system fell from internal division and weakness; the Bach system, lifeless but rigid, had to be pushed over from without.

Foreign affairs dominated the ten years of absolute rule. Absolutism had been established in order to conduct a strong foreign policy; and failure in foreign policy brought absolutism to an end. The Metternich system had broken down abroad as well as at home. Before 1848 the tsar refrained from action in the Near East in order to be allowed the privilege of sustaining the Austrian Empire; after 1848 the tsar sustained the Austrian Empire in order to receive a reward in the Near East. Conflict between Russia and Austria was difficult to avoid under any system of policy, once Russia occupied the Danubian principalities; it was made certain by Schwarzenberg's adoption of a new course. Confidence in Austria's strength was the essence of Schwarzenberg's policy. Metternich had feared that any European conflict would shake Austria to pieces; Schwarzenberg sought openings for a dynamic policy. In 1813 Metternich, after exploiting Napoleon in order to secure the survival of the Habsburg Empire, deserted him for Russia and the conservative cause; Schwarzenberg reversed this historic decision and thought Austria strong enough to go along with a new Napoleon. His foreign policy, too, had a Jacobin spirit: he despised the 'treaty system' of the Congress of Vienna, and hoped for gains in Germany and the Near East. In abandoning Metternich's conservatism, it is fair to say he had not much choice; it was imposed on Austria by the new dynamism of France and Russia, though Napoleon III and the elderly Nicholas I were both pale echoes of Napoleon I and the youthful Alexander I. The spirit of the Congress of Vienna had been lost before its territorial settlement was challenged; and Austria was caught between the pressure of Great Powers both in east and west. Russia moved on the Danube; Napoleon III dreamt of a new Kingdom of Italy.

Schwarzenberg devised a new policy; his failure was in not conducting it with new weapons. A policy of adventure could not be based solely on the Habsburg army; it needed demagogy, the appeal to German nationalism. Ten years later Bismarck solved the problem which had baffled Schwarzenberg: with the assistance of German nationalism he gave Germany, and the Habsburg Monarchy too, security against both Russia and France, and yet tied German liberalism to the service of the Prussian King. Schwarzenberg had Bismarck's daring and freedom from prejudice; he lacked Bismarck's master-weapon, the call to popular enthusiasm. War against Russia had been the programme of German and Polish radicals in 1848; yet

Schwarzenberg ruled as their conqueror. A forward policy in the Near East, bringing the scattered German urban communities under German political leadership, was only possible on the basis of German nationalism; this was the purpose for which Bruck had advocated the 'Empire of seventy millions'. Schwarzenberg tried to secure the Empire of seventy millions purely as a Cabinet manoeuvre and against German sentiment; this failed at the Dresden Conference in 1851, and his Near Eastern policy was thus doomed before it started. After 1867, when the Habsburg Monarchy had compromised with the master nations, Poles, Magyars, and Germans, it could follow an anti-Russian line; and every increase of their hold on the Monarchy made this line more pronounced. Schwarzenberg, ostensibly free from principle, sacrificed everything to the principle of absolute rule; this was the fundamental contradiction of his system.

Bismarck had, besides, another advantage: his influence over the King of Prussia was supreme, and his power virtually unchallenged. The Prussian conservatives and the Prussian generals disliked Bismarck's adventurous course; they were silenced, partly by the King's authority, partly by their awareness of the peril in which they stood. Schwarzenberg was always threatened by court influences, especially after Kübeck's success in 1851; and Buol,[1] who became Foreign Minister on his death in April 1852, had never the deciding voice. The great aristocrats, as out of date in foreign policy as in home affairs, still advocated Metternich's policy of conservative solidarity; the generals were obsessed with Italy, the only campaigning ground they knew, and believed that the Austrian army was no match for Russia. This was a characteristic absurdity: the diplomats based their policy on Austria's strength; the generals were convinced of her weakness.

The Crimean War forced the Habsburg Monarchy to the crisis of decision; and the contradictory decisions then taken determined her ultimate fate. Unable to opt for either east or west, Austria remained thereafter in a state of suspended animation, waiting for extinction. In the preliminary stages of the war, Buol achieved the highest Habsburg ambition: the Russian armies withdrew from the Danubian principalities, and these were occupied by Austria. The Danube

1. Pronounced Boo-ŏl.

was thus under Austrian control practically throughout its entire navigable length; Russia was cut off from the Balkans; and Austria was free to become the sick man's sole heir. This outcome could be consolidated only if Austria became the ally of England and France, and so transferred the war from the Crimea to Galicia; only there could great results be obtained, probably however, as the generals urged, at Austria's expense. Francis Joseph, on Buol's advice, sent an ultimatum to Russia; criticized by the generals, he promised them not to act on it. The war in Galicia, shrunk from in 1855, had to be fought by Austria in much less favourable conditions in 1914. Buol attempted to save something of his position by an alliance with Prussia; this, too, implied either a return to the conservatism of Metternich or an appeal to German nationalism, and Buol could make neither. Thus the Crimean War left Austria without friends. Russia ascribed her defeat to the Austrian threat to join the allies; the allies believed that Russia would have withdrawn without war if Austria had joined them at the beginning.

The Congress of Paris, which ended the war in 1856, marked in meeting place and in spirit the end of the system of Vienna. Austria was no longer a European necessity. England and France had checked Russia in the Near East without Austrian assistance; both, though for different reasons, looked favourably on Italian nationalism; and Russia and Prussia, again for different reasons, no longer cared for the conservative cause. France and Russia, late enemies, prepared to combine against Austria; this was a new version of Tilsit. Buol had hoped to win a French guarantee for the Austrian provinces in Italy; instead he had to hear Austrian rule denounced in full Congress by Cavour. He had hoped, too, to gain the Danubian provinces in permanent possession; instead, the Austrian troops had to withdraw, and within a year or two, the principalities turned themselves into independent Rumania with French and Russian encouragement. Still, though the Peace of Paris defeated the project for an Austrian Danube, it defeated the project for a Russian Danube also. Rumania became a no-man's-land, a neutral possessor of the mouth of the Danube and therefore more tolerable to both Austria and Russia than that it should be held by either. In the later Eastern crises of the seventies and eighties, Russia did not challenge the independence of Rumania; therefore the crises could be kept within the resources of diplomacy. Once Russia, and Rumania too, left the principles of 1856, the question of existence was raised for the Habsburg Monarchy; and the signal for this was the visit of Tsar Nicholas II to the King of Rumania at Costanza in June 1914. Francis Joseph reigned for sixty years after the Crimean War; and these sixty years were lived out in the shadow of the Peace of Paris.

The failure of foreign policy in 1856 was reinforced by the economic crisis of 1857; the retreat from military absolutism began. Martial law was at last lifted from Lombardy-Venetia, and Archduke Maximilian, the Emperor's brother, attempted as Governor to give expiring Austrian rule a spurious liberal air; there were conciliatory talks with the conservative Hungarian magnates and with the Greater German capitalists. All this marked a loss of nerve, not a change of system. In any case, the Austrian rulers insisted, as Metternich had done, that the danger came from without; and this time they were right, though without realizing how great the danger was. The isolation of Austria tempted Napoleon III to bring to life his dream of a new Bonapartist hegemony in Italy; and in 1858 he agreed with Cavour to expel Austria from northern Italy. Russia, anxious to see Austria humiliated and weakened, was ready to promise Napoleon neutrality. The Austrian rulers were still bemused by their former boasts of Austrian strength; faced with discontent in Lombardy, they could offer no answer other than a punitive expedition against Sardinia. At the last minute Buol lost confidence and sought support from the Great Powers. His appeals were in vain: no one believed now in the 'Austrian mission'. France was preparing to attack Austria; Russia desired the defeat of Austria; British opinion desired the victory of Italian nationalism. The only resource for Austria was in Germany. This, too, was beyond Buol: he could not make the demagogic appeal to German national feeling, and Francis Joseph would not even buy Prussian support by recognizing the Prince Regent of Prussia as commander-in-chief in North Germany. With inevitable logic, the Habsburg Monarchy rested on the army and on nothing else; and in April 1859 Sardinia was provoked to war by an ultimatum summoning her to disarm.

The Austrian army did not live up to its high claims. Radetzky had died in 1857. His incompetent successor, Gyulai,[1] owed his

1. Pronounced Dýul-u-y.

position to court intrigue; he could not be provoked into action even by a telegram from the Emperor's adjutant: 'Surely you can do as well as the old ass Radetzky.' The French had time to come to the assistance of Sardinia, and the first battle, Magenta, was fought on Austrian soil. Though indecisive, it completed the timidity of the Austrian commanders, who fell back on the fortified Quadrilateral. In June, the Austrians, attempting to repeat Radetzky's victory at Custoza, blundered into the French at Solferino; two antiquated military machines, both rusty, competed in incompetence, and the French, mostly by accident, held the field. Solferino shook the faith of Francis Joseph in the strength of his army; for the rest of his life, he expected it to provide defeats. In June 1859 his mind first showed its true stamp: he planned to retreat in the hope of recovering his position later. This, his first compromise, was tactical, not sincere, though, like many of his later compromises it proved lasting. He preferred direct negotiation with Napoleon III rather than the mediation of the neutral Powers, for these would impose a settlement which it would be impossible to challenge later. Napoleon III, on his side, had strong reason to compromise: unable to imagine the blinkered conservatism of the Habsburgs, he feared an Austrian appeal to German nationalism and wished to settle with Francis Joseph before war threatened on the Rhine. Thus, despite defeat, Austria obtained generous terms; she surrendered only Lombardy, and without its defensive Quadrilateral; and, retaining Venetia, remained an Italian Power, to her later embarrassment.

The great Italian conflict, so long foretold, had ended tamely. Still the system of military prestige was fatally shaken. The master-nations, despite the defeat of 1849, had shown their strength. Italian diplomacy had succeeded where Italian arms had failed, where indeed they failed even in 1859: Lombardy had been lost. Hungary had been an essential aid to Italy's success: troops, needed in Lombardy, could not be spared from the army of occupation in Hungary; Hungarian regiments had proved unreliable in battle; and, when Kossuth arrived at Napoleon's headquarters at Milan to organize a Hungarian legion, this had been the decisive threat pushing Francis Joseph to make peace. The war made German favour essential, too: the Empire could not go on without new loans, and the German capitalists of Vienna demanded constitutional concessions. The

Habsburgs were faced again with the choice of 1848: either they must share their power with the master-nations, or they must win the support of the subject peoples. This choice was the subject of the great debate between 1859 and 1867; though it was not difficult to foretell which choice the dynasty of the Counter-Reformation and of anti-Jacobinism would make.

CHAPTER EIGHT

THE STRUGGLE BETWEEN FEDERALISM AND CENTRALISM: OCTOBER DIPLOMA AND FEBRUARY PATENT, 1860–61

THE self-confident absolutism of Schwarzenberg and Bach had made concessions neither at home nor abroad: it dispensed with both internal support and foreign allies. The result was internal discontent and foreign isolation, and of these foreign isolation was the more decisive. In 1859, after the Peace of Villafranca, Austria was threatened on three sides: Napoleon III would return, sooner or later, to the support of Italian nationalism; Prussia was bidding for liberal national backing in Germany; Russia aimed to reverse, at Austria's expense, the verdict of the Crimean War. The Habsburg Monarchy had to compromise with one or other of its enemies. Genuine co-operation with Napoleon III was impossible; for the Bonapartist programme to which Napoleon was committed implied the full radical programme of 1848 – national Italy, national Germany, national Poland, and national Hungary – and the patronage of Napoleon would have ended for Francis Joseph much as it ended for his brother Maximilian. A radical foreign policy was ruled out; conservatism and liberalism remained. Conservatism implied a return to the principles of Metternich – the Holy Alliance abroad, and conciliation of the landed aristocracy at home. This was the line taken immediately after the Italian War, when Rechberg, a disciple of Metternich, succeeded Buol as Foreign Minister. Rechberg supposed that the Holy Alliance had been deliberately jettisoned by Schwarzenberg and his arrogant colleagues. In fact, it had decayed even before the fall of Metternich and was now beyond recall: conservative principle would certainly not reconcile Russia to the settlement of the Peace of Paris; and Prussia, herself threatened by rising German sentiment, dared not champion the lifeless German Confederation. Thus liberalism remained: a revival of Bruck's 'Empire of seventy millions', but this time fortified by an appeal to German liberalism, both within the Habsburg Monarchy and beyond. This, too, involved concessions greater than the Habsburg dynasty could ever freely grant. As a result, Austrian foreign policy oscillated from conservatism to liberalism and back again, with even an occasional longing glance towards Bonapartist radicalism; and at each oscillation home policy oscillated too, until an outcome was reached not by statesmanship, but by defeat in the war of 1866.

The course of constitutional experiment was, then, determined by foreign events. Francis Joseph wished to strengthen his diplomatic and military position; this was his sole motive of policy. His own view of the Empire had been expressed in the absolutism of 1851; and Schwarzenberg and Bach were the only ministers with whom he was ever in genuine agreement. When Bach, to conciliate popular feeling, was dismissed from the Ministry of the Interior in July 1859, he found a comfortable retreat as ambassador to the Vatican, the only discarded minister of Francis Joseph to have his fall broken. Henceforth Francis Joseph exploited ministers without identifying himself with them or caring for them; a policy, not immediately successful, would be abruptly jettisoned, and an all-powerful minister would find himself dismissed overnight without a word of gratitude or regret. In the strange twilight world of the Habsburg court the peoples of the Empire counted only as raw material. There was no new revolution, only sullen criticism and, in Hungary, passive resistance. In 1848 the peoples, or at least their most advanced elements, had voiced their demands: they had sought to secure their freedom, some by destroying the Empire, others by cooperating with it. Now the Emperor sought only to conciliate the peoples without lessening his position of power. The foundations of the Austrian Empire were discussed; the fortunes of the Empire swung violently into a federalist, and then back into a centralist channel;

but the discussions took place in the nominated Reichsrat or in the Emperor's study, and the decisions depended not on the wish of the peoples, but on the sudden autocratic resolve of Francis Joseph. There was no attempt to consult the peoples and no intention of taking them into partnership; they were regarded as tiresome, wayward children, and the only problem was how to put them in a good humour so that they would pay their taxes and serve in the army for the greater glory of the dynasty. Eisenmann, writing of the October Diploma, accurately describes all the constitutional experiments of Francis Joseph: 'Absolutism in bankruptcy put on a false constitutional nose in order to extract a few pennies from the public.'

Two groups at court competed for the Emperor's favour in 1859, as indeed they had competed ever since his accession – the German bureaucrats and the great landowning nobility. Each offered what they promised would be a fraudulent scheme: a method of working the Empire more smoothly without impairing the power of the Emperor. The bureaucrats, established by Bach, were in possession: though discredited by the failure of 1859, they still conducted the affairs of the Empire. Their leaders – Lasser, Minister of Justice; Bruck, restored as Minister of Finance; Plener,[1] who became Minister of Finance on the suicide of Bruck in 1860; Schmerling, who became Minister of State in 1861 – had all a vaguely liberal past. Lasser had been a leading member of the Kroměřiž parliament; Schmerling a spokesman of the liberal group in the Lower Austrian Diet before 1848, and head of the Austrian party at Frankfurt. Still, this liberalism was overshadowed by their devotion to the centralized bureaucratic state; and those of them who had left the Schwarzenberg government, as Bruck and Schmerling had done, differed from it only in thinking that the state would be still more centralized and still more bureaucratic, if a central parliament were added to it, a view held by Bach himself. Devotion to the Empire and experience in running it were their assets in the conflict for the Emperor's favour; their weak point was his fear that their German liberal outlook would lead to a 'constitution', that is, to the interference of the peoples in the exercise of his autocratic power.

The landed nobility had been the defeated party in 1849, defeated as emphatically as extreme radicalism. The Bach bureaucrats blamed

1. Pronounced: Plainer.

the nobility, and especially the sham liberalism of their Diets, for the revolution; and saw in their programme of provincial autonomy a parody of the radical programme of national states. The new centralization had deprived the nobility of all power in the localities; and the new absolutism trampled on historic rights as firmly as on popular sovereignty. There was no room for aristocratic idlers as officials: even Rauscher, Cardinal Archbishop of Vienna, was of plebeian origin. Only the court was safe from this levelling outlook, and there the historic nobility had maintained a foothold. As early as 1850 a group of loyal Hungarian magnates had dared to petition the Emperor for the restoration of their historic constitution. The self-confidence and political experience of the Hungarian nobles gave them an advantage over the others; and the 'Old Conservatives' at court, who had failed under Windischgrätz, were now led by Szécsen,[1] a Hungarian magnate loyal to the Emperor and yet, like every Hungarian magnate, a Hungarian patriot.

The Old Conservatives claimed to represent a common idea of aristocratic tradition; in reality history divided them. When Szécsen appealed to history and to the 'historico-political individualities' of the provinces, his history was real: he was appealing to the Hungarian tradition which had survived in full, indeed increasing, strength, until broken by violence in 1849. When the Bohemian nobles echoed Szécsen's phrases, they appealed not to history, but against history – against the unitary state of Maria Theresa and Joseph II which had made itself a reality at the expense of the Bohemian and German provinces. Szécsen and the Hungarian magnates had the solid backing of the Hungarian gentry and of a wider Hungarian 'nation'; Clam-Martinic[2] and the Bohemian nobility had no sympathy with Czech nationalism, and their political talk was nothing more than a clever trick to escape from the control of the lower-class bureaucracy instituted by the Bach system. The Old Conservatives at first won over Francis Joseph by their assurance that aristocratic Diets would guarantee him against a 'constitution'; they were lost as soon as he realized that the price was the destruction of the unitary Empire, and the bureaucrats were restored to favour when they persuaded the Emperor that their bureaucratic talent was great enough to preserve his power undiminished under a

---

1. Pronounced: Say-chen.   2. Pronounced: Clam-Martinits.

pseudo-constitution as they had preserved it in the difficult days of 1848.

The ten years of Bach's rule had extended the Imperial problem. Szécsen, a Hungarian, now led the Old Conservative nobility; such an amalgamation would have been unthinkable before 1848. Before 1848, and still more during 1848, Hungary had had a special position; there had been a practical 'Dualism' ever since the days of Maria Theresa. The autonomous county administration had never been challenged except in the reign of Joseph II, and the traditional forms of the Hungarian constitution had been, with interruptions, respected. The March laws of 1848 had been confirmed by the Emperor Ferdinand; and the Kroměřiž Assembly had not attempted to include Hungary in its constitutional work. Now, in 1859, Hungary had been ruled from Vienna for ten years exactly like the other parts of the Empire; and Francis Joseph was resolved not to give up Bach's principal achievement, this stupendous advance on the work of earlier Habsburgs. Discontent was dangerous only in Hungary, and Francis Joseph could maintain his power elsewhere, if only Hungary were once satisfied. To maintain Bach's work, Francis Joseph had to deny these facts, and the constitutional oscillations from 1860 to 1867 were all attempts to preserve the Bach principle by giving to Hungary only the concessions which the rest of the Empire received. Hungary never ceased to demand her constitutional Diet. One way of pretending to satisfy this demand was to give Diets to all the provinces, including Hungary; the other was to give the Empire a constitution, with a central parliament at Vienna. The first was the way of conservatism, of the pseudo-historic nobility; the second was the way of liberalism, of the middle-class German bureaucracy. Neither satisfied Hungary; she rejected both an Imperial parliament and provincial Diets, and demanded the unique position to which her unique history entitled her.

The war of 1859 discredited the Bach bureaucracy and the foreign policy with which they were associated. Rechberg, the new Foreign Minister, laboured to restore the Holy Alliance; Goluchowski, a Polish aristocrat, succeeded Bach. To show the new respect for the provinces, his title was changed to Minister of State, that is minister for the states or provinces, much as though the British colonies had been administered by the Home Secretary and that they were then conciliated by changing his title to Secretary for the Dominions. The change was no more than nominal. Goluchowski was an aristocrat, but he was a Pole; and his appointment was the first sign that the Habsburgs had made their peace with this historic nation, and the Poles with the dynasty. Goluchowski certainly desired autonomy, under aristocratic Polish control, for Galicia; he desired just as much the maintenance of a unitary Habsburg Empire to defend Galicia from Russia and Prussia, the real oppressors of the Poles. Nor could he favour a genuine revival of the Holy Alliance with these two repressive powers. In fact, in appointing Goluchowski, Francis Joseph had discovered a way of avoiding the unattractive alternatives that were presented to him. Goluchowski, though a conservative noble, was a centralist; though a centralist, not a German; though loyal to his nation, loyal, too, to the dynasty. The Polish aristocracy was the only class in the Monarchy which served the dynasty without conditions, except for the condition of autonomy for Galicia which it was easy to grant; and they remained to the end the most stalwart and reliable supporters of the Habsburgs. They had only one defect: they were not enough to run and finance the entire Empire.

Though the Habsburg Monarchy was once more threatened with a crisis of existence, Francis Joseph yielded with obstinate slowness. He proposed to make a fraudulent concession with the aid of the conservative nobility; yet the appointment of Goluchowski showed that the conservative nobility were to be defrauded too. In March 1860, the Reichsrat, vain relic of the Patent of 1851, was brought out of its obscurity to advise the Emperor on a change of system. It was to be 'reinforced' by members of the provincial Diets; since these did not exist, the thirty-eight extra members (two for each province) were nominated by the Emperor out of hand. Most of the members of the Reichsrat were now Old Conservatives, though there were enough bureaucrats on it to keep up a constant fire of criticism; and in July the Reichsrat submitted a majority report advocating the reconstruction of the Empire according to the principles of aristocratic federalism. This report was never considered by Francis Joseph. Action was forced on him by the needs of foreign policy. In pursuit of the Holy Alliance, he was to meet the Tsar and the King of Prussia at Warsaw on 21 October, and he wished to go armed with a declaration of conservative home policy. With the characteristic impulsiveness which, throughout his life, followed his long delays, Francis Joseph, who had evaded decision for more than a year, now demanded a settled constitutional draft within a week; indeed the general principles were settled during a single conversation with Szécsen in the train between Salzburg and Vienna. The outcome, intended to be a new fundamental law of the Empire, was the Diploma of 20 October 1860.

The October Diploma gave the victory to the Old Conservative nobility: it attempted to revive a historic federalism which had never existed. Henceforth laws were to be passed with the 'cooperation' of the provincial Diets and the Reichsrat; this was the sole concession to liberalism, and there was no suggestion that even in these harmless bodies the will of the majority would be decisive. Diets, packed by the landed aristocracy, were to be set up in the historic provinces; and these Diets were to possess legislative power over all subjects other than a limited number reserved to the Reichsrat, which was to meet occasionally with its membership increased to one hundred by representatives from the Diets – a trivial body to act as the legislature of a great Empire. Thus, in the middle of the nineteenth century, after three hundred years of the extension of Habsburg power and seventy years after the French Revolution, it was proposed to dismember the Habsburg Empire and to hand over the fragments to the landed nobility in exchange for the assurance that the nobility would preserve the Empire from liberalism. The Diploma, though drafted by a Hungarian, did nothing to conciliate Hungary: it expected the Magyars to be content with the position of Vorarlberg or the Bukovina. The sole concession to Hungarian right was the clause that, whereas regulations to be issued later would settle the composition of the other Diets, the Hungarian Diet 'should proceed according to its earlier constitution'. This concession, too, was valueless, for it could refer only to the traditional constitution, and this, in Hungarian eyes, had been superseded by a modern liberal constitution in 1848. In a final clause the authors of the October Diploma unconsciously confessed the falsity of the pseudo-historical doctrine which put Hungary on the same level as the other provinces; for this clause provided that, as the provinces 'other than the lands of the Hungarian crown' had 'for many years transacted many things together', these matters should be dealt with by the Reichsrat in the absence of the Hungarian members. In this grudging and accidental way the unitary state of Maria Theresa and Joseph II was allowed to continue a limited existence.

The October Diploma expressed the frivolity and shortsightedness of the Habsburg aristocracy, a class more dangerous to the Monarchy in loyalty than in disaffection. Szécsen and his Hungarian associates had an excuse: they cared only for Hungary. They realized that the Hungarians would not be satisfied with the restoration of their traditional rights – the 'earlier constitution' of the Diploma; yet they obstinately hoped that the Hungarians would be so far satisfied as to abandon passive resistance and to revive the traditional 'bargaining' with the King of Hungary within the framework of the October Diploma. The Bohemian nobility did not consider the Imperial problem at all; without political sense or experience of power, they were concerned only to erect a barrier against 'liberalism' and to free themselves from bureaucratic rule. The victory of Old Conservatism at once brought its ruin. The case against liberalism had a certain plausibility so long as it was confined to theoretical discussion; once practically expressed in the October Diploma, it became obvious that this policy would weaken the Empire and arouse the opposition of the German middle class without at all lessening Hungarian discontent.

Besides, the October Diploma was stillborn. It was contrived to give Francis Joseph a solidly conservative appearance at the Warsaw meeting; and the Warsaw meeting was a failure. Russia and Prussia could not be won back to the system of Metternich; both dreamt of foreign gains and flirted with liberalism. Alexander II, on the eve of emancipating the serfs and contemplating a liberal policy even towards the Poles, would resume friendship with Austria only in return for concessions in Rumania and the Black Sea; and these concessions Austria would not make. Even if she had, Alexander II would not, at this time, have given Austria any security against further threats from Napoleon III in Italy. Prussia, full in the short-lived liberalism of the 'new era', would not support Austria against Russia or France except in return for concessions in Germany; and these concessions, too, Austria would not make. The Metternich system had rested on a general acceptance of the *status quo*; and this was no longer accepted by any Continental Great

Power – not even by Austria. Since the Holy Alliance was beyond revival, Austria's only resource lay in an alliance with German liberalism: the 'Empire of seventy millions' to check Russia in the Balkans, an appeal to German nationalism to overshadow Prussia in Germany. As a result, Francis Joseph returned from Warsaw already disillusioned with the October Diploma and anxious to conciliate his German bureaucrats; and domestic events increased this anxiety.

Until October 1860, Austria had remained in practice a centralized absolutist state. With the October Diploma, electoral bodies had to be organized to prepare for the proposed Diets, and political discussion had to be tolerated. Thus the Diploma produced exactly what it had been designed to avoid – the expression of political opinion by the subjects of the Emperor. The Press had to be given some freedom; and this Press, entirely German or Magyar, voiced a universal rejection of the new system. The Germans, even the German nobles, regarded the greatness and unity of the Empire as their historic possession, a possession now to be destroyed for the benefit of the Bohemian nobility; and far from welcoming the provincial Diets, they preferred the preceding absolutism. The Hungarians, released from the rule of the 'Bach hussars' and with their county meetings restored, wiped out the events of the past eleven years. They refused to conduct the county meetings according to the traditional rules, and restored the regulations as created by the March laws; the county committees of 1848 were everywhere elected unchanged except for those members who had entered the service of absolutism and whose names were greeted with a unanimous cry of 'dead'. The county organization of 1848, however, supposed a responsible central government at Budapest; none existed, and the county committees would not accept orders from Vienna. There followed therefore a state of legalized anarchy more complete than anything under the old constitution. It was indeed obvious from the first day of the county assemblies that the Magyars would insist on the validity of the March laws, with their basic principle of personal union, and would refuse to recognize the unity of the Empire by sending members to the Reichsrat in Vienna.

Szécsen and his Hungarian associates would not admit the bankruptcy of their ideas. The political outbreak in Hungary they ascribed not to a fundamental rejection of the principles of the October

Diploma, but to distrust of the good faith of the Imperial government. The Hungarians, Szécsen argued, could have no confidence in the Imperial promise to restore the 'earlier constitution' when they saw the Diploma used in the rest of the Empire to promote aristocratic obscurantism; and Szécsen did not scruple to throw over his Bohemian allies in order to give Austrian rule a more liberal appearance. The Hungarian conservatives differed from the Hungarian liberals only in political outlook; they were not severed by race or nation, for the gentry, predominantly liberal, shaded into the magnates, predominantly conservative, and some even of the magnates were unshakably liberal. The Bohemian conservatives were severed from the Austrian liberals by both class and nation – the one exclusively noble and non-national, the other exclusively middle-class and German. Thus flirtation with liberalism did not shock Szécsen as it shocked Clam-Martinic. Besides at bottom Szécsen and his friends did not care what regime existed in non-Hungarian Austria so long as Hungary recovered her traditional constitution. Szécsen picked on Goluchowski as personifying the reactionary spirit of the October Diploma; at the same moment Goluchowski was attacked by the Bohemian nobility as failing to operate the Diploma, for – as a convinced centralist – he was devising electoral schemes to pack the Diets with bureaucratic agents of the central government and so rob them of the federal power theoretically promised to them. Yet the German bureaucrats, remembering that Goluchowski had superseded Bach, condemned him as a conservative aristocrat. Thus hated by Germans, Hungarians, and Bohemian nobility, Goluchowski was an easy victim, and was dismissed on Szécsen's prompting in December 1860.

Szécsen's new nominee as Minister of State was Anton von Schmerling, now cast for the task of giving the non-Hungarian lands a stronger 'dose' of liberalism in order to win the confidence of liberal Hungary. Schmerling's reputation as a liberal rested on his resignation from the Schwarzenberg government in 1851; there had been little more in this than the clash of two strong personalities. Schmerling's greatest achievement had been his successful resistance at Frankfurt in 1848 against the radical attempts to dissolve the Habsburg state. Schmerling was essentially a servant of the unitary state; he had been a judge or, in the revealing Austrian phrase, 'a judicial official', and saw little difference between the civilian and military servants of the Monarchy. His liberalism amounted at most to the view that it would strengthen the Monarchy to give the German middle classes a junior partnership, in which the German liberals would shoulder the blame and from which the Empire would reap the profit. He had no sympathy with the traditionalism of the Old Conservatives or with their view that the Hungarian constitution was an inalienable possession of the Hungarian 'nation'. He regarded the Hungarian constitution as forfeited by the rebellion of 1849, and the Bach system as the immutable foundation for any concession which the Emperor might deign to grant. His aim was focused on the 'Empire of seventy millions', not on conciliating Hungary; and, far from implementing the October Diploma, he meant to reverse its spirit and to restore the unitary state which Bach had built up. The Old Conservatives had now the argument from results used against them: the Bach system had taken ten years to fail, their system had proved bankrupt within two months. Immediate success was the only test applied by Francis Joseph, and by that test the Old Conservatives were condemned. Szécsen and his adherents had to acquiesce helplessly in the Patent of 26 February 1861, ostensibly a gloss on the October Diploma, in reality the restoration of the centralized state.

The February Patent kept only the names of the October Diploma. The Reichsrat, in the Diploma an enlarged Crown Council, swelled to an Imperial parliament; the Diets, in the Diploma provincial parliaments, dwindled into electoral committees for the Reichsrat with some say in local administration. The Reichsrat was given legislative power over all subjects not expressly reserved to the Diets, and these were few; it was given a true parliamentary appearance, with a nominated House of Lords and a House of Representatives three hundred and forty-three strong. The Hungarian Diet lost its importance like the rest; as a trivial concession, it was permitted, if it wished, to exercise its remaining powers according to the laws of 1848. Yet, curiously enough, at this moment of centralist victory, the Patent took a further step towards Dualism. The Diploma had vaguely mentioned the need for the non-Hungarian lands to transact certain classes of affairs together; the Patent made practical provision for this need and established, alongside the full Reichsrat, a 'narrower' Reichsrat which the deputies from Hungary would not attend. This clumsy device contained the implicit admission that the non-Hungarian lands were a unity, closer and more real than the theoretical unity of the great Empire; and it contained, too, the admission that the Hungarian lands were a similar Imperial unit and that Budapest ranked with Vienna rather than with Prague or Innsbruck.

Schmerling and his associates were, after all, practical administrators as well as being dogmatic centralists; and they knew that many things were done in Vienna for the non-Hungarian lands which were not strictly 'Imperial'. The 'narrower' Reichsrat was a confession of this. Still, they hoped to lessen this contrast between Hungary and the rest of the Empire by shifting some administrative affairs back from Vienna to the provinces; the Diets, having been called into existence, had to be given some occupation, and the Patent transformed them from local legislatures into instruments of administration. They ceased to resemble the State legislatures of the United States and became models for the English county councils. This was in line with contemporary liberal thought both in France and Germany which, inheriting rigid centralism from the French Revolution, attempted to moderate this by autonomous local government. Moreover, since the Diets had now administrative tasks, they needed a permanent existence, and the Patent provided for a 'Committee of the Diet' which should represent the Diet when this was not in session. Certainly, the bureaucrats of 1861 did not intend to transfer to the Diets administrative powers of any importance; still, as time passed, the sphere of local administration swelled, and a strange contrast resulted after 1867. In Hungary, traditional home of local autonomy, the central government encroached at the expense of the county committees and, by appealing to the national spirit, subdued them to its will; in 'Austria', pattern of the unitary state, provincial administration squeezed out the agents of the central government and, by enlisting national support, held Vienna at bay. When the Habsburg Monarchy fell in 1918, Hungary had become a centralized state, Austria was administratively a federation.

In 1861, the Diets mattered only as electoral colleges for the Reichsrat. The elections to the Diets were themselves a matter of great complication. The members of the Diets were elected by four separate groups of electors – great landed proprietors, the chambers of commerce in the towns, town constituencies, and rural constituencies. Each 'curia' operated as a separate group in returning deputies to the Reichsrat. For example, of the 54 Bohemian representatives, 15 were chosen by the curia of great landowners, 4 by the curia of the chambers of commerce, 1 by the representatives of Prague, 15 by the town representatives divided into eleven geographical groups, and 19 by the rural representatives divided also into eleven geographical groups. The packing was double: for their own sake, the Diets were packed in favour of property; for the sake of the 'Empire of seventy millions' they were packed in favour of the Germans. Electoral systems in every constitutional country were still twisted in favour of wealth and the towns; Bismarck, a conservative, first introduced universal suffrage and overweighted the countryside. This was the time, too, of the 'fancy franchises' even in England; and the university constituencies survived as an unsuccessful attempt at packing in favour of intellect. Still, in England, the abuses had a historical origin; in the February Patent they were artificially devised.

The unique feature of this 'electoral geometry' was its packing in favour of the Germans; the property qualification and overweighting of the towns would have done this in any case, since the Germans were the wealthy and the urban nationality, but the packing was also done deliberately in the town and country constituencies. No packing was necessary in the curia of great landlords: this was the dynastic class, ready to follow the Emperor's bidding – except in Bohemia – even if this meant favouring the Germans. Thus, in Carniola, a province almost exclusively Slovene, the curia of great landowners – a quarter of the Diet – remained solidly German thoughout. The chambers of commerce were German organizations by definition. Electoral geometry dominated the more open constituencies. The towns were favoured at the expense of the country; German towns and country were favoured at the expense of non-German town and country, especially at the expense of the Czechs. Thus a German town deputy represented 10,000 inhabitants; a Czech town deputy 12,000. A German rural deputy represented 40,000 inhabitants; a Czech 53,000. Moreover the town constituencies were rigged – Czech suburbs were cut off and thrown into the surrounding rural constituency, so that Prague, already largely Czech, had no more town representation than Liberec[1] which was safely German. In Moravia the towns, with a population of 430,000, had 13 deputies; the country, with 1,600,000, had 11. The most staggering achievement of electoral geometry was in Dalmatia, where 400,000 South Slavs had 20 representatives, and 15,000 Italians had 23. The Italians were the most subversive nationality, the South Slavs the most loyal; yet even this was overcome by the pull of one historic nationality to another. Still, the favouring of Italians in Dalmatia and of Poles in Galicia was a frill, a refinement; the essence of electoral geometry was its creation of a German majority in the Reichsrat. In exchange for this artificial preponderance, the Germans were to assist Schmerling in maintaining the unity of the Empire against the Hungarians and in extending Habsburg authority in Germany.

Yet not even the privileged Germans received a true constitution. The February Patent contained none of the provisions essential to a constitutional system. The phrase concerning the 'cooperation' of the Diets and Reichsrat in legislation was taken over from the October Diploma; there was nothing concerning the freedom of the Press, immunity of members, independence of the judiciary, or the responsibility of ministers; recruits for the army could be levied and taxes raised (though no new taxes imposed) without the consent of the Reichsrat; the Emperor nominated the president and vice-president of both houses; and in case of need the ministry could issue regulations without waiting for the meeting of the Reichsrat. Two days after the issue of the Patent, Francis Joseph demanded from his ministers 'a solemn promise to defend the throne against demands for further concessions from the Diets or the Reichsrat or from revolutionary mass movements'. He added: 'Especially the Reichsrat must not be allowed to interfere in foreign affairs, in the organization of the army, or in the affairs of the high command.' This sentence defined the political attitude from which Francis Joseph never wavered.

Schmerling's aim was to win the Germans for a Greater German foreign policy, the 'Empire of seventy millions'. He gave hardly a

1. Pronounced: Liberets. German name: Reichenberg.

thought to the Magyars, whom he had been called in to conciliate. Still it was obvious that the Magyars would not send representatives to a Reichsrat where their eighty-five deputies would be in a permanent minority. The February Patent anticipated this refusal and provided, in Clause 7, that, if a Diet failed to send representatives, direct elections could be held in the constituencies. This was a threat to appeal from the Magyars to the subject nationalities of Hungary, and so to disrupt the unity of the Hungarian lands; and this challenge ended any faint hope that the Hungarians might 'bargain' on the basis of the February Patent. Yet at the very moment when the February Patent jettisoned Szécsen's policy and destroyed his influence in Hungary, Francis Joseph consoled him for defeat by promising that Clause 7 should never be applied. For, after the failure of the Bach system, Francis Joseph never committed himself fully to any line of policy. He was determined not to be enslaved by an all-powerful minister and was, besides, sceptical of every policy. Faced with difficulties beyond his understanding, he was prepared to allow an energetic minister to try out some particular panacea, while he himself prepared a way of retreat for the moment when this panacea should fail. Feudal federalism had failed. Now Schmerling was given his chance to experiment with sham constitutionalism. Francis Joseph was not converted to sham constitutionalism, still less to real constitutionalism, nor even to the idea of taking the Germans into a junior partnership.

CHAPTER NINE

CONSTITUTIONAL ABSOLUTISM: THE SYSTEM OF SCHMERLING, 1861–5

THE Bach system followed a single pattern; the system of Schmerling rested on contradictions. The February Patent reversed the October Diploma, yet was formally a gloss upon it; and, while its spirit was centralizing, it made the provincial Diets essential as electoral bodies

and so gave them a greater importance than they had ever previously possessed. Neither Diploma nor Patent acknowledged the
Hungarian laws of 1848; yet, by providing for a Diet, they gave the
Hungarians full opportunity to voice their demands and to organize
opposition to government from Vienna. Hungary was more dissatisfied, and Hungarian dissatisfaction more effective; this was the
combined achievement of Szécsen and of Schmerling. The legal
position of Hungary defied definition. Schmerling and his supporters
held that nothing had changed except that Hungary, like the other
provinces, had been allowed to hold a Diet; the Old Conservatives
maintained that the traditional constitution, detroyed by Kossuth,
had been restored, though they admitted that the legal and social
changes made during the Bach period should remain until the Diet
provided otherwise; the overwhelming majority of Hungarians dismissed as illegal everything which had taken place since the outbreak
of civil war in the autumn of 1848. They passed a sponge over the
work of Bach, and it was small consolation that the same sponge
wiped out the deposition of the Habsburg dynasty by Kossuth and
the rump parliament at Debreczen.

Unlike Francis Joseph, the Hungarians had learnt from the events
of 1849. Kossuth had tried to establish Great Hungary by whipping
up Magyar frenzy; instead he had brought Hungary to disaster, and
even now could only offer from exile the remedy of Habsburg defeat
in a new war with Napoleon III. This policy of alliance with Italian
nationalism and the spirit of the French Revolution was played out;
for both had lost such force as they once possessed. The new line in
Hungary was to conciliate the national minorities, while maintaining
the principle of Hungary as a national state; and ten years of Habsburg absolutism had made this policy possible. The German
middle classes of the towns now looked to the Magyar gentry for the
liberal system which comprised their political ambition, and even
Serb and Slovak intellectuals had more hope from Budapest than
from Vienna. Kossuth was displaced as Magyar leader by Deák.

Francis Deák, like many of the leaders of the English revolution in
the seventeenth century, combined in himself the two sources from
which his class drew its strength: he was both landowner and
lawyer. He was near enough to the soil to be spared the fancies of the
magnates who frequented the Vienna court; he had enough ex-

perience of the world to escape the dead negations of the uneducated country squires. He was a master of legal manoeuvre; yet, a strange thing for a lawyer, was himself without ambition. His sole aim was to find a secure place for historic Hungary in the modern world; and his common sense told him that the Magyars could not maintain Great Hungary against both the subject peoples and the Habsburgs. Defending his policy he said: 'We must admit that by ourselves we are not a great state.' He knew, as Kossuth did not, that Hungary had become great only in association with the Habsburg Empire; he knew also, as the Old Conservatives did not, that Hungary had remained great only by ceaseless resistance to Habsburg encroachment. His caution and tactical skill led him to conciliate the other nationalities, and so to prevent any renewal of the events of 1848. Still, he had no more sympathy with their claims than Kossuth and no vision of any true cooperation between peoples of different nations. His concessions were tactical, and he, too, intended to 'magyarize' all the inhabitants of Hungary, though by more insidious means. This evil lay at the root of his policy and ultimately poisoned all his great achievement. Deák's moderation was calculated; and the moderation of his followers was more calculated still – it sprang only from their experience of the 'Bach hussars' and lessened as the memory faded.

The Diet, when it met in April 1861, refused to behave as the traditional Diet of Old Conservative dreams. Elected on the representative franchise of 1848, it claimed to be a parliament, not a Diet, and asserted its continuity with the parliament of 1848; yet for this much was lacking – there was no responsible ministry and neither Croatia nor Transylvania was represented. The Old Conservatives had not a single member in either house. Most of the magnates and a minority of the lower-house gentry looked to Deák; the majority of the gentry, led by Koloman Tisza,[1] were still 'Kossuthites', with no programme beyond resistance. There could be no question of sending delegates to the Reichsrat in Vienna, as prescribed by the February Patent; the only question was of the method by which protest should be made against the illegality of Diploma and Patent. Tisza and his followers argued that, since the Diet was an illegal body and Francis Joseph an illegal ruler, they should limit themselves to

1. Pronounced: Tissa.

resolutions; Deák answered that, as Francis Joseph was in fact exercising the powers of King of Hungary, they should proceed by the traditional method of an address to the Crown. Enough members of the 'resolution' party abstained to give Deák's proposal a majority, and later the entire 'resolution' party accepted Deák's lead. The extremists were not converted to moderation; they used Deák's skill and high character only as a means towards their own ends.

Deák's address, though humble in form, was uncompromising in substance: it asserted the legality of the laws of 1848 and refused to negotiate with the King until these were restored. This ended Old Conservative hopes of a return to the traditional 'bargaining' between King and Diet. It was useless for them to advise Francis Joseph to make a conciliatory answer which should pave the way to agreement; agreement was obviously impossible. Szécsen and Vay, the two Hungarian ministers, were dismissed. Their places were taken by two Hungarians so long absent from Hungary as to have become, or so it was believed, loyal Austrians: Forgács[1] had been Governor of Bohemia, and the diplomat Maurice Esterházy, having forgotten Magyar and never mastered German, employed French as his normal language. On Schmerling's proposal the Hungarian address was answered by an ultimatum: the Diet must appoint delegates to the Reichsrat without delay. When this was refused, the Diet was at once dissolved. Before it separated, the Diet passed unanimously a resolution that the first tasks of a free Hungarian parliament would be to satisfy those demands of the nationalities which did not conflict with the political and territorial integrity of Hungary; to establish political and civil equality for all religions, including the Jews; and to abolish all remnants of feudalism. Deák, mistakenly, credited the Imperial ministers with some political skill; and he provided in advance against any Habsburg appeal to the non-Magyars or to the lower classes in Hungary, an appeal never in fact made.

Schmerling was not fit to be Deák's opponent. His only advance on Bach was a more conscious appeal to the Germans in the Empire, and this turned him more than ever against the other nationalities. The moment for his *coup de théâtre* had now arrived. On 23 August he read in the Reichsrat a declaration of policy in which the acts of the

1. Pronounced: Fúrgãtch.

ministry were throughout described as the acts and resolutions of the Emperor; when he reached the sentence, 'The constitution of Hungary was not only broken by revolutionary violence, but forfeit in law and also abolished in fact', he was interrupted by a storm of applause from the German left and centre. Ten days later the Reichsrat passed a resolution supporting Schmerling's Hungarian policy. This was a symbolic act: the Germans abandoned their earlier liberal principles and entered into an alliance with the dynasty which was never afterwards completely broken. The spirit of the October revolution of 1848 was extinguished until its artificial revival in the dark days of October 1918.

The decay of German liberalism was to exercise a decisive influence on the history of Europe. Before 1848 liberals everywhere had been convinced of the ultimate victory of their ideas; instead, in 1848, the revolution had failed and success remained with the despised dynasties. In France too the revolution of 1848 failed; this failure was only an episode in a century of revolutions, and the success of Napoleon III did not prevent the rise of Gambetta or Clemenceau. In Germany the revolution of 1848 was a solitary event, and the German liberals resigned themselves to failure. Some liberals, the most stalwart, left Germany for the free land of America; a few turned to revolutionary Socialism; and some remained liberals, though without hope. Most worshipped success and were ready to leave the dynasties in power if the dynasties would accomplish some of the objects of the liberal programme; so the Austrian German liberals went over to the Habsburgs in 1861, and so the Prussian German liberals abdicated to the Hohenzollerns in 1866. The surrender was not deliberate; the liberals genuinely persuaded themselves that the dynasty had been converted to liberalism. The Bach system had depended on German middle-class bureaucrats; with a sort of Jacobinism it overrode class privileges and local rights. It transformed the Austrian Empire into a great Free Trade area, enormously enhancing the importance of Vienna as a financial and commercial centre. Schmerling removed the remaining German scruples; he gave them a parliament and offered them in foreign policy the 'Empire of seventy millions'. The Habsburgs seemed to have become the standard-bearers of Greater Germany. This won over not merely the Austrian Germans, but many Germans from outside Austria as well. Between 1861 and 1866 moderate liberals in Germany occasionally looked to Prussia, as likely to achieve some modest practical result; the former radicals of 1848 became supporters of Austria. There is a startling illustration. In October 1848 the left of the Frankfurt parliament sent two delegates to sustain the Vienna revolution. Both fell into the hands of Windischgrätz. One, Robert Blum, was executed; Froebel, the other, also sentenced to death, was reprieved and fled to America. This same Froebel returned to Vienna as a pamphleteer in Schmerling's service; and gave the first impetus to the meeting of the German princes at Frankfurt in 1863 – last Habsburg bid for the headship of Germany.

The Austrian Germans were absorbed in the German problem; they had neither time nor understanding for the problem of the Austrian Empire. Themselves without historic background, they condemned all traditions as necessarily conservative, and in opposing Hungary thought that they were sustaining the same revolutionary cause as the French radicals had sustained against the Vendée. By the accident of history, the Germans enjoyed 'national' freedom (that is, the use of their language), even when the dynasty was most reactionary; they could not therefore understand the demands of the other nationalities for national freedom, especially as these demands were directed more against their own cultural monopoly than against the power of the dynasty. They were willing to give up their provincial patriotism in Tyrol or Styria for the sake of a great Austria; why could the others not do the same? Besides, the national movements were truly tainted with reaction and conservatism. The non-historic nationalities lacked an urban middle class and everywhere accepted the alliance of the local nobility. Even the Hungarian movement talked a historic, legal language repellent to modern liberalism and seemed concerned only to maintain the privileges of the Magyar aristocracy. In the 1860s federalism had little to recommend it. The United States were plunged in civil war; the German Confederation was no more than a barrier against liberal aims; and in Austria the October Diploma, practical expression of federalism, had been unashamedly a device for reviving political feudalism. The German liberals, disillusioned as to their own strength, sought allies; and they had to choose, or so they supposed, between the dynasty, which – with all its past faults – had just granted a constitution and would maintain Austria as a great German state, and a policy which would disrupt the Empire for the sake of the conservative nobility.

The liberals were aware of the constitutional defects of the February Patent and meant to remedy them. Only, lacking all sense of history or of rights based on the slow development of law, they never grasped its basic defect: it was an act of Imperial absolutism, granted of grace as a temporary device and one which could be revoked at will. The Reichsrat had not attained its position by struggle; therefore, despite its parliamentary appearance, it was a body without power. The Germans thought that, since they were in a majority in the Reichsrat, the ministry depended on them. In fact, since their majority rested on 'electoral geometry', they depended on the ministry. The Germans received an artificial majority in a sham parliament; in return they gave up their liberal principles, barred the way against cooperation with the other peoples of the Empire, and committed themselves to support the dynasty whatever its policy. In a word, they destroyed the possibility of the growth of any Imperial conception other than as the instrument of the dynastic will to power. The Germans were more politically adult than the other peoples of the Monarchy; the responsibility which rested on them was therefore the heavier and their decision the more criminal. For the decision taken in 1861 was the doom of stability and peace in central Europe.

Schmerling believed that he had achieved a great stroke by cementing the alliance between the Germans and the dynasty; in reality, he had done no more than return, with a greater display of phrases, to the system of Bach. In Hungary the system of county autonomy was once more suspended, and the Bach administrators, supported by a large army of occupation, returned to their posts. Schmerling intended to let Hungary come to her senses; then she could have once more the limited Diet of 1861. 'We can wait!' was the sum total of his Hungarian programme. This the Empire could not do: the only reason for the constitutional experiment of 1861 was the need for quick results. The Bach system would, no doubt, have destroyed Hungarian separatism and created a united Empire, if it had been maintained unshaken for two or three generations; it had been shattered by foreign war within ten years, and now the foreign situation was more threatening than it had been in 1859. Everyone knew that the Schmerling absolutism in Hungary could not be maintained for long, even Schmerling and his colleagues described it as provisional; and the Magyars had become far more confident as the result of the proceedings in the Diet. Was it likely that they would succumb to Schmerling where they had held out against Bach? There was a balance between dynasty and Magyars implicit even in the system of Schmerling: neither could destroy, but neither could be great, without the other. The balance could be overset only by calling in the non-historic, Slav, peoples. National arrogance forbade this to the Magyars; the alliance with the Germans forbade it to the dynasty. Yet there was no other way in which Schmerling could succeed.

It was obvious from the start that there was no room in the Schmerling system for the Czechs, who had been the principal losers by the overthrow of the October Diploma. At once inexperienced and ambitious, the Czech leaders made in these years decisions as fateful and as mistaken as the decisions of the Germans. Czech nationalism could have been, from the start, a programme of democratic rights: the Czechs were not burdened, like the Magyars, with a great aristocracy, nor, like the Germans, associated with the Imperial past. Palacký, with some wavering, had put forward a pure national programme at Kroměřiž, advocating the redivision of Austria into new national units. This had asked too much of the other Czech leaders. The weaker their present position, the more it needed reinforcement with historic rigmarole; and thus the sons of Czech peasants presented themselves as claimants to the inheritance of the dead Kingdom of Bohemia. A national programme would have meant the loss of Silesia, now mainly German and Polish; it would have endangered Moravia, where the Czech majority was still dormant; it implied even the partition of Bohemia. After all, national frontiers, like natural frontiers, are advocated only when they involve an accession of territory. A new Czech national unit larger than historic Bohemia could have been created if it had included the Slovaks of Hungary; and this idea had been aired by some extremists at the Slav Congress in 1848. The events of 1848 made the Hungarian frontier immutable. Economically it counted for less; politically and above all culturally it counted for far more, and there was never after

1848 that free movement of Slav intellectuals to and fro across the Hungarian frontier which was a normal feature of the Austria of Metternich. Besides, the pressure of Magyar nationalism drove the few Slovak intellectuals away from their former Czech links. The first Slovak literary forms had been deliberately based on the peasant dialects of western Slovakia, as being nearer to Czech; these forms were strange to the bulk of Slovak peasants, and to save them from magyarization the Slovak intellectuals of the sixties adopted instead the dialect of central Slovakia. Thus to meet the Magyar danger the Slovaks were driven to become a separate nation; and the more rigid the Hungarian frontier the more clearly defined the Slovaks became. In 1848 it was still possible to imagine a change in the Hungarian frontier; after Kossuth the frontier seemed eternal, and was accepted as such by the dynasty and even by the Czechs.

Since Hungary could not be dismembered, its example was followed; and the Czech intellectuals aped the Hungarian assertion of traditional rights, though they had no traditional rights to assert. The Hungarian example led the Czech intellectuals, too, to ally themselves with the feudal aristocracy, who also – though for very different reasons – demanded an autonomous Bohemia. This alliance was cemented in the period of confusion which followed the publication of the October Diploma: the nobility patronized Czech culture, the intellectuals espoused the rights of the Bohemian Crown. The bargain was as bad as that which the Germans made with the dynasty. The nobility, divorced from the people of Bohemia, cared nothing for Czech emancipation, which could only mean the emancipation of their own peasants; Clam-Martinic and his fellows wanted simply an artificial feudal state which they could run without interference from bureaucracy or liberalism or modern industry. The Czech leaders had to talk the language of feudal conservatism; and they had to abandon the economic grievances of their peasants in order to make a common front not only with the Bohemian lords but with the anti-liberal aristocrats from the German lands as well. Yet the Bohemian nobility, despite their talk of the rights of the Crown of St Wenceslaus, could not conceive of a system in which the court of Vienna was not the centre of their existence; and, on their prompting, the Czech leaders agreed, under protest, to attend the Reichsrat. This gained them nothing except to make them the target of German abuse; when they withdrew from the Reichsrat in June 1863, this too achieved nothing except to demonstrate their weakness as compared with the Magyars. When the Hungarians boycotted the Reichsrat they reduced it to the 'narrower' Reichsrat of the Patent: without Hungary the great Empire could not exist. When the Czechs withdrew, the only result was to make the course of business smoother; in fact even the Bohemian Diet was not brought to a standstill by Czech abstention – the German members were merely left in a stronger position to resist Bohemian autonomy. The Czechs thus lost both ways: the aristocratic programme of 'historico-political individualities' lacked all basis of reality and so could not be exacted from the Empire by conflict; their alliance with the nobility prevented any cooperation with the German liberals, or even with the other Slav peoples.

Schmerling's alliance with the Germans barred him, too, against any appeal to the subject peoples of Hungary. These helot peoples – first denied an existence by Kossuth and then subjected to the centralism of Bach – could be won for whichever side offered them a measure of national existence. Under the protection of the army of occupation Serbs and Slovaks both revived, though in more modest form, the national claims of 1848. But the Bach system had destroyed their faith in Vienna, and they appealed, though with little success, to the Diet at Budapest. Their suspicions were well founded. The Habsburgs, most conservative dynasty of the nineteenth century, could not work with peasant peoples against the Magyar lords, who, however rebellious, possessed a tradition and a history. The German liberals, themselves in conflict with the Czechs, could not support the claims of more backward races who had even less comprehension of the needs of a great Empire. The Serb and Slovak deputations to Budapest bore witness to the skill of Deák and to the political incompetence of Schmerling.

Croatia and Transylvania, the *partes adnexae* of Hungary, were handled with the same incompetence. Croatia had been the keypoint of Habsburg recovery in 1848; it received as reward the destruction of its historic position and the rigour of the Bach hussars. The Old Conservatives who overthrew the Bach system cared nothing for Croatia, for, as Hungarian patriots, they supported historic rights only when these worked in favour of Hungary; and the October Diploma was operated in Croatia only as an after-thought. The Croat gentry took Hungary as their model. They, too, rejected the theory of the October Diploma as a free gift, demanded all the legal rights of their Diet of 1848, and refused to send delegates either to Vienna or to Budapest. Deák once more showed his wisdom: he announced that Hungary did not insist on the validity of the incorporation of Croatia into Hungary in 1848 and offered the Croats 'a clean sheet' on which to write the terms of their new partnership. Schmerling was merely enraged by the appeal to historic rights: the Croat Diet was brusquely ordered to send dele-gates to the Reichsrat and, on its refusal, abruptly dissolved. Schmer-ling was glad to see it go; despite his boasting in the Reichsrat, he did not want the Croats in Vienna, where they would have strengthened the Czech opposition against his loyal, subservient Germans.

The greatest confusion was in Transylvania. In 1848, the Transyl-vanian Diet had voted its own abolition and the merging of Transyl-vania into Hungary; at the same time, the Rumanians, previously without votes or indeed legal existence, were given a limited fran-chise. If historical doctrine meant anything, then the October Diploma, with its guiding principle of a return to 1847, implied the revival of the Transylvanian Diet; on the other hand, if Transylvania was to be treated as part of Hungary, then the Rumanians should receive the franchise which had been part of the incorporation of 1848. The Old Conservatives tried to have it both ways. As Hun-garian patriots, they would not surrender what Hungary had gained; as reactionary landowners, they opposed the enfranchise-ment of the Rumanian peasants. Thanks to their resistance, the Transylvanian Diet did not meet until November 1861. Here was safer ground for Schmerling to practise his doctrine of a united Empire. The Rumanians, backward and helpless, would obey the central government and would use their votes to swamp the Magyars and Széklers in favour of the loyal Saxons; even if a few Rumanians were returned, they had no Slav sentiment to bind them to the Czech conservative opposition. In 1863 Saxon delegates from Transylvania appeared at the Reichsrat, and Schmerling was able to proclaim that it was now the full Reichsrat of the united Empire. In fact, this united Empire had the support only of the Germans; all the other peoples were either silent or in opposition.

Schmerling presented the Austrian Empire as a German state; the logical consequence was an Austrian bid for supremacy in Germany. This logic was lacking at the Habsburg court. While Schmerling evoked German national feeling, Rechberg, the disciple of Metternich, remained Foreign Minister and attempted to revive the conservative alliance with Prussia. Schmerling's threats helped Bismarck to power in Prussia, and Bismarck was ready to face a conflict; Rechberg kept out of Schmerling's hands the weapon of nationalist enthusiasm without which this conflict could not be fought. In 1863 Schmerling won Francis Joseph for the idea of a reform of the German Confederation under Austrian leadership. The practical expression of this policy was the meeting of the German princes at Frankfurt in August 1863, last gathering of Germany under the presidency of the Habsburgs. Schmerling's success was illusory: Rechberg, not Schmerling, accompanied Francis Joseph to Frankfurt and kept the discussions on safe conservative lines. Still, Schmerling could have done no better: as a servant of the dynasty, he thought only of cooperation with the other German dynasties, and this gave no satisfaction to the deep-seated feeling of German nationalism. Moreover the King of Prussia, greatest of German princes, refused to come to Frankfurt, and the German princes would do nothing without him. In the autumn of 1863, Prussia finally rejected the Austrian demand for inclusion in the Zollverein, which Rechberg had made for the sake of conservative solidarity and Schmerling for the sake of the 'Empire of seventy millions'. This was the decisive moment in German, and so in Austrian affairs; henceforth conservative and liberal policy led alike to war.

For this war Austria lacked allies. Francis Joseph would never surrender the remnant of his Italian lands, though this was at all times the price of Napoleon's support. The Polish revolt in the spring of 1863 completed the estrangement with Russia. While Bismarck made effective gestures in favour of Russia, Austria made futile gestures in favour of the Poles, mainly to keep the support of the Polish aristocracy in Galicia, Schmerling's only allies other than the Germans. Besides, new crowns always tempted the Habsburgs, and Francis Joseph dreamt, even now, of a Habsburg Kingdom of Poland. Yet he would not work whole-heartedly with the western Powers, England and France; and thus forfeited the last chance of escaping from isolation. There was the same confusion in the question of Sleswig-Holstein, which arose early in 1864. Schmerling insisted that Austria must help to liberate the Duchies in order to satisfy German feeling: Rechberg ensured that she acted only in cooperation with Prussia, thus offending the liberal enthusiasm to which Schmerling wished to appeal. In August 1864, Rechberg, too, had his brief moment of success. Faced with the complications of the Sleswig-Holstein question, Bismarck, perhaps not sincerely, made a last attempt to return to Metternich's conservative partnership. The Schönbrünn agreement, drafted by Bismarck and Rechberg, was an alliance against 'the revolution' – against German liberalism, against Italy, and against Napoleon III. The proposed alliance offered Austria a revival of the Italian hegemony which Metternich had made the centre of his system; the implied price, however, was the recognition of Prussia as an equal in Germany, and this Francis Joseph had always refused. Besides, alliance against the revolution did not extend to Hungary; and Bismarck made it an essential condition that Austria 'should shift her centre of gravity to Budapest', ignoring that this meant abandoning the German cause in south-eastern Europe – or perhaps advocating it for that very reason. Most of all the Rechberg–Bismarck pact gave Austria no security against Russia in the Near East; yet a pacific Russian policy in the Balkans had been the necessary basis for Metternich's system. In truth, there was no chance of reviving the Holy Alliance after the Punctation of Olomouc and the Crimean War; and both Francis Joseph and William I of Prussia rejected their advisers' draft. William would not act as Austria's satellite; Francis Joseph hoped to gain the advantages offered by both Schmerling and Rechberg without committing himself to either. Slow-witted, obstinate, and ambitious, he grasped on all sides at prizes which evaded him, and supposed that the postponing of decisions was the essence of policy.

After August 1864 Rechberg's policy had failed as completely as Schmerling's after August 1863. The only question was which would fall first. Schmerling had the last satisfaction of seeing his rival go in October 1864. Austrian foreign policy now abandoned all effort at principle and fell back on dynastic selfishness. Mensdorff, the new Foreign Minister, was a great noble, but, being a soldier, supported a strong central authority. He had accepted office only at the military command of the Emperor and, without faith in his own judgement or capacity, looked for guidance to Esterházy, the Minister without Portfolio. Esterházy was that worst of counsellors, a despairing conservative, his vision sharpened by certainty of defeat; he could see the dangers in every policy and salvation in none. He had no sympathy with Schmerling's appeal to German liberalism, and no hope in Rechberg's conservatism. He believed only that the dynasty should defend its greatness and should go down with honour; therefore he refused to soil this honour by trying to buy off any of the enemies who threatened the Habsburg Monarchy. In short he combined Metternich's opinion of Austria's weakness with Schwarzenberg's policy of isolation, which had been based on a belief in Austria's strength.

Esterházy was exactly the man for Francis Joseph. Both desired to preserve the greatness of the Empire; both believed that it could not be done. Both were convinced of the irresistible strength of Austria's enemies; both refused to stain their conscience by negotiating with any of them. The rise of Esterházy threatened Schmerling; for Esterházy, though an expatriate, was still a Hungarian, and through his influence the Old Conservatives began to recover their lost ground at court. Moreover, by the end of 1864, Schmerling was being deserted even by his German supporters. At first the Germans had hailed Schmerling as 'the father of the constitution' and had looked to him for help in remedying the defects of the February Patent. It soon became clear the Schmerling had no sympathy with liberal principles and that he regarded the debates of the Reichsrat as a troublesome interference with the smooth working of the bureaucratic machine. Besides, he owed his position to his having convinced the Emperor that the February Patent lacked all the qualities of a true constitution. Liberal faith in Schmerling revived with the Frankfurt meeting and with the first Austrian moves in the Sleswig-Holstein affair; it collapsed again when Austria acquiesced in a course of policy repugnant to German national sentiment. The Germans in the Reichsrat at last realized that the dynasty had not been converted to liberalism, as they had so blindly assumed in 1861; and they looked round for allies to enforce liberalism upon the dynasty. Since the Germans would not renounce the artificial predominance given them by 'electoral geometry', this ally could only be Hungary; and the Germans thus returned to the idea of the German radicals in 1848 – Magyar domination in Hungary was the price they would pay for German domination in the rest of Austria. The Germans would no longer support Schmerling's attempt to break Hungarian resistance; and in the winter session of 1864–5 they threatened even the grants needed for the military establishment. Francis Joseph had agreed to the February Patent only on condition that the Reichsrat would not tamper with the army; this condition was now infringed, and therewith Schmerling's fall made certain.

Developments in Hungary gave Schmerling the final blow. In the spring of 1865, with war approaching, even Schmerling could wait no longer and proposed to summon the Hungarian and Croat Diets once more. This was a barren proposal: the Hungarians, who had refused the Imperial demands in 1861, were not likely to surrender to a government much more nearly threatened by war. The only result of a meeting of the Diet would be to strengthen Hungarian resistance and to discredit the Empire in the eyes of Europe. This was Deák's opportunity. Between 1861 and 1865 he, too, had been content to wait, though with more justification; and had lived retired on his estates without expressing any political opinion. Now his contacts with the Old Conservatives at court told him that Schmerling was doomed and that the time had come to hold out to Francis Joseph the prospect of a compromise. Deák's influence had grown steadily in Hungary during his four years of silence; and it was completed at this very moment by Kossuth's change of line in emigration. Kossuth had now despaired of a new revolutionary war in alliance with Italy and Napoleon III; and, driven on by hatred of the Habsburgs, stumbled at last on the only policy which could give central Europe stability without the Habsburgs. Late in the day he began to advocate a free Danubian Confederation of Hungary with Serbia, Rumania, and Croatia – even if the price was a federal capital at Belgrade. This was to ask the Magyars to accept Slav peasants as equals, and the followers of Kossuth at once answered: 'Better Vienna than Belgrade!' By a fitting irony the one wise proposal that Kossuth ever made destroyed at a blow his influence in Hungary.

The way was thus clear for Deák, and in a series of newspaper articles in April and May 1865, he put forward his programme for a compromise: once the legal constitution was restored, Hungary would recognize the needs of the Empire and would provide for them on a basis of equality with the Austrian lands. Here was a programme on which Francis Joseph could negotiate. He had no 'system' for his Empire; he was determined only to maintain the greatness and armed might of the dynasty, and was indifferent as to the doctrine on which this greatness should rest. Deák's articles at once brought Francis Joseph on a visit to Budapest; for the first time he behaved strictly as King of Hungary, avoided all mention of the Empire, and declared his intention of meeting the legitimate wishes of the Hungarian people. The attempt to break Hungarian resistance was ended; and on 30 July 1865, Schmerling and the ministers who supported him were dismissed from office.

CHAPTER TEN

THE END OF OLD AUSTRIA, 1865–6

SCHMERLING had failed to break the resistance of the Magyars and had lost control of the Germans. Francis Joseph, though now starting on a different path, was still far from the idea of surrendering his power to either the Magyars or the Germans. The latest pronouncement of Deák seemed to offer some hope of a bargain which would leave the greatness of the Empire unimpaired; and in the west the alternative to sham constitutionalism, in the Emperor's eyes, was not real constitutionalism, but no constitution at all. Both Magyars and Germans were disqualified from office: a bargain had still to be struck with the Magyars, and the Germans were tarred with liberal 'disloyalty'. The only alternative was the conservative nobility, the men of the October Diploma, and the new ministry was a 'Ministry of Counts'. This was not a simple return to the situation in 1860: then the Hungarian magnates had been in the ascendant, and federalism had not counted for much with Golu-

chowski, the Minister of State; now the Hungarian Old Conservatives had disappeared, and federalism had to be practised more
seriously in order to counter the demands of the German liberals.
Belcredi,[1] the new Minister of State, was a Moravian noble, not a
Pole, and for him the pseudo-historical plans of the conservative
party were a reality. Belcredi was a man of courage and of long
administrative experience; like all the best Austrian nobles he cared
deeply for the greatness of the Empire, but he genuinely believed that
this greatness could be best served by restoring to the nobles a
position which they had never in fact possessed. Francis Joseph
thought only of Hungary and supposed that the appointment of
Belcredi would make agreement with Hungary easier; Belcredi
imagined that he had been appointed to carry through a federal
transformation of the Empire and so render concession to Hungary
harmless. This misunderstanding caused ultimate disappointment
for both Emperor and minister.

It was easy for Belcredi to reverse the policy of Schmerling.
Schmerling's worst offence in Hungarian eyes had been the admis-
sion of the Saxons from Transylvania to the Reichsrat. This was now
undone. The Transylvanian Diet, favourable to Vienna, was
dissolved, and a new one, packed in favour of the Magyars, elected;
its sole task was to vote the incorporation of Transylvania into
Hungary. The Czech boycott of the Reichsrat was approved, and
Francis Joseph announced his intention of being crowned King of
Bohemia as well as King of Hungary. The Reichsrat was closed.
More, the entire February Patent was 'suspended', on the ground
that it could not operate in one part of the Empire while the Emperor was negotiating about its amendment with another part of the
Empire. The conservative nobility welcomed the disappearance of
the February Patent and the defeat of the German bureaucrats
which this implied; and Francis Joseph was delighted by the ending
of its 'constitutional' threat. Yet Hungary was the real gainer. The
Austrian lands lost all public voice and could not be played off
against Hungary; instead of Hungary bargaining with 'Austria',
she bargained directly with the Emperor. The Habsburgs and the
Magyars became equals; and this guaranteed victory to Hungary in
advance.

1. Pronounced: Bell-crayd-ee.

Once the Schmerling system had been destroyed, Belcredi's political resources were exhausted. He had nothing better to offer than Schmerling's policy of waiting: Schmerling waited for the Hungarians to accept the February Patent, Belcredi waited for them to accept the October Diploma. The Hungarians would accept neither: they demanded throughout the restoration of the constitution of 1848, with only such modifications as they themselves should voluntarily propose. This demand was renewed when the Hungarian Diet met once more early in 1866. The Belcredi ministry offered Hungary only the restoration of county autonomy and a Diet with some administrative powers; Deák demanded a responsible ministry as provided by the laws of 1848. Deák sought to make this demand acceptable to the Emperor by outlining the arrangements with the rest of the Empire which this responsible ministry would carry in the Hungarian parliament. A committee of the Diet, under Deák's guidance, defined the common affairs of the Monarchy in which Hungary would share and proposed that these should be settled by Delegations from the Hungarian and Austrian parliaments. These Delegations marked a considerable advance on the deputations which Deák had originally proposed: they were to be independent bodies, not bound by instructions and not responsible to the two parliaments which nominated them, and in case of disagreement they were to sit as a single body and reach a decision by a majority vote.

This arrangement, keystone of the Dualism created in 1867, seemed to give up the independence of Hungary on which Deák had always insisted; for foreign policy, and the military needs springing from it, would be imposed on the Hungarian parliament by a majority of the Delegations, and there would not be ministers of foreign affairs and of war responsible to the Hungarian parliament. It was the decisive breach with Kossuth's Hungary of 1848 and the decisive concession to the Imperial demand for greatness. Yet it was not as a concession, but as an increase of Hungarian power, that it was justified. The Hungarian Delegation, held together by Magyar solidarity, would always vote as a unit; the Austrian Delegation would be split into Germans and Slavs, so that Hungary would impose her will and policy upon the entire Empire. This argument would never have occurred to Deák, whose vision was limited to the internal affairs of Hungary and to the assertion of the rule of law. That Deák accepted the argument and made it his own was the first sign of influence of Julius Andrássy, now to be decisive in the making of Dualism. Andrássy, as a young dashing magnate, had been a close adherent of Kossuth in 1848, had been hanged in effigy by the executioners of Francis Joseph, and had accompanied Kossuth into exile. He had returned and made his peace with the dynasty, when he realized the futility of Kossuth's schemes to overthrow the Habsburgs with foreign revolutionary aid. Now he became Deák's principal adviser, and Deák had already decided that he should be the first Prime Minister of free Hungary.

The two men made good partners. Deák understood Hungarian law and the art of parliamentary tactics; Andrássy knew the great world and the art of diplomacy. Each represented in different form the Hungarian adaptation to the modern world which preserved Great Hungary until the twentieth century. Deák was the ideal type of the petty noble who had emerged from his *comitat* to become a parliamentary statesman and who had developed his devotion to the traditional institutions of Hungary into Magyar nationalism; Andrássy was the ideal type of magnate who had left the Imperial court for the Budapest parliament and who had also become, in his way, a Magyar nationalist. But much of this nationalism was play-acting: the magnates still aspired to play a great role in Europe, and Andrássy's deepest ambition was to be Foreign Minister of a powerful Austrian Empire, not to be Prime Minister of Hungary. Both men were moderate, Deák from wise judgement, Andrássy from harsh experience. Both men desired to compromise with the Emperor and to conciliate the nationalities – enough at any rate to keep them from acting as allies of Vienna. Andrássy, however, was in a hurry: he wanted to display his diplomatic talents to Europe and gave a cynical twist to Deák's love of tactical manoeuvre. Andrássy was the perfect intermediary between Deák and the Emperor. Francis Joseph was estranged by Deák's probity and by his legal pedantry; Andrássy conciliated him by his impatience to be done with internal affairs and his desire to see the Empire, in some new form, play once more a great part in Europe. Deák and Andrássy would both have been shocked by the later violence of Magyar nationalism; yet both based their moderation on tactics and so prepared the way for its overthrow. The Hungarian was yet to be born who would accept the Slavs and Rumanians as equals.

In the spring of 1866 the Belcredi ministry was far from accepting the plans of Deák, even with the bait which Andrássy had tied to them. Like Schmerling, they had come to regard the Hungarian Diet as a subversive body. As so often in human affairs, men, brought to office to pursue one policy, found themselves in a short time pursuing its opposite. The Belcredi ministry had been appointed to strengthen the Empire for a war against Prussia by settling with Hungary; as the war with Prussia came nearer, they put off a settlement in the hope that a victory in war would make concession unnecessary. Mensdorff and Esterházy had nothing which could be called a foreign policy – nothing except an assertion of all Austria's claims and a refusal to seek allies by the slightest concession. They would not appeal to German national feeling against Prussia; at the same time they would not restore the conservative partnership by recognizing Prussia as an equal. They would not make concessions to the 'revolutionary' Napoleon III; they would not conciliate the tsar by concessions in the Near East. They would not buy Italian neutrality by surrendering Venetia, and dreamt, even now, of restoring the settlement of Italy as it had existed before 1859. Old Austria committed a brainless suicide; and Bismarck went to war in order to impose on Austria a decision which her rulers were incapable of making for themselves. The Austrian ministers feared victory as much as defeat; for victory would compel Austria to become without reserve the leading German power and so cause the eclipse of the cosmopolitan Austrian nobility. Esterházy, who contributed to the war more than any other expressed their outlook: 'I hate this war; for, whether we win or whether we lose, it will no longer be the old Austria.' As in 1859 and again in 1914, Francis Joseph and his advisers were set on war and equally set on defeat.

At the last minute, after Italy had made a military alliance with Prussia, the Austrian government decided to surrender Venetia, despite their previous protests of principles. The offer was refused by Italy. The Austrian ministers were now as obstinate in concession as they had been earlier in refusal. Since Italy would not accept Venetia, it should go to Napoleon III. On 12 June 1866 they bought the neutrality which Napoleon III had neither intention nor ability to abandon by promising to surrender Venetia, whatever the outcome of the war, and by agreeing to a French protectorate of the Rhineland. Thus, even before defeat, the paramount Power of Germany and Italy abandoned both. Aristocratic incompetence and dynastic pride made defeat certain. Archduke Albrecht, the best general of the Monarchy, could not, as a member of the Imperial house, be exposed to the risk of defeat. He was therefore removed from Bohemia, the decisive theatre of war, to Venetia, which was being defended solely for the privilege of surrendering it; and a second-rate soldier, Benedek, was sent to Bohemia. Albrecht won an empty victory over the Italians at Custoza. Benedek blundered over Bohemia until attacked on two sides and his army routed by the Prussians at Sadova[1] on 3 July 1866. Austria had still great powers of resistance. Archduke Albrecht, recalled from Italy, organized a new defensive front on the Danube and challenged Prussia to a long war. This was not necessary. Bismarck aimed to preserve Austria, not to destroy her; and pushed on peace negotiations the harder in order to avoid the mediation of Napoleon III or Russian demands for a reward in the Near East. By the Peace of Prague (23 August 1866), Austria lost Venetia and was excluded from Germany; she remained a Great Power.

The Austria which emerged from the war of 1866 was created by Bismarck as much as the Austria which emerged from the Napoleonic Wars was created by Metternich: created, that is, not in its internal balance, but in its significance as a Great Power. Metternich's Austria was a European necessity; Bismarck's Austria was a German necessity, or rather a Prussian necessity. It was the essential barrier against Greater Germany, against the Pan-German programme which would swamp the Prussian Junkers. And since many others were opposed to Greater Germany, Austria was welcome for them also. It was better than Greater Germany for the Czechs, the Poles, and the Slovenes; in the international field, it was better than Greater Germany for France. Moreover, the alternative to Greater Germany, if the Austrian Empire fell, or perhaps its accompaniment, would be Pan-Slavism and the extension of Russian power; therefore the Austrian Empire was welcome for England and even for conservative Russians who disliked Pan-Slavism. Dominant in Germany

1. German name: Königgrätz.

The
HABSBURG
MONARCHY
1815-1918

0   50   100   150
Miles

PRUSSIA

SAXONY

Elbe

Prague

BOHEMIA

MO

B

BAVARIA

Danube

Inn

Linz

UPPER
AUSTRIA

Salzburg

LOWER

VIENN

AUSTRIA

Bratis

VORARL
BERG

Innsbruck

SALZBURG

TYROL

CARINTHIA

Graz

Klagenfurt

 STYRIA

Dr

SWITZ'L'D

A L P S

Ljubljana

CARNIOLA

Zagre

LOMBARDY

Milan

VENETIA

Venice

GOR

TRIESTE

ISTRIA

RIJEKA

Save

CROATIA

Pulj

D

B

I T A L Y

A

D

R

I

A

Mountains

Military Frontier

Cracow annexed   1846
Lombardy lost   1859
Venetia   "   1866
Bosnia and
Hercegovina annexed 1908

J.F.Horrabin

and Italy, Austria had challenged too grossly the nationalist dogmas of the time; excluded from Germany and Italy, Austria served to postpone the raising of the great questions in central and eastern Europe from which the Powers still shrank. Italy resented the existence of Austria; but Italy was without power, except when associated with the grievances of others, and within a few years Austria, with Bismarck's assistance, supervised Italy's policy almost as closely as in the days of Metternich. The Russian expansionists whose eyes were fixed on Constantinople resented the existence of Austria; but they were in a minority, and the decision went against them in Russian counsels, except for a few weeks in 1878, until the destruction of Bismarck's Europe in 1914. Everyone else wanted Austria to be kept going. After the war of 1866 the Habsburg Monarchy was undoubtedly a Sick Man; this very fact won her European tolerance and even support.

Metternich had recognized the danger of becoming solely a European necessity; and had sought, with little success, a 'mission' which should make the Empire acceptable to its peoples and so less dependent on the favour of others. The search for a mission was renewed after 1866, with little more success than in the days of Metternich. The Magyars, indeed, found a mission for Austria in the furthering of Magyar hegemony in Hungary; and this suited Bismarck's need. Bismarck revived the German alliance with the Magyars which had been part of the Frankfurt programme in 1848. Only he improved on it: Frankfurt had sought Magyar aid for Greater Germany, Bismarck used Hungary as an ally against it, and this policy was the more welcome to the Hungarians. Still, it could not be Austria's sole mission to serve the ambition of the Magyars, who were hardly one fifth of her population. The Germans still hoped that the Habsburg Empire would further German cultural and economic supremacy in south-eastern Europe, or at any rate within the Empire. This did not fit so easily into Bismarck's system. Bismarck could not allow the revival of German Austrian strength and therewith a renewed danger of the 'Empire of seventy millions'; on the other hand, he could not allow the Austrian Empire to lose its German character and so become eligible as the ally of France or even of Russia. In fact, Bismarck wished to preserve Austria as she was in 1866 – defeated, but still German; and the suspended animation of Austrian politics in the age of Dualism was largely the result of German needs. Certainly Germany would have resisted any real Austrian attempt to follow the only mission which could have justified her existence: the discovery of a way of cooperation between peoples of different nationalities, not based upon the hegemony of a privileged nation or class. Not that Bismarck, still less any other German statesman, understood the nature of the Austrian problem. The Poles were the only Slav minority of whom Prussian politicians had experience, and these they ruled by force without serious effort to conciliate them. Force alone would not do in Austria; this had been the decisive lesson from the experience both of Bach and Schmerling. Francis Joseph was reluctant enough to accept the aid of the Magyars; he would certainly not place himself in the hands of the Germans also – especially as these would acquire real force only with a Greater German programme, detestable alike to Francis Joseph and to Bismarck. Still, without a free cooperation of the peoples Greater Germany was certain. The only alternative was Russian hegemony in central and eastern Europe; and in the outcome the subjects of the Habsburgs experienced first one and then the other. This was the measure of Habsburg failure.

CHAPTER ELEVEN

THE MAKING OF DUALISM, 1866-7

IN August 1866, immediately after defeat, the Magyars offered themselves as partners. Deák declared that they asked no more after defeat than before it; he meant by this that their highest ambition had now become capable of practical achievement. Andrássy, coming to Vienna to confer with the Emperor, spoke already as an Imperial statesman. He had very different views on Austria from the Old Conservatives who had hitherto provided the link between the Emperor and Hungary. Andrássy desired an Austria centralized, liberal, and German, just as Hungary would be centralized, liberal, and Magyar. This was a revival of the idea of 1848, except that the partnership was now between Budapest and Vienna, instead of between Budapest and Frankfurt, so that there would still be room for the dynasty. The Germans and Magyars were to be the two 'Peoples of state'; as for the others, Andrássy said: 'the Slavs are not fit to govern, they must be ruled.' Dualism as a partnership between Magyars and Germans was a favourite idea, or more correctly a favourite misunderstanding, in the following years; it was far from being the intention of Francis Joseph. He had brought himself to make concessions to the Magyars in order to avoid making concessions to any other groups; and he certainly did not intend to surrender his power to the German liberals. Andrássy's clever talk in favour of the German Austrians offended Francis Joseph and actually restored the position of Belcredi, which had been shaken by the lost war; for Belcredi combined support, somewhat grudging, of Dualism with resistance to liberalism. In July 1866, Francis Joseph, still needing support against Prussia, seemed ready to accept all Hungary's demands; in August, with the signing of the Peace of Prague, the immediate crisis was ended, and Andrássy returned to Budapest empty-handed.

The Hungarian demands had been clearly stated. Belcredi now planned that the other provinces of the Empire should be brought artificially to formulate similar demands, so that Hungary should lose her unique position. The provincial Diets had therefore to be recalled and induced to claim privileges which they had not exercised for centuries or often never possessed. If, however, the Diets were elected on the existing franchise, they would not claim these privileges; for 'electoral geometry' would produce German majorities in favour of a strong central parliament. The electoral system had to be made anew, and unreliable, that is centralist, officials hastily replaced by federalist nobles. Belcredi, operating conservative policy more thoroughly than ever before, ran the more sharply against its great contradiction: he was proposing to challenge both the bureaucracy and the German middle class throughout the Empire by breaking the bonds of the unitary state as it had existed for more than a century, yet his conservatism debarred him from seeking allies other than the great nobility. Belcredi meant to manufacture Slav majorities in the Diets, but he did not wish these majorities to represent popular movements. He objected to the German majorities of Schmerling as liberal, not as German; and he turned to the Slavs as conservative, clerical, and respectful to the nobility. The Slavs were conservative and clerical from immaturity; and as they grew into political consciousness, they, too, became liberal and demanded the Rights of Man. Thus the only political allies of Belcredi were not a serious force; and as they became a serious force, they ceased to be eligible as allies. Belcredi had to hope that the landed nobility would suddenly develop administrative skill and that the German bureaucrats would be loyal enough to assist in dissolving the unitary state which they had themselves created.

Belcredi had, however, only a few months in which to demonstrate the failure of Old Conservatism for the last time. He had seemed the only alternative to the German liberals. In October 1866 Francis discovered a German and in a way a liberal, who was not associated with the German liberals of the Empire. Beust,[1] who now became Foreign Minister, had been for many years Prime Minister of Saxony and a leading opponent of Bismarck in the German Confederation. His appointment announced a policy of revenge against Prussia: Beust had no reason for political existence except his hostility to Bismarck, and his very appearance in office was a provocative reassertion of the connexion between Austria and Germany. Beust was no Metternich equipped, or handicapped, with a political philosophy; his stock-in-trade, like that of all the statesmen in the unreal petty German states, was smartness – the clever phrase and the quick result with no thought of the consequences. Beust had no 'views' about the Austrian Empire. Naturally he regarded it as a German state, since he had been dealing with it as such for years; but he had no emotional attachment to any particular policy – the tradition of the unitary Empire which dominated the bureaucracy, the pseudo-historic ambitions of the nobility, the dynastic 'mission' to protect the subject peoples, were alike indifferent to him. His only concern was somehow to settle the internal affairs of Austria, so that it would once more inspire confidence abroad and he could proceed to build up an anti-Prussian coalition. He therefore looked straight at the central fact which bureaucrats and nobles, Schmerling and Belcredi, had alike evaded: the only important thing was to settle

1. Pronounced: Boyst.

with Hungary, and the only way of doing it was to give the Hungarians what they demanded. His grasp of this truth brought him success where his predecessors had all failed and made him, on the Imperial side, the creator of Dualism. Yet this very success in internal affairs doomed his foreign policy. He gave the Magyars, and to a lesser extent the Germans, a voice in the affairs of the Empire; and these were the two peoples who would never support a war of revenge against Prussia. The Magyars knew that they owed their success to the defeat of Austria in 1866; the Germans, despite their resentment against Prussia, would not go against the German national state. Thus, by a supreme paradox, the political system devised by an exponent of war against Prussia ensured the permanence of Bismarck's work.

It never occurred to Belcredi that a 'foreigner' would settle the Austrian problem behind his back. He went slowly on his way, provoking the provincial ambitions of the non-Hungarian lands. Even Belcredi, with his dislike of a central Reichsrat, realized that the individual Diets were not imposing enough to impress Hungary; on the other hand he would not revive the February Patent which had been 'suspended' in September 1865. He therefore fell back on the clause of the October Diploma, which provided for occasional meetings of the non-Hungarian lands in an 'extraordinary Reichsrat'. He could thus escape the electoral provisions of the February Patent. The Diets would be instructed to elect their delegates by a simple majority instead of each curia voting separately; and the result would be a Slav-conservative majority in the Reichsrat instead of the German liberal majority produced by 'electoral geometry'. Negotiations with Hungary could thus be dragged out indefinitely. Meanwhile, Croatia could be encouraged to make demands against Hungary and thus to weaken Hungary from within.

While Belcredi methodically prepared his version of 'electoral geometry', Beust acted. He visited Budapest and established close agreement with Andrássy: both men thought in terms of foreign policy and both regarded with impatience the dogmatism of Belcredi, the hesitations of Francis Joseph, and even the probity of Deák. Beust, once satisfied of the possibility of an agreement, persuaded Francis Joseph to abandon the traditional method of 'bargaining' between King and Diet; the Hungarian leaders were regarded as a responsible government, according to the laws of 1848, and came to Vienna for direct negotiation. This was the decisive step, for in agreeing to a responsible government Francis Joseph had acceded to the Hungarian programme and had to accept concessions from the Hungarian ministers instead of they from him. The negotiations at Vienna were of a strange, illegal character: Andrássy and his colleagues already spoke for Hungary, and the Austrian ministers, though technically still Imperial ministers, spoke merely for the non-Hungarian lands, for the lesser Austria as created by Dualism. Francis Joseph, once convinced that the Hungarian proposals would leave him in control of the army and of foreign affairs, was in a hurry to finish; as always, impatience followed his prolonged hesitation, and he jettisoned old obligations and advisers. In December 1866, a Croat deputation came to Vienna offering to cooperate with the Empire on an equal footing with Hungary; they were brusquely told that the services of Jellačić were not regarded with favour as they had been in 1848 and that they must settle with Hungary as best they could. Belcredi was still able to issue a Patent on 2 January 1867, for the meeting of an 'extraordinary Reichsrat'; this was a vain expedient. He and the other Austrian ministers could only listen to the Hungarian proposals and sadly acquiesce, knowing that the Emperor had already made his decision. On 7 February 1867, Belcredi and 'the Counts' were dismissed; and Beust was left alone, with a few officials, to wind up Old Austria. In this characteristic way, Dualism was manufactured helter-skelter; and the constitution of Austria-Hungary determined by a Saxon politician and a Magyar aristocrat.

The intention of all Austrian ministers, of Schmerling as well as of Belcredi, and the original intention of Deák, had been a settlement between the two 'Imperial halves'. Hungary had certainly been consulted; and Dualism did not become effective until transformed into a law of the Hungarian parliament in March 1867. The other, nameless 'half' had no voice: Francis Joseph had settled without it. To wait for the consent of a non-existent Reichsrat seemed unnecessary; besides, the Reichsrat might dispute points which Hungary had already accepted. The Hungarians, however, insisted that the non-Hungarian lands must approve the settlement, though they could neither alter nor reject it. Beust therefore revived the February Patent, which had been designed for the entire Empire, and applied it casually to the 'half'; the 'narrower Reichsrat' of the Patent became henceforth the 'ordinary Reichsrat' of constitutional Austria. This device ran up against the last relics of Belcredi. The Diets, elected under his management in November and December 1866, were federalist or conservative; and five of the most important[1] refused to acknowledge the February Patent or to send members to the Reichsrat. These recalcitrant Diets were abruptly dissolved, and the 'electoral geometry' of Schmerling revived with such force that a German majority was manufactured even in Bohemia. Czechs and Slovenes continued to boycott the Reichsrat without avail. It had the appearance of a respectable parliament; and completed the formalities of Dualism by accepting the settlement as a 'constitutional law' in December 1867.

Dualism was exclusively a 'compromise' between the Emperor and the Hungarians. The Hungarians agreed that there should be a single great state for war and foreign affairs; Francis Joseph handed over the internal affairs of Hungary to the 'Magyar nation'. The Hungarians also agreed that there should be a customs union with the rest of the Monarchy, to be renewed every ten years. There were thus three separate organizations: the permanent 'common monarchy', which still presented a great Habsburg Power to the outer world; the temporary economic union of Austria-Hungary; and the two separate states, Austria[2] and Hungary. The 'common monarchy' was confined to the Emperor and his court, the Minister

1. Bohemia and Moravia with Czech-conservative majorities; Carniola with a Slovene majority; Galicia, with a Polish majority; Tyrol, with a majority of German conservatives. Even electoral geometry could not destroy the Slovene majority in Carniola, where the Slovenes were 98 per cent of the population, and the Diet was dissolved afresh. Electoral geometry was also useless in Galicia, and the Poles were bought off by the promise of a special position.

2. Technically the 'Empire of Austria' still meant the whole; and Austria-Hungary, to use a British analogy, is not 'England-Scotland,' but 'Great Britain-Scotland'; and 'the common Monarchy' was a Hungarian device to avoid the hated word 'Empire' or 'Reich'. The non-Hungarian lands had no name: they were 'the other half of the Empire' or, strictly, 'the lands represented in the Reichsrat'. They were loosely called 'Austria', and I shall henceforth use this convenient description, though it was not legal until 1915.

for Foreign Affairs, and the Minister of War.[1] There was no common Prime Minister and no common cabinet. Beust, given the title of Imperial Chancellor in honour of his achievement in disrupting the Empire, attempted to exercise an authority superior to the two state ministries, and was imitated by a later Foreign Minister, Kálnoky;[2] these attempts were successfully resisted by the Hungarians. Unofficially and without constitutional authority, the Crown Council of the Emperor acted as a common cabinet: it was attended by the two Prime Ministers, the common ministers, a few Archdukes, and the Chief of Staff. They could do no more than advise the Emperor; and decisions on 'great policy' remained in his hands. This had been the motive of Francis Joseph in making the compromise: in foreign affairs he was still supreme.

The common monarchy had, however, constitutional expression in the Delegations. Each Delegation had sixty members. In Hungary the House of Magnates by direct vote elected twenty, of whom one had to be a Croat; the House of Representatives by direct vote elected forty, of whom four were elected by the Croat members. In Austria, twenty were elected by direct vote in the House of Lords; forty were elected in the House of Representatives by electoral colleges of members from the various provinces and returning a number of delegates proportionate to the size of the province – varying from ten for Bohemia down to one for Tyrol or Vorarlberg. Thus, the Hungarian Delegation represented the unitary state of Hungary, with a feeble gesture of recognition towards Croatia; the Austrian Delegation was a last version of the Estates General of conservative dreams. Hungary, which had two fifths of the population and paid one third of the taxes of the Monarchy, had in decision an equal voice. The Delegations deliberated apart; once they had agreed to the demands of the common ministers, the two state parliaments had to provide the necessary money and contingents of

1. The third common minister, the Minister of Finance, had no serious function. He could only present the expenses of the common monarchy to the Finance Ministers of Austria and Hungary, and these had to devise the necessary taxes. Being unemployed, he became the odd-job man of the Monarchy; for example, he was put in charge of Bosnia and Hercegovina when these were occupied in 1878.

2. Pronounced: Kahlnockee.

men without dispute. In case of disagreement, the Delegations were to meet and vote together in silence; this was the highest expression of the common monarchy. In practice, the Hungarians resisted this infringement of their sovereignty, and it was never exercised. This, too, suited Francis Joseph; since the Delegations remained deliberative, decision rested with him. Here, too, the Hungarians, by refusing to cooperate with the other peoples of the Empire, restored power to the Emperor.

The surrender of sovereignty did not extend to economic affairs, and in these the Delegations had no say. They were settled by direct negotiation between the two parliaments. Many common institutions, such as postage and coinage, created in the days of Bach, were allowed to survive; and, after much wrangling a single National Bank was created in 1878. The two principal topics of dispute were the 'quota' – the share of common expenses – and tariff policy; and over these a crisis arose every ten years. Hungary originally contributed only 30 per cent and, though her share was finally raised to 34·4 per cent, the price was paid in a tariff policy increasingly favourable to Hungarian interests. Austria, as she developed into an industrial state, needed cheap food; Hungary insisted on high wheat duties in the interests of the great estates, and, since Austrian industry dared not lose the free Hungarian market, the Hungarian threat to abandon the commercial union usually succeeded. Still, the Austrian parliament sometimes jibbed, and the 'compromise' had then to be forced through by irregular means; this was, for instance, one cause of the great political crisis in Austria in 1897. In fact, the decennial economic bargain provided in Austria-Hungary the same regular explosion as the septennial army grant supplied in Imperial Germany: in both each recurring crisis seemed to question the very basis of the state.

There remained the two constitutional states, Austria and Hungary. The Hungarian constitution rested on the 'March laws', with the single modification, in internal affairs, that the Palatine, or Viceroy, disappeared and the King exercised his constitutional functions directly; this was a practical modification, created by the railway which had brought Vienna within four hours of Budapest. This new Hungary was a unitary state, greater than old Hungary had ever been: it included Transylvania and also the 'military frontiers', the lands of southern Hungary which had been controlled by the Austrian army since their liberation from the Turks in the eighteenth century. This gain brought in hardly any Magyars: the colonists, introduced under Maria Theresa, had been Slovaks, Germans, Rumanians, and Serbs. These, especially the Serbs, had fought fiercely against Hungary in 1848; now, abandoned by the Emperor, they were anxious for reconciliation. Deák, too, was committed to concession. The result was the Nationalities Law of 1868, striking departure in theory from the chauvinism of Kossuth. This law attempted to reconcile the Magyar national state with the existence of other nationalities in Hungary: it gave rights to minorities, it did not create a multi-national state. The minorities could conduct local government in their own language; in non-Magyar counties, they were to hold the chief administrative posts; and in the state schools, any nationality, living together 'in considerable numbers', must be able to receive education in their own language 'up to the point where higher education begins'. An admirable law, except that it was not operated in any single particular.

Deák's Hungary, too, did not attempt to renew Kossuth's incorporation of Croatia. Instead there was a 'compromise', negotiated between the two Diets. Croatia, deserted by the Emperor, had in fact to accept whatever terms Andrássy and Deák offered; still, the defects of the compromise were due to the political backwardness of Croat leaders rather than to Magyar bullying. Croatia preserved her separate existence, her language, and her Diet; she paid a fixed proportion of the common expenses of the Kingdom of Hungary, and the Croat Diet elected forty representatives to the Hungarian parliament, who were entitled to speak in Croat and took part only when the affairs of 'greater Hungary' were being discussed. There was open failure only on one point: the Croats claimed Rijeka,[1] the Hungarians insisted that it be a free city. Since the Croats held out, the Hungarians took Rijeka by a cardsharper's trick: when the compromise was presented to Francis Joseph for approval, they pasted a Croat translation of their Magyar version over the Croat statement that no agreement could be reached. There was a deeper flaw in the bargain. Hungary in 1866 possessed a modern constitution, Croatia only the traditional constitution with all its faults; and

1. Pronounced: Ree-yehka. Italian name: Fiume.

besides, with the abdication of Francis Joseph in the internal affairs of Hungary, could no longer play off Vienna against Budapest. The finances were settled at Budapest; and the bewildered Croat gentry could never determine whether the common expenses which they were called upon to meet were in fact expenses of 'greater Hungary' or of Hungary proper with which they had no concern. There was no responsible ministry. The Governor of Croatia, hitherto appointed by the Emperor, was now appointed and dismissed by the Hungarian Ministry; and the Croat Diet had only the traditional function of barren opposition and complaint. It was forbidden to communicate with Vienna; and even the Governor could communicate with the Emperor only through the Minister for Croatia at Budapest. In fact, like the nationalities in Hungary, the Croats were dependent on Magyar good will.

In Hungary there could be a return to the 'March laws'. In Austria the February Patent would not do even for the Germans. Beust was ready to meet them. With his long experience of constitutional play-acting as Prime Minister of Saxony, he knew that liberal concessions did not involve any shift of real power so long as they did not lead to parliamentary control over the executive, and these liberal concessions were all that the German liberals demanded. They thought it the duty of liberalism to protect the individual from the state and could not imagine a state under popular control, least of all under their own; as in Germany, the state was still something remote, *die Obrigkeit*, 'authority'. To take over responsibility for the running of a great state is a terrifying prospect for anyone except a hereditary dynasty or a hereditary governing class grown accustomed to the idea. In England nearly three hundred years passed (roughly from the beginning of the reign of Elizabeth to the end of the reign of George III) before the English landowning and commercial classes would take the plunge; in France the bourgeoisie, after the great Revolution, resorted to every kind of desperate expedient for avoiding responsibility – empire, revived monarchy, sham monarchy, sham empire – until the failure of all left them with no escape from responsibility in the Third Republic, and even that perished from lack of a true governing class. In Austria, as in Germany, the dynasty had not been overthrown and had no intention of relinquishing power; and the liberals were content with a series of 'constitutional laws', added as glosses to the February Patent.

These constitutional laws, even now, did not transform the February Patent into a system of responsible government; and the way was left open for the revival of Imperial autocracy in case of emergency. Still, they created a system of individual freedom more genuinely liberal than in either Hungary or Imperial Germany. There was equality before the law, civil marriage, freedom of expression, freedom of movement. The Concordat of 1855 was undone, state control of the Roman Catholic Church re-established, and education freed again from clerical control. There were balanced budgets and stable currency for more than thirty years. The police state of Metternich still existed (as, for that matter, France was a 'police state' even in the Third Republic), but it was a police state exposed to public criticism and confined to civilized behaviour. The Austrian citizen after 1867 had more civic security than the German and was in the hands of more honest and more capable officials than in France or Italy; in fact, he had an enviable existence, except that the state lacked national inspiration, and the dynasty could find no 'mission' to replace this. The German liberals offered a certain liberalism even in national affairs, and postulated a rather vague language equality in schools and public offices. The constitutional article left ambiguities to be disputed in the future; for it spoke both of the 'provincial language' and of the 'language usual in the province'. The Czechs argued that Czech and German were the two 'provincial languages' of Bohemia and that therefore Czech could be used in schools and official matters throughout Bohemia; the Germans answered that Czech was not the 'language usual in the province' in the exclusively German areas. In the Bohemian Diet the German majority, who were also the liberal leaders in the Reichsrat, passed a decree forbidding the teaching of a second compulsory 'provincial language'; they knew that all Czechs would learn German and wished to protect themselves from having to learn Czech. Still, despite these tricks, Austria had, from the start, a more liberal system of national policy than Hungary, and gave the nationalities an increasing chance of development in the following years.

The worst flaw in the liberal constitution-making of 1867 was the failure to reform the system of electoral geometry. The German liberals did not even attempt to extend the franchise in the towns, which, being predominantly German, would still have returned a German majority. The liberals of the Reichsrat were only eager, in the contemporary phrase, 'to climb on to the driver's seat of the state coach'; and it escaped their attention that they were not allowed to hold the reins. Beust's most prized performance was the appointment of an allegedly parliamentary ministry in January 1868. This was not a true responsible ministry, where the leader of a party is appointed Prime Minister and then chooses his colleagues. The ministers were chosen by Francis Joseph on the advice of Beust, and they were chosen as individuals, not as a party group. The ministry had no common programme and no common responsibility; the ministers intrigued against each other and one of them said of Herbst, the Minister of Justice: 'He criticizes us all, and regrets ceaselessly that he cannot attack the Minister of Justice as well.' This 'bourgeois ministry' seemed a liberal triumph after the 'ministry of Counts;' but Bach and many of his associates had also been of humble origin. Decision remained with the Emperor and with a few ministers whom he trusted; and most of the ministers were merely heads of administrative departments. Political affairs were now discussed without restraint and the German Austrian, at any rate, felt himself free; yet at bottom there had been little more than a return to the Bach system of rule by German middle-class officials with a liberal past – only these officials no longer needed to attend mass or to defer to the opinions of the higher clergy. In theory Austria-Hungary had become a partnership of two constitutional states, the one based on German, the other on Magyar hegemony. Behind this constitutional cloak there remained the Habsburg Monarchy, an Empire where indeed the ruler had surrendered some of his immediate control over internal affairs, but where he still exercised supreme power and where the many unsolved problems still gave him infinite room to manoeuvre for the maintenance of this power.

CHAPTER TWELVE

LIBERAL FAILURE:
GERMAN ASCENDANCY IN AUSTRIA, 1867–79

DUALISM followed a series of political expedients and was not meant to be the last of them. Francis Joseph had accepted it in haste as the necessary prelude to a war of revenge against Prussia, and repented of the bargain as soon as he had made it. His resentment was less against the Magyars than against the Germans. Though the Magyar success was greater, it was not thrust under the Emperor's nose: Budapest was four hours away, and the Magyar ministers, though liberals, were aristocrats, familiar figures at court. The Reichsrat, ineffective as it was, caught the Emperor's attention every time he left the Hofburg; and the liberal ministers, with all their subservience, were pedantic middle-class lawyers with anti-clerical views. As a result, German liberal rule, though harmless and loyal, was constantly threatened and lasted only ten years; Magyar hegemony was left undisturbed until it had doomed the Empire. There was a further consideration. German rule could be moderated or overthrown by playing off the other nations of Austria, and especially the Czechs, against the Germans; the settlement with Hungary could be challenged only if Czechs and Germans were reconciled, and any real concord among the peoples of Austria, though it would weaken the Magyars, would endanger also the supremacy of the Emperor. In internal, as in foreign affairs, Magyar hegemony was the price which Francis Joseph was willing to pay for the preservation of his own power; and since this Magyar hegemony brought the Habsburg Monarchy to destruction, Francis Joseph was the maker of his own ruin.

In 1868, after the creation of the bourgeois ministry, the immediate need of Imperial policy was to bring the Czechs back into practical politics, in order to play them off against the Germans. The Czech leaders had been driven to despair by the revival of Schmerling's electoral geometry: they had feared disaster if Austria remained a German power, they encountered disaster even though Austria was excluded from Germany. Rieger, principal Czech leader, followed wild courses: talked Pan-Slavism in Russia, and spoke of 'the mother city of Moscow'. Russian tsardom was at this time neither willing, nor indeed able, to disrupt the Habsburg Monarchy. Besides, Pan-Slavism estranged the Bohemian aristocracy, Rieger's only allies. In 1868 the Czech intellectuals and the Bohemian aristocrats renewed their alliance: Pan-Slavism was discarded and political demands formulated on the Deák model. The eighty Bohemian absentees from the Reichsrat made a declaration of their aims: they asked for equal national rights for the Czechs in Bohemia, and for a reform of the electoral system; they demanded also the unity of the lands of St Wenceslaus and the same independence for this 'great Bohemia' as Hungary possessed. The Czech leaders were bewitched by the Hungarian example. They saw, quite rightly, that the Magyars had achieved their national freedom by associating it with historic rights, and they supposed that the way to achieve the national freedom of the Czechs was to claim the historic rights of Bohemia. They did not see that the historic rights of Hungary were real, the historic rights of Bohemia imaginary, and that in claiming them the Czechs were taking up an added burden, not acquiring a new weapon. Still, the Declaration put them back into the political market, though the price they asked was too high.

The Declaration had been, in part, prompted by Taaffe,[1] the deputy Prime Minister, with whom the bourgeois ministers were saddled, as Schmerling had been saddled with Rechberg. Taaffe was a true 'Emperor's man:' an aristocrat of Irish origin, now German in the sense that his estates were in Tyrol. With Irish ingenuity, he could adapt himself both to the German liberals and to the Czech intellectuals, and got on with them as well as with the Emperor himself. He was tactful, considerate, not without intellectual interests. He had the defects of his class: he relied on time, rather than on energy, to provide solutions; he was sceptical of everything, including his own ability; and though he genuinely wished to conciliate the peoples of Austria, he did not for one moment believe that they were fit to share in the government of the Empire. Free from German dogmatism, he was ready to work for a system of

1. Pronounced: Tahfe.

national equality; on the other hand, having no estates in Bohemia, he escaped the barren conservatism of Bohemian 'historic' rights and had no sympathy with federalism. His practical aim was that the Czechs should acknowledge the unity of Austria by attending the Reichsrat, in return for fair treatment in Bohemia; and this aim was acceptable to the German ministers, who, after the disasters of the previous years, would also pay a good price for the recognition of Austrian unity.

The offer was rejected by the Czech politicians. Leaders without followers, they dared not abandon their noble allies. Unlike the nationalities of Hungary, they asked for more than tolerable treatment. They insisted that the Czechs were Bohemians as the Magyars were Hungarians; so indeed they were both in Czech and German. They were tied to the history which they had themselves revived and claimed to be the 'people of state' in Bohemia, not a minority in Austria. This was not a simple conflict between Czech and German; it was a clash between the historic Kingdom of Bohemia and the equally historic 'Holy Roman Empire of the German Nation' which had included Bohemia. The Czechs could no more be content with minority rights in Bohemia, which they claimed as their own state, than the Germans, accustomed to regard Bohemia as part of the Reich or at any rate as part of the German state of Austria, could be content later with minority rights in Czechoslovakia. Moreover, the Czech spokesmen spoke for few besides themselves: they were not sustained by a large following of nationalists, eager for jobs in the bureaucracy; and therefore the sharing of official posts, the fighting point of practical nationalism, hardly concerned them. Indeed, if they had achieved their Kingdom of Bohemia, they could not at this time have found Czechs qualified to administer it. As always, the less popular support a national movement has, the more extreme are its demands. A generation later, when there really was a conscious Czech nation, the historic rights of the Kingdom of Bohemia counted for much less in its political existence and admission to state employment for much more. Most of all, in 1868, the Czechs, conscious of their own weakness, had no faith in German good will. As Imperial ministers, the German liberals appeared conciliatory; as members of the Bohemian Diet, these same Germans treated the Czechs with contempt and, intoxicated with their artificial majority, withdrew in a body to the bar whenever a Czech rose to his feet. At heart, every German, from the Frankfurt liberals of 1848 to Hitler, regarded Bohemia as a German protectorate. To escape this, the Czechs might seek the protection of the Habsburg Emperor; they were unwilling to combine with the Germans and impose constitutional government on the Emperor.

The negotiations of 1868 led to nothing. Rieger, again in despair, vainly sought help from Napoleon III, himself in desperate need of help from the Habsburg Monarchy. The German ministers seemed indispensable; and early in 1870 proposed to break the Czech boycott of the Reichsrat by instituting direct election to the Reichsrat in the constituencies. This ended Taaffe's hope of further conciliation and drove him from office. Just at the moment of success, the German liberals were ruined by the failure of Beust's foreign policy. Beust had aimed to build up a European coalition against Prussia. Napoleon III and Francis Joseph met at Salzburg; Beust attempted to mediate between Italy and France over the question of Rome; and Austria was paraded as a German state, for the sake of feeling in Germany. This was a barren pretence. Beust sought German support against Prussia, but the object dearest to German liberalism was the unification of Germany, and that was being achieved by Prussia. The Germans in Austria were ready to take part in the pretence, since it guaranteed their privileged position in Austria, and, besides, they wished to restore the connexion with Germany which had been broken in 1866. For the Germans outside Austria, Beust offered no attractions: he proposed that they should ally themselves with the national enemy in order to satisfy his personal vanity.

The Franco-Austrian alliance was, however, wrecked on the question of Rome. The Austrian generals would not face a new war against Prussia, unless secure from an Italian attack; Italy would not enter the alliance unless the French troops were withdrawn from Rome; Napoleon III could not give up the protection of the Pope, which was the last remaining point of his prestige. Beust, a Protestant from Saxony, would have had no scruples in abandoning the Papacy; the deep-rooted loyalty of the Habsburg House to the Catholic cause tied his hands, and the tradition of the Counter-Reformation deprived the dynasty of its last chance to recover its German position. Negotiations dragged on throughout 1869: declarations of friendship were made and military missions exchanged in a futile attempt to impress Bismarck. Nothing was settled; and when the Franco-Prussian war broke out in July 1870, France and Austria were not in alliance. If Prussia won, Beust would never have his revenge on Bismarck, and he was ready to run the risk of war. He received no support. The generals feared defeat; the German ministers were enthusiastic for Bismarck despite his exclusion of Austria from Germany; and Andrássy, as Hungarian Prime Minister, resisted a war which must either reverse the verdict of 1866 – and so destroy its sequel, the compromise of 1867 – or else lead to a new Austrian defeat. Germans and Magyars could have been overriden if Beust had been able to create a European coalition; as it was, he had not fulfilled the conditions of his employment. After all, it was too much to expect to find the victorious rival of Bismarck in a vain, super-ficial diplomat, ruined by long years as Prime Minister of a petty German state. Austria-Hungary remained neutral and accepted Bismarck's Germany as the predominant Power in Europe. Only the Bohemian Diet expressed sympathy with France and protested against the annexation of Alsace-Lorraine; a gesture of moral support more challenging to the Germans than useful to France. It was repaid, with equal futility, by French expressions of sympathy in 1938.

Once the policy of revenge was abandoned, Francis Joseph was no longer committed to the German liberals; indeed, he could even challenge the compromise with Hungary. In the autumn of 1870 he turned once more to Taaffe. Taaffe's attempts at conciliation failed with both Czechs and Germans: the Czechs believed that they were in sight of complete victory, the Germans would not negotiate with the man who had displaced them. Since Francis Joseph would not again employ the German liberals, there remained only two alterna-tives: the dogmatic Austrian centralists, still led by Schmerling, or the federalizing aristocrats whose last representative had been Belcredi. The Magyars insisted that they would never tolerate Schmerling as Prime Minister of Austria; and this Hungarian interference in the affairs of Austria made Francis Joseph the more resolved to appoint a ministry which would recognize Bohemian rights and so deprive Hungary of her unique position. In February, 1871, a 'ministry above the parties' came into office, federal in programme, yet – despite liberal outcry – mainly German in

membership. Hohenwart, the Prime Minister, was a German aristocrat, who believed that federalism would strengthen the Empire. The
intellectual leader of the ministry was Schäffle,[1] the Minister of
Commerce, a German who was not even an aristocrat. Schäffle, a
radical from Baden, was one of the few Germans who had possessed a
genuine idealism in 1848 and who had retained it in the years of
failure. Though a radical and a Protestant, he had become Professor
of Political Economy in the University of Vienna and taught the
economics of social welfare in the high age of *laissez faire*. His German
patriotism was devoted to a spiritual tradition, not to the worship of
Prussian force; and he believed that this tradition could be renewed
in the Habsburg Empire, if the Empire were purged of racial
domination. Schäffle was almost the first to grasp the class division
of the nationalities; and he advocated universal suffrage as a weapon
at once against liberalism and against the German monopoly. With
the limitless confidence of the idealist, he believed that the Germans
would quietly accept the loss of their privileged position and that
universal suffrage would make Austria universally contented and so
capable of challenging Magyar hegemony also. Universal suffrage
was too daring a doctrine for Francis Joseph, and Schäffle had to be
content with a meagre extension of the franchise – enough, however,
to give the Czechs control of the Bohemian Diet. Still, Schäffle's
ideas took root in Francis Joseph's slow-moving mind and came to
unexpected fruition thirty-five years later.

The principal object of the Hohenwart–Schäffle government was
a compromise with Bohemia; and the Czech leaders supposed that
the moment had come for them to repeat the success of Deák and
Andrássy. They were ready to agree to generous terms for the
German minority in Bohemia; and, not being saddled with an
educated class anxious for official jobs, would, unlike the Magyars,
have kept their promise.[2] Their aim was centred on a revived King-

1. Pronounced: Sheff-le.

2. Czech and German were both to be official languages. The 'subsidiary
language' was to be legal in any commune where it was the language of one fifth
of the electors and also in Prague. This favoured the Germans. Being richer than
the Czechs, they could more often ensure their one fifth minority of electors;
moreover they were not one fifth of the electors of Prague. One third of the members of the Diet were to be 'Bohemian' (i.e. Czechs), one quarter German, again a
proportion more favourable to the Germans than their numbers warranted.

dom of Bohemia, with its own government and all the other rights possessed by Hungary. The unity of the lands of St Wenceslaus was to be restored by putting Moravia and Silesia under Prague, as Transylvania and Croatia had been put under Budapest. Despite the superficial parallel, there was basic difference. Moravia and Silesia both resisted the Czech programme, as Transylvania and Croatia had tried to stand out against the Magyars. The Magyars could subdue Transylvania and even Croatia of their own strength, once Imperial force was withdrawn; the Czechs needed Imperial force to reduce Moravia and Silesia. Moreover, it was one thing for the dynasty to desert Rumanians or Slovaks; quite another for it to dragoon the Germans, in possession, though a minority, of Moravia, and a majority in Silesia. For this nation provided the officials, the capitalists, the intellectuals for the entire Monarchy; provided the capital city and even, in a sense, the Emperor. Besides, the Czechs themselves confessed, in their 'Fundamental Articles', that the Kingdom of Bohemia could not carry equal weight with the Kingdom of Hungary. Instead of proposing a trialism of Bohemia, Hungary, and 'Austria', the shrunken, nameless 'Imperial third', they proposed a federal system for all the Imperial lands except Hungary, with the Reichsrat transformed into a 'Congress of Delegates' from the provinces. Dualism would survive, except that the Austrian Delegation would be directly elected by the provincial Diets. The Czechs could not really imagine the disruption of the unitary state created by Maria Theresa; besides, they were committed to their conservative noble allies in the German provinces. Yet federalism, as Palacký had seen at Kroměříž, had no national sense unless there was a creation of new national divisions. This idea was totally unacceptable to the conservative nobles and, implying the destruction of 'historic' Bohemia, equally repugnant to the Czechs themselves.

Even without federalism and without the revival of 'Great Bohemia', the Fundamental Articles aroused German resistance. The elder Plener, Finance Minister under Schmerling, expressed the German position: 'The wishes of the Czechs in Bohemia are a sentence of death to the Germans. These wish, and must wish since they are a minority in Bohemia, to form a whole with the Germans of the other provinces through the central parliament. . . . We could sacrifice the Ruthenes [=Little Russians] to the Poles, the Slavs and Ruman-

ians to the Magyars, because Ruthenes and Slovaks can be polonized
and magyarized – but Germans can't be czechized.' The alleged
danger to the Germans in Bohemia produced what was to be later a
usual feature of Austrian politics, riots in the streets of Vienna. Hohenwart, who only understood the court and parliamentary intrigue,
and Schäffle, the idealist of the study, were at a loss how to proceed.

This was Andrássy's opportunity. He had always realized that a
settlement in Bohemia would destroy Hungarian predominance in
the Empire and shake Magyar control even within Hungary. The
Czechs, elevated to the rank of an Imperial nation, would no longer
be indifferent to the condition of the Slavs in Hungary; and their
attack on Magyar supremacy would be supported by those Germans
who remained loyal to the Empire. On the other hand, the Germans
who rejected equality with the Czechs would seek to destroy the
Habsburg Monarchy, and the inevitable result would be the subordination of Hungary to Greater Germany – unless Russia came to the
rescue of her Slav brothers, which would be even worse. Confident
that difficulties would arise, Andrássy retired to a remote country
seat and waited for an appeal from Francis Joseph. The appeal came;
and when Andrássy arrived in Vienna after a show of reluctance, the
game was already won. Andrássy spoke with contempt of the
Bohemian programme and compared the proposed election of
the Austrian Delegation by the provincial Diets to electing the
Hungarian Delegation by the county meetings – an arrogant depre-
ciation of the 'historic' provinces. He said to Hohenwart: 'Are you
prepared to carry through the recognition of Bohemian state rights
with cannon? If not, do not begin this policy.' Hohenwart dared not
answer him. The Czechs were given no opportunity of 'bargaining',
as Deák had bargained in 1865. When they rejected Hohenwart's
first offer of autonomy for the lesser Bohemia, Francis Joseph lost
patience and succumbed to Andrássy's opposition. Negotiations were
broken off, the Hohenwart ministry dismissed, and in October 1871
Francis Joseph returned to the bourgeois ministry of German
liberals as the only alternative.

Hohenwart's policy could have been carried through only at the
price of new conflict with the two nations whose opposition had
weakened the Empire for twenty years. The Czechs lacked as yet the
numbers, the unity, and the wealth to be formidable. They were

mistaken, no doubt, to insist on the unity of the Bohemian lands; their real mistake was not to be strong enough to use threats, the only argument which Francis Joseph could understand. Yet the Germans, too, did not owe their return to office to their own strength. They had been imposed on Austria by the Magyars. These were the victors of 1871 : they perpetuated national conflicts in Austria and so ensured their own predominance at the very moment when changed foreign circumstances made it less necessary. Beust had failed and was now dismissed; he was succeeded as Foreign Minister by Andrássy, who thus attained the position which he had coveted ever since his return from exile. Andrássy diverted the Emperor to foreign politics; and there was no more talk of a coronation in Prague or of a revision of the settlement of 1867.

The new bourgeois ministry, contemptuously tolerated by Francis Joseph and Andrássy alike, had lost all liberal fervour. It was content to maintain the unity of the constitutional state. Schäffle's modest reform of the franchise had given the Czechs a majority in the Bohemian Diet, and this now refused to elect members to the Reichsrat. In 1873, therefore, the ministry instituted direct elections from the local constituencies to the Reichsrat and, at the same time, increased the numbers of the Reichsrat to give it a more respectable parliamentary appearance. This change made nonsense of the Czech policy of abstention; and already some of the younger Czechs began to condemn the rigid demand for state rights. This new generation was unmoved by the historic enthusiasm of the Czech pioneers and thought in practical terms of bureaucratic position. They might have been won over to the unitary state by conciliatory treatment. Instead, the German ministers insisted on the German character of Bohemia and ruled it almost as severely as Hungary had been ruled by the Bach hussars.

The Germans made concessions only to one nationality. Beust had already promised Galicia administrative autonomy, as part of his tactics in building up a majority for the settlement with Hungary; and the Poles had distinguished themselves by their resistance to any similar autonomy for others, especially during the negotiations with Bohemia. In 1871 they received the reward of a special Minister for Galician Affairs. Henceforth the Poles controlled the administration of their own province, yet had their representative in the central

G

government. They made such good use of their privileges that, before the fall of the Empire, they succeeded in turning themselves into a majority in Galicia – a feat never accomplished by the Magyars in Hungary. In 1846 there had been two and a half million Little Russians[1] in Galicia and under two million Poles; in 1910, at the last Imperial census, there were four and three-quarter million Poles and only just over three million Little Russians. This was the most startling achievement of a 'historic' nation even in the Habsburg Monarchy. Yet the Poles accomplished it with much less ruthlessness and dishonesty than the Magyars in Hungary. The Little Russians were allowed schools and even newspapers; what they lacked was intellectual leadership free from the Uniate Church. The few Little Russian intellectuals were not even sure to what nation they belonged. At one time they dreamt of emancipation by Great Russia; later they were seduced by the fantasy of an independent 'Ukraine', a project as much anti-Russian as anti-Polish. And since the tsarist government could never decide whether to encourage the Little Russian feeling as a weapon against the Habsburg Monarchy or to suppress it as a danger to tsardom, the Little Russians received none of the inspiration from beyond the frontier which the Serbs or Rumanians of Hungary drew from the independent kingdoms of Serbia and Rumania.[2]

1. These people call themselves 'Rusin'. The official name, both in Galicia and in Hungary, was 'Ruthene', which is dog Latin for Rusin. A later attempt to differentiate them from the Russians led to the invention of a 'Ukrainian' nationality; Ukraine is merely Russian for the frontier – the equivalent of the Welsh and Border Marches – and the Ukrainians are the people of the frontier. The Russians call the inhabitants of central Russia ('Russki') Great Russians and the men of the frontier Little Russians; both are Russians, related at any rate as closely as the Anglo-Saxons of England and the Anglo-Saxons of lowland Scotland. The Little Russians of Galicia largely belonged to the Uniate Church (an amalgam of the Roman Catholic and Orthodox Churches); this certainly divided them from the Great Russians and the orthodox Little Russians in Russia, but it divided them from the Roman Catholic Poles still more.

2. There were other reasons for the Polish success. The census of 1846 was conducted by Imperial officials, mostly German; the census of 1910 by Poles. In 1846 only those who claimed to be Poles were counted as Poles; in 1910 all were counted as Poles who did not claim to be something else. As well, in 1910 most Jews were counted as Poles. This was not dishonesty, but a liberal inclusion of the Jews in 'the people of state'.

The Poles contrasted their privileged position in Galicia with the harsh Germanization to which the Poles were subjected in German Poland and with the dead weight of tsarist absolutism, more hateful from its Russian character, in Russian Poland. To protect themselves from either they wished to preserve the Habsburg Monarchy. At the same time, they regarded Galicia as the model for the Polish state in some unimaginable future, and wished to preserve the Habsburg Monarchy in such a form that Galicia could be cut off from it at a moment's notice. Goluchowski, Governor of Galicia and former Minister of State, said: 'We are a part of Poland, and to create a federal organization would be to put an obstacle in the way of our future.' The Poles were thus the most loyal of Austrians and un-selfish advocates of a strong central Power (so long as this did not extend to Galicia). For the moment, they allied themselves with the German liberals and broke the Slav boycott of the Reichsrat. They were unreliable allies: they were loyal to the Emperor, not to the Germans, still less to liberalism, and would readily support any system of government which the Emperor favoured, once they were satisfied that it would not endanger the special position of Galicia.

The first blow to German supremacy, and still more to German self-confidence, came from the economic crisis of 1873, which shook German liberalism both in Austria and in Germany as severely as the economic crisis of 1857 had shaken the system of Bach. German liberalism had committed its fortunes to the success of *laissez faire*: it had confidently believed that, given peaceful conditions and free-dom from governmental interference, there must be an era of un-bounded prosperity. The collapse of 1873 exposed the falsity of the German economic, and so too of their political, ideas. The great German middle class felt that their humiliation to the Hungarians and their subservience to the Emperor had been in vain, if they were not to receive an economic reward. The German political leaders, capitalists or the associates of capitalists, were discredited by the financial scandals, which, as always, accompanied the collapse of economic optimism. The other nationalities, particularly the rising Czech capitalists, blamed the Germans, who possessed the appearance of power. *Laissez faire* had failed, and there was a general readiness to return responsibility to the dynasty, which alone was ready to bear it. After 1873 the German upper middle class put its liberal principles in the background and concentrated on the defence of capitalist interests. More, since it looked to the state to promote these interests, it abandoned the distrust of state power which had been the strongest element in its liberalism.

German hegemony in Austria, however, ended, as it began, with events in foreign affairs. Andrássy aimed to preserve the Austria–Hungary of 1867 and the European order that went with it. Now that the Habsburg Empire had been remodelled, he, who had fought against Russia in 1848, returned to the policy of Metternich and restored the conservative alliance with Russia and Germany. This alliance, the first League of the Three Emperors, paraded the danger from the International as Metternich had paraded the danger from radicalism after 1815. Like the Holy Alliance, the League of the Three Emperors depended on a negative Russian policy in the Near East; and in 1875 upheavals in the Balkans, worse than the Greek revolt of Metternich's day, made it impossible for Russia to stand aside. The Eastern Question was reopened, and therewith the existence of the Habsburg Monarchy endangered almost as much as that of Turkey itself. Andrássy knew this. He said in 1876: 'If it were not for Turkey, all these [nationalistic] inspirations would fall down on our heads. . . . If a new state should be formed there [i.e. in the Balkans] we should be ruined and should ourselves assume the role of "the Sick Man".' He tried to impose reforms on Turkey in an effort to keep Russia neutral. The Turks were not impressed by the show of European disapproval. They knew that Bismarck would keep Germany out of Near Eastern affairs and that France was too weak to have any foreign policy except to avoid war; in England Disraeli, the Prime Minister, spoke violently in favour of Turkey; in Austria-Hungary the Magyars, with anti-Slav frenzy, clamoured against Russia, and the City of Budapest presented a sword of honour to the Turkish general who defeated Serbia in the war of 1876. In fact, the Turks counted on British and Austro-Hungarian support in war against Russia. This course was without attractions for Andrássy. He feared the strain of war even against Russia alone; and he feared equally a victory, which would restore Habsburg confidence and so undo the effects of the defeat of 1866.

Since Russia was determined to impose reform on Turkey and war was thus inevitable, Andrássy next strove to keep Russian aims within modest limits. This was the object of the Zákupy[1] agreement of 1876: Russia was to be content with Bessarabia, the strip of territory along the Danube which she had lost in 1856. Russia was prepared for a partition on the grand scale. If she could acquire Constantinople and the shores of the Black Sea, she was quite willing for Austria-Hungary to establish her hegemony over Serbia and the Western Balkans down to Salonica. For Austria-Hungary partition was impossible. It would place the mouth of the Danube and the exit from the Black Sea, which was still her most important economic route, under Russian control; it would saddle her with Slavs, unmanageable after their long resistance to Turkish oppression. Most of all, the penetration of German Austrian capital in the Balkans, especially the nascent Orient Line from Belgrade to Constantinople, depended on a united Turkey and would be ruined by partition. Andrássy, like Metternich, had to rely on the conservatism of the tsar: this was his only resource against Pan-Slavism. He had one other asset: in 1876 Bismarck warned the tsar that Germany could not allow the destruction of Austria-Hungary. Even this was a doubtful asset: Bismarck had no objection to the partition of Turkey and, unlike Andrássy, would not have regarded it as equivalent to the destruction of the Habsburg Empire.

As a result, Austria-Hungary watched, in neutrality, the Russo-Turkish war of 1877–8. This caution offended Francis Joseph, who, along with the generals, his closest advisers, desired a strong assertion of Imperial power. Andrássy obstinately maintained his precarious balance. The crisis came in February 1878, when the Russians, made careless by victory, imposed a Pan-Slav peace on Turkey. Andrássy would not acquiesce in the Russian terms; on the other hand, he avoided an alliance with England, which would have committed him to war, until the Russian surrender made it an empty formality. The Russians, shaken by the efforts of 1877, shrank from a great European war; withdrew their extreme terms; and allowed the results of their victory to be undone at the Congress of Berlin. The Berlin settlement gave Turkey, and so Austria-Hungary, another generation of existence. Yet it did not rest on either Turkish, or Austro-Hungarian, strength. It sprang from the Russian belief that British, and perhaps even German, power would support the two

1. German name: Reichstadt.

ramshackle Empires. Both were European necessities, with all the disadvantages which that involved.

One problem remained. Bosnia and Hercegovina,[1] the two Turkish provinces where the revolts had started in 1875, could not be put back under Turkish rule. Russia had constantly pressed them on Austria-Hungary, to tempt her into setting the example of partition. For this reason Andrássy had tried to avoid the offer; on the other hand, he could still less afford their union with the Slav state of Serbia. At the Congress of Berlin he squared the circle. The Great Powers solemnly persuaded Austria-Hungary to become responsible for the two provinces: though placed under Austro-Hungarian administration, they remained part of the Turkish Empire, and Andrássy actually hoped that they could be handed back to a reformed Turkey within a generation. A further piece of Turkish territory, the Sanjak of Novi Bazar, remained under Turkish administration, with an Austro-Hungarian garrison. This, too, was Andrássy's device; it demonstrated, he hoped, that the fortunes of Turkey and Austria-Hungary were now interlocked.

Bosnia and Hercegovina had not been annexed; therefore they could not be included in either Austria or Hungary. They became instead the only territorial expression of the 'common monarchy' and thus the last relic of the great Habsburg Monarchy which had once directed a united Empire. The two provinces were the 'white man's burden' of Austria-Hungary. While other European Powers sought colonies in Africa for the purpose, the Habsburg Monarchy exported to Bosnia and Hercegovina its surplus intellectual production – administrators, road builders, archaeologists, ethnographers, and even remittance-men. The two provinces received all the benefits of Imperial rule: ponderous public buildings; model barracks for the army of occupation; banks, hotels, and cafés; a good water supply for the centres of administration and for the country resorts where the administrators and army officers recovered from the burden of Empire. The real achievement of Austria-Hungary was not on show: when the Empire fell in 1918, eighty-eight per cent of the population was still illiterate. Fearful of South Slav nationalism, the Habsburg administrators prevented any element of education or of self-government. Kállay, the common Finance Minister who

1. Pronounced: Hertsegovina.

directed the administration of Bosnia and Hercegovina for more than twenty years, forbade there the circulation of the *History of Serbia* which he had himself written. One 'historic' people called to another; and the Magyars, especially, favoured in the two provinces the Mohammedan hegemony, which had almost destroyed the Magyar nation three hundred years before. The Mohammedans were the large landowners, and Habsburg administration therefore preserved the feudal system of land tenure which had been the worst feature of Turkish rule. Even the public buildings were in a bastard-Turkish style, truly expressive of the Imperial spirit. For the Christian majority there was only one change: they could no longer revolt against their rulers. This discharged the 'mission' of the Habsburg dynasty.

The acquisition of Bosnia and Hercegovina finished the career of the German ministers. They had resented their exclusion from foreign affairs, as absolute as during the Crimean war in the days of absolutism. Conscious of their precarious artificial majority, they resisted the adding of any Slavs to the Empire; and the German ministers actually voted against Andrássy's policy in the Delegations. This was a breach of the implied bargain which Francis Joseph had made: the Germans were claiming to interfere in foreign affairs which the Emperor had reserved for himself, and, besides, were criticizing the one success which interrupted his record of failure. Francis Joseph was resolved to have done with them; and Andrássy, who had helped them to office, was naturally not inclined to support them. Changed political circumstances in Germany also counted against the German Austrians. Bismarck, too, broke with his liberals in the course of 1878 and created a new conservative coalition: the mounting force of German sentiment was increasingly difficult for him to control, and he preferred the revival of Habsburg loyalty to the danger of Pan-Germanism. By a necessary evolution, Bismarck, maker of the lesser Germany, became patron of an Austrian government favourable to the Czechs.

Last of all, the events of 1878 ruined Andrássy too. Success, though limited, had, as he feared, restored prestige to the dynasty; and Francis Joseph resented Andrássy's thwarting of his wishes in the interests of Magyar hegemony. Yet, absurdly enough, the Magyars also resented Andrássy's moderation. Andrássy, before he resigned, gave Habsburg fortunes one further decisive twist. In October

1879, he concluded with Bismarck an alliance between Germany and Austria-Hungary, and so gave Habsburg foreign policy the stable base which it had lacked since the breakdown of the Holy Alliance. The Austro-German alliance lasted for forty years and, before it collapsed, drew the partners into a war for the mastery of Europe. Yet it was designed by Bismarck, and by Andrássy too, to prevent war, not to prepare it. Its only concrete clause promised German assistance to Austria-Hungary in case of a direct attack by Russia. This was the least price that Bismarck could pay to prevent Austria-Hungary looking to England and France for support and so reviving the 'Crimean coalition'. This must have restored a 'western' character to the Habsburg Monarchy and revived its German ambitions; Bismarck's Germany would have been isolated or left with Russia as sole partner – lamentable alternatives. Still, the price was modest; after 1878, Russia was in no condition to contemplate war even with Austria-Hungary. The real significance of the alliance was in what it left out: it did not promise German support for Habsburg ambitions in the Balkans. The 'Empire of seventy millions' was, in some sort, at last achieved; not, however, in the form in which its originators had conceived it. Bruck, Schwarzenberg, and Schmerling had intended a Greater Germany, incorporating even Hungary; Bismarck and Andrássy perpetuated German disunity and the independence of Hungary. The 'Empire of seventy millions' would have promoted Germany hegemony in southeastern Europe; the Austro-German alliance bound Austria-Hungary to a conservative policy in the Balkans and preserved the Turkish Empire. The alliance expressed Bismarck's view: 'The Balkans are not worth the bones of a single Pomeranian grenadier.' It was, too, Andrássy's last *tour de force*: Hungary shifted her alliance from Vienna to Berlin, from the Germans of Austria to the Germans of the Reich, less exacting and more reliable partners. The Austrian Germans were abandoned both by Germany and by Hungary; their political hegemony lost its sanction, and Francis Joseph could recover his authority by balancing above the nationalities. At the general election of June 1879, Imperial influence was used against the Germans, and the German liberals lost their majority. In August 1879, Taaffe became Prime Minister. German hegemony in Austria was ended.

CHAPTER THIRTEEN

HABSBURG RECOVERY:
THE ERA OF TAAFFE, 1879–93

THE appointment of Taaffe restored political independence to the
Emperor. Taaffe thus defined his own position: 'I do not belong to
any party and am not a party minister; I am a minister appointed
by the Crown and, if I may use the expression, an Imperial minister
(*Kaiserminister*). The will of the Emperor must, and will, be decisive
for me.' Taaffe aimed to conciliate the nationalities; 'None of the
various nationalities is to obtain decisive predominance.' In return,
the nationalities were to accept the unity of Austria and their representatives were to attend the Reichsrat. Instead of obeying a party
majority, he manufactured a government bloc, 'the iron ring'. His
simplest appeal was to loyalty; good Austrians supported Taaffe, as
Taaffe had obeyed the Emperor's command to form a ministry. This
appeal brought over the great landowners and the Poles, who had
formerly sided with the ruling Germans; for these had no political
principle other than conformity with Imperial wishes – so long as
these did not threaten their social privileges. Taaffe won, too, the
support of the German Roman Catholic peasantry, who had disliked
the centralism and anti-clericalism of the German liberals. Taaffe
achieved even more: he persuaded the Czechs, and so also the
Slovenes who followed the Czech lead, to return to the Reichsrat and
to swell the 'iron ring'.

Rieger had found it increasingly difficult to hold his people to the
policy of boycott after the failure of 1871. A Czech nation was
coming into existence. The Czechs had once more a culture, with
writers and musicians who could stand comparison with the greatest
names of other nations.[1] In 1881 a Czech national theatre was built

1. In a review of the first version of this book, the great Austrian historian A. F.
Příbram, then living as a Jewish refugee in England, strongly condemned this
suggestion that Dvořák and Smetana could stand comparison with Brahms and
Wagner. There could not be more curious evidence of the German claim to superiority of culture.

by popular subscription; and a separate Czech University created in Prague. The new Czech middle class had little sympathy with Rieger's aristocratic associates and none with their 'historic' programme. The Bohemian nobles disliked rule by bureaucrats and so demanded Bohemian home rule; the new Czech generation wished primarily to substitute Czech bureaucrats for German and did not mind going to Vienna in order to accomplish this substitution. In 1878 Rieger was already in retreat. He worked out new proposals for a compromise with Fischhof, one of the few Germans (in reality a Jew) who still believed in the spirit of Kroměříž. This 'Ennersdorf programme' proposed a Nationalities Law, no more electoral geometry, and Czech attendance at the Reichsrat in order to support a revision of Dualism; the provinces were to be given administrative autonomy on the pattern of Galicia – a modest demand since the days when Bohemia claimed equality with Hungary.

Taaffe completed the Czech conversion. He made Czech and German the two languages of the 'outer service'[1] in Bohemia. In return the Czechs agreed to enter the Reichsrat. They, too, scrambled on to the driver's seat of the state coach and helped to push the Germans off. The historic rights of Bohemia received only the empty acknowledgement of a declaration, made by the Czechs at the opening of every session until the end of the Monarchy, that they disputed the authority of the Reichsrat over Bohemia. In reality, Rieger accepted the unitary Austrian state and supplanted the German liberals as the party 'loyal to the constitution'. In 1882 the Czechs received a further reward: the franchise was lowered to bring in the 'five-florin men', clerical German peasants and Czech peasants and shopkeepers. Thereafter the Czechs continued to support Taaffe in the hope of securing the entry of Czech into the 'inner service'.

The pact between Taaffe and Rieger was a great victory for the unity of constitutional Austria. Instead of trying to disrupt Austria, the nationalities competed for jobs in the Austrian bureaucracy and sought the favour of the central government. In theory Taaffe hoped to achieve a final settlement between the conflicting national claims; in practice he aimed 'to keep all the nationalities in a balanced state

---

1. That is, in the contacts of executive and judicial officials with the public. The 'inner service,' that is the correspondence of officials with each other, remained exclusively German.

of mild dissatisfaction'. In this queer mockery of a constitutional system Taaffe developed unrivalled dexterity. The government majority was held together by administrative concessions – a new road here, a new school there; and the established party leaders, bargaining with the Prime Minister and hurrying importantly down the corridors of the vast parliament house, ceased to press for any fundamental change of system. The need for a settlement was not forgotten; some time in the future the national conflicts would be settled, and a united Austria would insist on a revision of the compromise with Hungary. Meanwhile, the Emperor was satisfied; Taaffe was satisfied; the party leaders were satisfied. Besides, if ever agreement was reached between the nationalities, the Reichsrat would want to make parliamentary government a reality and there would be an end of Taaffe, the *Kaiserminister*. Every now and then Taaffe would sound the Czech and German leaders to see whether they were nearer agreement; he did not attempt to drive them. With more justification than Schmerling, Taaffe, too, could wait. Like many Austrian statesmen, from Metternich onwards, Taaffe had little hope of ultimate success; it was enough to get to the end of a session without worrying what would happen at the end of a decade.

Yet Taaffe's system of 'muddling along' gave Austria a stability and calm such as she had not enjoyed since the days of Francis. For a decade bitterness went out of public life. Nobles and bureaucrats, old enemies, were reconciled. The bureaucrats had still a great state to administer; Taaffe was a guarantee that they would administer it in a spirit favourable to the nobility. The bureaucracy itself was no longer composed of German ex-liberals of 1848; it included ambitious men of all nationalities who saw in the Austrian state a worthy outlet for their abilities. A new 'Austrian' conception was born – an Austria of devoted state servants who carried a standard of law and hygiene even to the remote Bukovina. Moreover, despite Taaffe's insistence on acknowledgement of the central Reichsrat, the provinces were given increased functions of administration; for Austria, with its existing tangle of electoral complexity, could carry the tangle of a dual administration as well. Thus, by 1914, Bohemia, though still without home rule, had in Prague an administrative machine almost as large as the Imperial machine in Vienna and larger than the British civil service which in London conducted the affairs of the United Kingdom and of the British Empire. Like the 'cultural automony' of Metternich and of later dictators, Taaffe's 'administrative automony' was a substitute, harmless it was hoped, for political freedom.

In the Taaffe era, Austria-Hungary recovered, too, greatness and independence as a European Power. Kálnoky, who became Foreign Minister in 1881, was certainly the most successful and probably the ablest of the Foreign Ministers of Francis Joseph; with estates in both parts of the Monarchy, he regarded himself as an Imperial statesman, not as a servant of the Magyars. He had no faith in Russia's good intentions in the Balkans; and, though drawn by Bismarck into a renewed League of the Three Emperors in 1881, meant always to create a new coalition against Russian expansion. Bismarck imposed, too, a reconciliation between Austria-Hungary and Italy, the Triple Alliance of 1882 : the Habsburg Monarchy grudgingly acknowledged the existence of national Italy, and received in return the assurance of Italian neutrality in case of war with Russia. Kálnoky held out, however, against the Italian attempt to be admitted as a partner in the Balkans. His own policy was expressed in the secret treaty with Serbia, made in 1881, which transformed Serbia into a Habsburg protectorate; and Austria-Hungary openly displayed this protection when Serbia was defeated by Bulgaria in the war of 1886. In fact, Milan, the dissolute Obrenović[1] king, was prepared to sell his kingdom to the Habsburgs. Kálnoky thought it not worth buying : he had already the advantages of Serb dependence without the national troubles which the inclusion of Serbia in the Monarchy would involve. An ever greater success was the alliance with Rumania in 1883, an alliance underwritten by Bismarck : this secured the principle of an independent Danube.

A new period of crisis opened in the Near East in 1885. Kálnoky rejected Bismarck's advice to carry through a partition with Russia. He kept his hold on Serbia, yet resisted similar Russian claims in Bulgaria. With none of Andrássy's reservations, he sought the alliance of England and virtually achieved it in the second Mediterranean agreement of December 1887. England provided a fleet ready to enter the Black Sea; Austria-Hungary provided an army ready to

1 Pronounced: Obrenovich.

attack Russia from Galicia; Italy, the third partner, provided the link between the two real Powers. This was an alliance less dangerous to Bismarck than a revival of the 'Crimean coalition', and he helped, in fact, to promote it. Still, he could not allow it to come to war with Russia; and, early in 1888, published the text of the Austro-German treaty as a warning, especially to the bellicose Hungarians – with whom Andrássy had now associated himself – that Germany would not support Austria-Hungary in a Balkan war. Besides, Bismarck did not like partners who were too independent; and Kálnoky, despite his success, might have experienced some awkward surprises if Bismarck had not fallen from power in 1890. Ever more dominated by his fear of the 'Empire of seventy millions', Bismarck might have partitioned the Habsburg Monarchy with Russia rather than have helped Austria-Hungary to conquer the Balkans; and this attitude led him to emphasize more strongly than ever Germany's indifference to the fate of the Germans in Austria.

The Austrian Germans were thus the losers in the Taaffe era both at home and abroad. They still wished to be great both as Germans and as Austrians. They thought that the prestige of Imperial Germany should give them predominance over Czechs or Slovenes, who had no great national state to write their name large in Europe; yet a citizen of Vienna, the capital of a great Empire, had no desire to be put on an equality with a citizen of Munich, Dresden, or Weimar, capitals of petty states with their destinies determined from Berlin. Moreover, German had been for centuries the only language of literature and culture; and it was impossible for the Germans to understand the desire of other nations for a literature and culture of their own. Many of the Germans were themselves 'converts', and these especially resented the refusal of others to follow their example. One of the German liberals, himself Czech by birth, expressed this outlook in 1885: 'If the Czechs in Bohemia are made into Germans, that is in my view no deadly sin, for they rise from a lower level to the sunny height of a highly civilized nation. But to seek to czechize the Germans in Bohemia is quite another thing; that would be a disgrace unheard of in the pages of world history.'

The German opposition was voiced in the Reichsrat by elderly liberals, discredited by their barren years in office and mouthing threadbare liberal phrases in which even they did not believe. These were men who had failed in everything: failed as revolutionaries, failed as ministers, failed even in their speciality of destructive parliamentary criticism. With naïve economic determinism, they identified German interests with the upper middle class and resisted any extension of the suffrage. As elsewhere, in Germany, in France, and in England, there was no future for a capitalist liberal party; and the German liberals became a party of straight capitalist interest. Its few members represented 'pocket boroughs' – the chambers of commerce with their artificial German majorities. They had no mass support, even from the Germans, and dwindled down to a few Austrian centralists, defending the Empire in the interests of German Austrian capital.

The younger German leaders were unwilling to be divorced from the masses; for, after all, there were German masses, as well as the masses of the subject peoples. These German radicals had not experienced the failures and disappointments of the preceding thirty years. They had not learnt the strength of the dynasty after 1848; had not attempted to govern Hungary against Magyar opposition; had not known a Bismarck who excluded them from Germany. They ascribed the decline of German predominance to the timidity of their leaders and to the treachery of the dynasty which had abandoned the 'people of state'. These younger Germans echoed the phrases of the radicals of 1848, though without the sincerity and nobility which had sometimes redeemed the radical cause. In their ambitious moments they aspired to re-create the German monopoly in the Empire which had allegedly existed for two hundred years and which had at any rate been secured for a few years by Bach and Schmerling; in their more desperate moments they were ready to destroy the Empire in order to preserve the German areas, generously interpreted, from Slav interference. The first was predominantly the outlook of the Germans in Vienna, who had no practical experience of Czech or Slovene encroachment; the second became the expression of the threatened Germans on the 'racial frontiers', where Slav awakening was putting them in a minority. Even on the racial frontiers unbridled nationalism was the policy of a minority, and usually of a discreditable minority: the schoolteacher who was passed over for a Czech with a better degree, the signalman who caused an accident and was reprimanded by his Czech superior, the lawyer who lost his case before a Slovene judge – these were the standard-bearers of their race.

The new German radicalism was first expressed in the programme drafted at Linz in 1882 by three young men, all destined to play great, though very different, parts in the Austrian history of the next thirty years – Georg von Schönerer,[1] Viktor Adler, and Heinrich Friedjung.[2] All three belonged to the class of the 'free intelligence' and were untainted by the connexion with great industry which had discredited the older liberals; Adler and Friedjung were Jews, though both regarded themselves as German nationalists. Adler was a sincere radical, faithful to the spirit of 1848; he had national pride without national arrogance and soon abandoned nationalism for the cause of international Socialism. Friedjung was a writer of genius, the greatest historian whom Vienna has ever produced, his scholarship marred only by an assertive violence: he was soon driven from the German nationalist party by the anti-Semitism which became its dominant note, yet, with characteristic obstinacy, remained a fanatical German nationalist until his death. Schönerer, the only German of the three, aspired to be the Kossuth or Parnell of the German Austrians: empty-headed and vain, he had a gift for evil and destructive phrases and a taste for the howlings of the mob. The anti-Semitism which he invented enabled him to steal the German nationalist movement from more sincere or more generous radicals. Yet anti-Semitism was, for Schönerer, only a first step: the hatred which he directed against the Jews, as being the readiest and most defenceless target, he meant to turn later against the other nationalities of the Empire and even against Germans who were not wholehearted in their nationalism.

The Linz programme sought to return to the heroic age of German supremacy. Like the radicals of 1848, these radicals had no difficulty in recognizing the claims of the 'historic nations'. Galicia was to become a separate unit under Polish rule; Dalmatia to be handed over to its tiny Italian minority; with a parody of the October revolution, the Linz radicals would agree to personal union with Hungary, or even add Galicia and Dalmatia to Hungary, in return for Magyar support of the Germans in Austria. Again, as in 1848, the Austrian Germans invoked German backing: Imperial Germany

1. Pronounced: Shurn-er-er.   2. Pronounced: Freed-young.

was to intervene and to compel the dynasty to transform Austria into a unitary German state as the price of continuing the Austro-German alliance. Finally, as in 1849 if not in 1848, the Linz radicals were not sincere in their concessions even to Hungary: once Austria had become a German state, Germany and the German Austrians would support the dynasty in overthrowing the compromise with Hungary. Thus, stripped of its radical phrases, the Linz programme proposed to return to the system of Schmerling, with Bismarck as its guarantor instead of its enemy.

When the Linz radicals called on Germany for support, they confessed that the German Austrians had neither the strength nor the cultural superiority to maintain their monopoly in Austria. They assumed, too, that the German Austrians had voluntarily renounced the German national state, that Germany would come to their assistance at the first call, and that therefore they should be rewarded for not destroying the Habsburg Empire. These assumptions were false. The German Austrians had not renounced Germany; they had been deliberately excluded from Germany by Bismarck, and he had no intention of seconding their ambitions, still less of destroying Austria-Hungary. Bismarck feared Greater Germany, which would be beyond the power of the Prussian Junkers to master; and he feared, too, a blatant German hegemony in Europe, which would provoke a European coalition in resistance. The maintenance of an independent Austria-Hungary was the central point of Bismarck's policy: independent, certainly, of Russia or of France, but independent, too, at any rate in appearance, of Germany. As a consequence, it was in his interest to minimize the German character of Austria-Hungary. After all, he knew that he could always assert German control if it were necessary. The Linz programme invited him to assert German control unnecessarily and was therefore without attraction.

The German nationalists sensed their isolation, though they ascribed it to the subtlety of the Habsburg dynasty, not to the refusal of their hero Bismarck. While they continued to demand German supremacy in Austria, their day-to-day policy became resistance to Slav encroachments in their own national areas. One of their leaders expressed this policy: 'In Czech Bohemia let them do as they like; in German Bohemia we shall do as we like.' This was not at all the Linz programme; it was a denial of the unitary Austrian state, of which the Germans had been previously the great upholders. Administrative division of Bohemia was, in fact, very much what the moderate Czech leaders desired, once they abandoned their devotion to state rights. The Old Czechs were, however, also losing control of their national movement. The Czechs, too, had their radicals who knew nothing of the defeats and disappointments of the last thirty years. The Young Czechs saw Czech strength and consciousness increasing every year and were confident that they could win all Bohemia; they rejected the division of Bohemia into Czech and German areas, even though this would have brought immediate gain. The programme of state rights was revived, no longer a device of aristocratic conservatism, but the expression of radical nationalism.

The moderate Czechs and Germans in the Reichsrat were forced together by the danger from their own radicals. The German liberals could no longer defend the unitary state, when this was discarded by the German radicals; the Old Czechs needed a practical success, to silence the criticism of the Young Czechs. In 1890 a committee of Czechs and Germans, under Taaffe's presidency, reached at last the practical agreement for which Taaffe had waited. They proposed, quite simply, that provinces of more than one nationality should be divided administratively according to national distribution, and that the provincial bodies (courts of appeal, administrative centres, and so on) should be duplicated. In this way, for example, fifteen out of forty-one judges in the Bohemian Supreme Court would still not be required to know Czech.[1] Competing nationalities were to be bought off by creating enough bureaucratic posts to satisfy both. This clumsy scheme could work only where a nationality desired simply to be left alone. An arrangement of this kind satisfied the Italians in Tyrol: the Italian areas were marked off and placed under an Italian-speaking administration, only nominally subordinate to the provincial authorities in Innsbruck. The Italians cared nothing for Tyrol: they wanted to join the Italian national state and accepted autonomy *faute de mieux*. Moreover they lived in a compact area on

1. At this time the High Court in London had twenty-one members. Yet the Bohemian Supreme Court was merely a provincial body, one of a great number. This gives a measure of the prizes for which the nationalities fought and of the weight of bureaucracy which had to be created in order to satisfy them.

the fringe and made no claim to Innsbruck, the provincial capital. Even so, the later Italian demand for education in their own language at Innsbruck University led to violent, and successful, German opposition;[1] yet the Italians were a 'historic people' whose claim to culture could not be disputed, even by the Germans.

In Bohemia the compromise of 1890 was rejected by both Czechs and Germans. The Germans would not renounce Prague, despite their own claim for an exclusively German area; and so insisted on the unity of Bohemia, though the logical conclusion of this was that they should become a tolerated minority. The Young Czechs also insisted on the unity of Bohemia, as a preliminary to the demand that all Bohemia should be Czech. After all, both Czech and German radicals grew strong by fighting each other and would lose popular support if they were once separated. Taaffe's policy of waiting had been successful for the wrong reasons. He had thought to show the political leaders the folly of radicalism; instead radicalism threatened to destroy them. Mild dissatisfaction was turning into violent dissatisfaction; and the Reichsrat leaders tried to save Taaffe from himself. Their conciliation was testimony to the increase of national hostility, not to its decline, and it ruined them. At the elections of 1891 Rieger was denounced as a traitor, and his followers were routed by the Young Czechs; the German liberals, though nominally composing the opposition, had to be brought in by the strenuous exertion of government influence. Taaffe realized that the electorate was getting out of control; he drew the conclusion that the middle-class nationalists should be swamped by the introduction of universal suffrage.

It was common doctrine among nineteenth-century conservatives that nationalism was a middle-class movement from which the aristocracy and the masses were both free; and, if government could not be kept as an aristocratic monopoly, the masses should be called in against middle-class nationalism and liberalism. An Imperial appeal to the backward peoples was not new: at bottom it was the conception which had brought victory to Radetzky in 1848. In 1871 Schäffle, a half-socialist radical, had won the aristocrat Hohenwart

1. The Italians of Tyrol were offered instead education in Italian at the University of Trieste. It occurred to no one, not even to the Italians, that Trieste, too, would one day be claimed by Italian nationalists.

for the idea of using the subject peoples against the Magyars and Germans. In 1893 Steinbach, another social economist, won Taaffe for the idea of using the votes of the masses against the intellectuals of every nationality. Francis Joseph was persuaded by a simpler argument. Alarmed by the growth of Social Democracy in Austria and unwilling to shake the feeble fabric of Austrian constitutional life by the repressive measures which Bismarck had used in Germany, he hoped that universal suffrage would make the Austrian workers more contented, or at any rate less revolutionary.

Taaffe had no parliamentary party; he had only the backing of interest groups, the 'iron ring' of clericals, landowners, and Poles. These supported him as the Emperor's minister; and their support was conditional on his doing nothing to endanger their privileges or their existence. The substitution of universal suffrage for the four-class electorate which Taaffe proposed in 1893 threatened his own side as much as the liberal opposition: the 'iron ring' was asked to commit suicide out of loyalty to the Emperor, yet this loyalty was nothing more than a defence of their own position. The great land-owners feared a parliament of peasants; Hohenwart, the ideas of Schäffle long forgotten, objected to 'the transference of the political balance from the propertied to the unpropertied classes'. The Poles would lose much of their own province, Galicia, to the Little Russians. Only a few clericals believed that the Church would master universal suffrage as it had survived so many political systems. Taaffe's most reliable supporters, the Old Czechs, had been dispersed in the elections of 1891; and the Young Czechs, dependent on middle-class votes, were ready to make common cause even with the German liberals against this threat to their existence.

The coalition against Taaffe was encouraged, and perhaps organized, by Kálnoky. The two years after the fall of Bismarck had been the heyday of Habsburg predominance in the Balkans. England and Austria-Hungary stood close together, as nearly allies as they could be without England's actually entering the rumoured 'Quadruple Alliance'. German policy followed a 'new course'; openly anti-Russian, it offered Austria-Hungary unreserved support in the Balkans. In 1889 William II, German Emperor, said to Francis Joseph: 'The day of Austro-Hungarian mobilization, for whatever cause, will be the day of German mobilization too.'

Bismarck's reservations had been abandoned, and with the result that he foresaw: once Germany committed herself to action in the Balkans, decision passed from Berlin to Vienna. Kálnoky's dominating position was, however, shaken by the return of Gladstone to office in July 1892. The Liberal ministry repudiated the Mediterranean Agreements and regarded Austria-Hungary with suspicion. Gladstone himself never wavered from the judgement which he had made in 1880: 'There is not a spot upon the whole map, where you can lay your finger and say, there Austria did good.' It would confirm liberal suspicions and complete the estrangement if Taaffe were now allowed to play in the interests of Austrian conservatism the trick with which Disraeli had dished the Whigs in 1867. More seriously, the withdrawal of England in the Near East increased Kálnoky's need of Germany. Himself unable to shake British negations, he looked to Germany to cajole or compel England back to a more active line. If all inducements failed, then Austria-Hungary would need the direct support of Germany in the Balkans all the more.

The German government was in a strange, short-lived mood of democratic policy. Caprivi, Bismarck's successor, sought the favour of the German Progressives and Socialists; even his support of Austria-Hungary in the Balkans revealed his return to the Greater German radicalism of 1848. Vienna and Berlin could not separate their fates, despite declarations of independence on both sides. In 1848 the fall of Metternich had shaken the Prussian monarchy; in the sixties Schmerling's Pan-Germanism had compelled Bismarck to become a German nationalist; in 1879 Bismarck's breach with the National Liberals had opened the door to Taaffe also. Now, with Caprivi, friendship between the Berlin government and the democratic parties made it impossible for Taaffe to survive in Vienna. Kálnoky could not count on German support if the Austrian government was openly conservative, clerical, and anti-German. Besides, Caprivi was the only German minister since 1848 friendly to the Poles; this again worked to Taaffe's disadvantage. Kálnoky cared nothing for the German Austrians; he cared much for German backing. Since Caprivi played as a demagogue for radical support, Kálnoky played for radical support in Germany also. This was, after all, a game in which he had nothing to lose; for, as

Bismarck had seen, German radicalism, being Greater German in outlook, must always favour Vienna rather than Berlin. Thus Kálnoky, for the sake of his foreign policy, needed a liberal government in Austria, ostensibly constitutional, and supported by the Germans and the Poles. Perhaps, too, he was glad to overthrow an Austrian Prime Minister and thus to show that as 'common' Foreign Minister he was the heir of the Chancellors, a minister superior to all others.

The final blow to Taaffe came from Francis Joseph; for it was on Imperial support, not on the 'iron ring,' that he ultimately depended. Francis Joseph often followed contradictory policies; the deepest contradiction of his own mind was towards the Germans. In some sense, they were his principal opponents, and he never ceased to resent their attempts to tamper with his prerogative. On the other hand, he was himself German, inheriting a headship of Germany which had lasted for centuries: his proudest memory was of the meeting of the princes at Frankfurt in 1863, and the defeat of 1866 was his greatest humiliation. Besides, his heavy mediocrity made him a perfect type of German *Biederkeit*, which Schnitzler defined as a mixture of stupidity and guile. He revealed his German obtuseness in his few unguarded remarks. Thus, when it was first suggested to him that he should appeal to the Croats by being crowned King of Croatia, he replied in shocked surprise: 'But I am a German prince.' And it did not endear him to the Czechs when he said complacently during a visit in 1868: 'Prague has an entirely German appearance' – this was his notion of highest praise. Francis Joseph had been glad to see the German liberals out of office and outmanoeuvred by Taaffe in the Reichsrat; he was alarmed at the accusation that universal suffrage would destroy them. Besides, the Young Czech rejection of the compromise of 1890 seemed to imply a threat both to the Germans and to the Monarch.

For Francis Joseph there was something worse. The coalition of German liberals, Poles, Young Czechs, and great landowners had come together only in opposition to universal suffrage; if it maintained itself, it would impose on him a 'parliamentary' ministry. The sole reason for Taaffe's existence was to prevent a parliamentary ministry; he was failing to do so, and Francis Joseph had to employ other means. He used the method which he had often used before in dealing with the historic peoples, and which he was to use again: he threatened to cooperate with the masses, unless his power was left intact. If the parliamentary leaders attempted to impose a government upon him, he would support Taaffe and somehow carry universal suffrage; if they would become ministers on his terms, 'electoral geometry' should remain untouched. The politicians did not want power; they wished only to preserve the privileged position of their nation or class. Eagerly they accepted the Emperor's terms. Taaffe was dismissed in November 1893; and a coalition ministry, ostensibly parliamentary, followed. The ministry, like Taaffe's, owed its existence to the will of the Emperor. The subject peoples had been again shown a distant prospect of equality; as always, the offer had been no more than a tactful move by the dynasty to maintain its power. Taaffe had given Austria a breathing-space of fourteen years; it had not been used to good purpose. Now, for the last time, the dynasty and the Reichsrat were offered a new opportunity; the outcome was to shake constitutional Austria to the foundations. Within a few years everyone would regret the easy days of the 'iron ring' and Taaffe's 'muddling along'.

CHAPTER FOURTEEN

THE YEARS OF CONFUSION: FROM TAAFFE TO BADENI, 1893-7

THE fall of Taaffe brought Austrian politics to a standstill. His system had fitted Austrian circumstances perfectly, and no one knew what could take its place. The parliamentary groups, accustomed to threaten Taaffe as a preliminary to bargaining, had at last carried out their threat; they had no ambition to replace him. The Emperor had let him go without understanding the causes of his fall and without any conception of an alternative. A new *Kaiserminister* would be useless; he would merely continue Taaffe's system without Taaffe's sleight-of-hand. Yet there was no other system which the Emperor could adopt, for the opposition to Taaffe had been united only in negation. Francis Joseph, who had in fact decided the fall of Taaffe, therefore shouldered the responsibility on to the Reichsrat: since it had refused to tolerate an Imperial ministry, it should have a sham-parliamentary ministry and show whether it could do any better.

In a curious, perverted way the events from 1893 to 1897 repeated, as parody, the events of 1848 and 1849. Taaffe had been a more cynical, trivial Metternich, dependent on Imperial support and preserving Imperial power by balancing between nationalities and classes. In November 1893, the Imperial support had been withdrawn and a political intrigue tolerated, rather as the court had tolerated the 'Imperial revolution' of 13 March 1848. With Taaffe gone, as with Metternich gone, the dynasty was at a loss, and sullenly thrust the problem on to its subjects, as though they alone had caused all the trouble; finally, losing patience, it called on a man of violence – in the first case Schwarzenberg, in the second Badeni[1] – to rescue it from its own failure and to restore order by resolute action. The analogy cannot be pressed too far: the events of 1848 were real, the events between 1893 and 1897 were play-acting, a deliberate performance by selected actors unaware that anything real was at stake. Yet behind the inflated phrases and the vain personalities, there was a real background: constitutional Austria was being ruined on the boards of the Reichsrat theatre, and this determined the destinies of millions in central Europe and beyond.

Taaffe was followed by a ministry which claimed to be parliamentary, a ministry composed of the party leaders, and therefore in theory more nearly constitutional. In reality, the parties had never accepted the constitution and could find no basis of agreement. Each party remained an 'interest group,' aiming to exact concessions for its particular cause from the minister of the day and then willing to vote on general questions in the government majority. The parties were united neither by loyalty to the Empire nor by common political outlook; they had not even been able to develop a common tactic of opposition. The Poles and the great landowners were in parliament to see that the government did nothing to injure their privileges, Galicia and the great estates; the Germans, theoretically liberal, exerted themselves only to maintain the position of the

1. Pronounced: Baw-de-nee.

Germans as 'the people of state'; the Young Czechs intended to cause increasing difficulties until they secured recognition of the unity of Bohemia on a Czech basis. No genuine government could be formed from a coalition of these diverse, irresponsible elements. The solution was characteristic of the Austrian constitutional farce: the buying of parties was transferred from the Reichsrat to the ministry. The party leaders entered the 'coalition' ministry and there continued their conflict with each other, ceaselessly threatening to resign and to throw their party vote in opposition unless their sectional demands were met. There was no attempt to create a coalition programme or to reach an agreed settlement of the questions which had defeated Taaffe. The political auction of Taaffe's day was continued; there was no longer an auctioneer, and the bidders competed to occupy his empty desk in turn. Government ceased; and, as in pre-March, administration took its place. Feebleness and confusion at the centre is a luxury which only a state held together by an iron frame of bureaucracy can afford; and Austria, in its last twenty years of existence, survived only in its vast body of state servants. These continued to function and to keep the state in being, long after political life had disappeared. The contradiction bewildered contemporary observers in the early twentieth century; for it is difficult to believe that a great tree, strongly supported by iron trusses, is dead, merely because it produces no leaves.

The two years of the pseudo-constitutional ministry were dominated by barren controversies, significant only as a means of buying or losing votes for the government coalition. One of these disputes was bound to prove decisive; and, by chance, the decisive dispute was over the grammar school at Celje,[1] a question which in itself revealed all the maladies of Austria and all the tangles of national controversy. The province of Styria, in which Celje lay, had a German majority and was exclusively German in its northern part; in the south the market towns were German in a Slovene countryside, and as migration from the countryside gradually increased the town population, these towns too became increasingly Slovene. The Slovenes began to demand that the towns should satisfy their cultural needs, and in particular that education in the state grammar schools should be in Slovene as well as in

1. Pronounced: Tsil-yi.

German. This demand was persistently refused by the Styrian Diet, with its old German majority; and the Slovenes had to make their demand through the Reichsrat, where they were supported by the Czechs. In 1888 Taaffe established Slovene classes in the grammar school at Maribor,[1] the largest town in southern Styria. Thus encouraged, the Slovenes next demanded Slovene classes in the grammar school at Celje, a smaller town farther in the Slovene area where German preponderance was already shaky. Celje stirred passions as Maribor did not. Maribor was still genuinely German and would remain so even though Slovene children were educated in their own language; once Slovenes received secondary education in Celje, no one in Celje would use German as his cultural language and Celje would be lost. Similar battles were being fought in endless villages and small towns of Bohemia by the rival school-unions of Czechs and Germans; Celje happened to distil the rivalry of Germans and Slovenes in Styria, and so became the symbol of the conflict between Slavs and Germans throughout Austria.

Taaffe bought Slovene votes for the budget of 1888–9 by a promise of Slovene classes at Celje; with characteristic ingenuity he evaded his promise, and the fall of Taaffe in 1893 found the classes in the grammar school of Celje still conducted exclusively in German. Then came the coalition ministry, hastily collecting its majority by the widespread distribution of miscellaneous promises; among these, it confirmed the promise made to the Slovenes as far back as 1888. When the ministry began to carry out its promises, the difficulties of the Celje grammar school became overwhelming. If Slovene classes were created, the Germans – not merely the representatives of Styria, but the entire German bloc – would withdraw from the government; if Slovene classes were not created, the Slovenes would withdraw and would carry the Czechs with them. The question of Celje dominated Austria politics throughout 1894. The Germans refused 'to abandon the pioneers of German culture in the south'; the Slovenes refused to be satisfied with the government offer of a grammar school, exclusively Slovene, in some other town where the Germans had no traditional footing. No compromise could be reached. In June 1895, the government carried a grant for Slovene classes in the Celje grammar school through the Reichsrat; the

1. German name: Marburg.

Germans withdrew from the ministry, and the parliamentary coalition broke up. Thus ended the last attempt at constitutional government in Austria. Henceforth Austria was ruled by Imperial agents, some extracting a grudging toleration from the Reichsrat, most disregarding it.

Constitutional Austria decayed and perished from the irresponsibility of the political leaders. Most of these politicians admitted the need for a strong Empire, and none, except the German extremists, had any wish to destroy it; only, lacking faith in themselves, they never appreciated that the Empire depended on them. They inherited from previous generations a reliance on 'authority', and did not recognize that, once ministers, they became 'authority'; they supposed that to become a minister was merely to secure a stronger bargaining position for their particular interest. Besides, Austria suffered from the legal tangle of operating three constitutional systems – the October Diploma, the February Patent, and the 'constitutional laws' of 1867 – piled one on another, with their contradictions unresolved. The provinces acquired increasing administrative autonomy every year; they were not used, as even their feudal patrons had intended, to keep national conflicts within provincial limits. Instead the national groups were induced to acknowledge the central state by being allowed to transfer their provincial disputes to the Reichsrat. As always, the Habsburg state sought recognition, even at the price of being torn to pieces. The German minority in Celje called to the Germans throughout Styria; and these enlisted the support of Bohemian Germans, the Germans of Vienna, and even Germans from the Bukovina. The Slovene majority in Celje, thwarted by the German majority in Styria, called to the Slovenes of Carniola; and these enlisted the support of the Czechs and of Little Russian representatives from beyond the Carpathians. The Reichsrat, despite its name, was an assembly of conflicting national groups, not an Imperial Council; even the great landowners, ostensibly Austrian, supposed that Austria and the great estates were synonymous. The irresponsibility of the political leaders encouraged, even compelled, the Emperor to keep the real authority in his own hands; yet only responsibility could have sobered them. The national conflicts, which ruined Austria, were evidence of the universal belief that Austria was eternal. Every year the Emperor became more determined not to share his power with irresponsible politicians; every year the politicians, denied a share of power, became more irresponsible.

In another way, too, the Austrian state suffered from its strength: it had never had its range of activity cut down during a successful period of *laissez faire*, and therefore the openings for national conflict were far greater. There were no private schools or hospitals, no independent universities; and the state, in its infinite paternalism, performed a variety of services from veterinary surgery to the inspecting of buildings. The appointment of every schoolteacher, of every railway porter, of every hospital doctor, of every tax-collector, was a signal for national struggle. Besides, private industry looked to the state for aid from tariffs and subsidies; these, in every country, produce 'log-rolling', and nationalism offered an added lever with which to shift the logs. German industries demanded state aid to preserve their privileged position; Czech industries demanded state aid to redress the inequalities of the past. The first generation of national rivals had been the products of universities and fought for appointments at the highest professional level: their disputes concerned only a few hundred state jobs. The generation which followed them was the result of universal elementary education and fought for the trivial state employment which existed in every village; hence the more popular national conflicts at the end of the century.

For an educated man state employment lay ahead in every career except journalism and, to some degree, the law; yet these two independent professions were the most dependent on nationalism. Both helped to create the national struggle and both lived by it. Both were exclusively urban professions; both, therefore, in old Austria exclusively German professions, so much so that in Hungary where there were not enough educated Germans the Jews had to take their place. Nationalism broke in when the peasants, able to read and write, wished to read newspapers and when, emancipated, they wished to go to law. Before the national awakening, an aspiring Slovene who wished to be a journalist could find employment only on the local German paper, where he was at a disadvantage with his German colleagues. Once the peasants and unskilled workers could read, they would accept a second-rate Slovene paper, and even former Germans could make a career as Slovene writers. Thus the

Slovene leader in Carinthia for more than a generation bore an un-
mistakably German name. In Trieste the Slovene leader had an
Italian name, the Italian leader a Slav name; both climbed higher
and won more applause than their abilities would have merited
if they had remained with their own people. Nationalism made
the fortune, or at least the fame, of lawyers also. A litigious, half-
literate Rumanian peasant would prefer a bad lawyer who could
speak Rumanian to a thoroughly trained lawyer to whom he had
to stammer in German. The national lawyer was the centre of the
national movement in every small town: he alone could advise his
people and find a tribunal before which to publicize their claims.

The majority even of professional men were conscientious and
hard-working. Nationalism was the resort of the men with a grievance – the manufacturer with his profits declining, the university
student who failed to get a degree, the surgeon who bungled an
operation. Few men succeed in life to their satisfaction; many therefore felt at one time or another the appeal of nationalism. The
industrial workers and agricultural labourers, though not the rich
peasants, were still 'below nationalism' at the end of the nineteenth
century. They still accepted 'authority', though more doubtfully
than in the days of Radetzky. Austria was becoming industrialized:
heavy industry overshadowed the traditional crafts of Bohemia, and
iron-works were established in the mountain valleys of Carinthia and
Styria. Factories are the death of tradition and of respect. The
peasant touched his forelock to the lord and thought of the Emperor
as a greater lord, infinitely remote; despite Kudlich's work in 1848,
he was 'owned'. The factory owner touched his hat to no one; the
factory worker, though he might touch his cap to the employer, was
not owned by him, and organized trade unions to curb his power.
Towns and villages were not severed; and lack of respect spread
from one to the other. The masses were no longer unconsciously
Austrian; they were not yet consciously nationalist and might perhaps have been won for Austria, if Austria had had something to
offer them.

The traditional 'Austrian' classes were the territorial nobility and
the bureaucracy, once enemies, now reconciled. Both were debarred
by position and outlook from contact with the peoples. The nobles
regarded the Austrian people as an extension of their own peasantry,

their only function to keep the nobility in luxury; the bureaucrats knew the people only as an object of administration and would no more ask an Austrian spirit of the masses than of their own desks. Besides, the binding link for these 'Austrian' classes was loyalty to the Emperor; and all their energy had gone into the fight against 'liberalism', the threat to the Emperor's independent power. Francis Joseph himself had not hesitated to manoeuvre between the nationalities and even to encourage their rivalry; his sole aim had been to resist any interference with the army and with foreign affairs – the two decisive demands of any real liberalism. At last, in the nineties, the price of defeating liberalism became clear: to preserve the Habsburg army from parliamentary control the middle classes had been diverted into national struggles, and these national struggles now threatened to disrupt the Austrian state and even the Habsburg army. Loyalty to the Supreme War Lord was a good enough cause for the nobility who served as officers; good enough for the bureaucrats who collected the taxes for the army; and good enough for the illiterate peasants who had once made up the rank and file. It was not good enough for the industrial and intellectual middle classes, nor for the industrial workers; it was not even good enough for the peasants once they received an elementary education.

Francis Joseph was an Emperor without ideas; this was his strength and enabled him to survive. Yet, by the end of the nineteenth century, ideas made a state and kept it going; since the Habsburg Monarchy could not perform a nationalistic transformation act, as the Hohenzollern monarchy had done, an 'Austrian idea' had to be found. The phrase was everywhere; the translation into practice never took place. The dynasty had one traditional idea, despite its temporary abandonment by Joseph II: alliance with the Roman Church. The Counter-Reformation had saved the Habsburg dynasty from early extinction; and until the end the House of Austria shared a universalist character with the Papacy. Francis Joseph had early used his absolute power to undo the settlement of Joseph II and to restore the Roman Catholic Church as an ally against liberalism; and Taaffe had renewed the alliance after the anti-clericalism of the bourgeois ministry. It was not a perfect alliance. The princes of the Church were 'Austrian' and the clergy of the German country districts were ready to rally their peasants against liberal Vienna; still, the Church could not afford to estrange the rising nationalities, especially with the challenge of the Orthodox and Uniate Churches, both easily national, before its eyes. The Church had existed before the Habsburgs and would exist after them; though it favoured the dynasty, it had also to take precautions against the future.

Nevertheless, the 'Austrian idea' in its last version – an idea which in shaky form survived dynasty and Empire – was of Roman Catholic manufacture. The Christian Socialist party, organized by Lueger,[1] was the first real attempt of the Church to go with the masses, more democratic – and more demagogic – than the Centre, its German counterpart. Christian Socialism appealed to the traditional clericalism of the peasant and yet freed the peasant from dependence on the landowner; more, despite the peasant's hostility to the town, it brought the peasants into alliance with the shop-keepers and artisans who were threatened by the advance of great industry. In fact, the Christian Socialist party was the Austrian version of the Radical party in France (or even of Lloyd George radicalism in England), except that it worked with the Church instead of against it. It aimed to protect the 'little man' from limited companies and trade unions, from banks and multiple stores, and also from great estates and mechanized farming. It sought to divert the rising political passions into channels not dangerous to the Church: it was anti-liberal, anti-Jewish, anti-Marxist, anti-capitalist. The leaders of the movement knew exactly what they were about: though they appealed to base passions, especially anti-Semitism, they supposed that they could always control the passions which they evoked. Lueger declared, 'I decide who is a Jew,' and firmly protected any Jew who kept clear of liberalism and Marxism. Seipel, a later leader, said of his party's anti-Semitism: 'That is for the gutter.' He had no inkling that the gutter would one day murder his successor. Christian Socialism was an attempt to touch pitch and not be defiled. As the party of the 'little man', it was Imperial 'by appointment'; its supporters knew the value of the Archdukes' custom. Traditional Austrians were at first shocked by the Christian Socialist demagogy; and in the nineties Francis Joseph four times refused to confirm Lueger as

1. Pronounced: Loo-ee-ger.

Mayor of Vienna. In 1897 he was accepted; and the dynasty acknowledged that it had found a new ally.

In the nineties, as the national storm was rising, another great universalist movement established itself in Austria and brought yet more unexpected support to the universalist Empire and dynasty. In 1889 Viktor Adler united the scattered Marxists of Austria in the Austrian Social Democratic party. This was the year, too, of the founding of the Second International; and Marxism had already drifted far from the intentions of its founder. Marx's political strategy sprang from the failure of 1848. With penetrating vision, he saw the reluctance of the German liberals to take over the responsibility of government. This reluctance he ascribed to their fear of losing their property, and believed that the working classes, having no property, would be free of the reluctance. Marx was a revolutionary first and last. He did not preach revolution in order to achieve Socialism; he became a Socialist in order to achieve revolution. Though he recognized that a Socialist party must win the confidence of the masses by leading them in the day-to-day struggle over wages and working conditions, his aim was focused on the moment when the Socialists would seize power and bring existing society to an end. The German Social Democrats, the greatest 'Marxist' party in the world, soon relegated this seizure of power to the distant future; and the Austrian Social Democrats followed the German example. Like the liberals whom they denounced, they too shrank from responsibility and left the dynasty to shoulder the tasks which they found overwhelming. As the Christian Socialists were demagogic, so the Social Democrats were revolutionary, only in phrase.

Marxist Socialism was in theory universal: it preached the unity of the working classes who knew no fatherland and imagined a Socialist Europe without state wars or national hatred. For it, as for the traditional governing classes, nationalism was exclusively middle class; national conflicts it regarded as the device of rival capitalists to use the power of the state against foreign competitors and to divert the working classes from an attack on their real enemy. In practice, Marx was imprisoned in the revolutionary psychology of 1848: he recognized only the claims of the historic nationalities, though in this case historically revolutionary – the Germans, the

Poles, the Italians, and the Magyars.[1] He dismissed Slav nationalism as a reactionary fraud. He adopted the Polish thesis that the Ruthenes – the Little Russians of Galicia – had been 'invented' by the Habsburgs as a weapon against the revolutionary Poles; he endorsed the opinion of Engels that the Czech and Croat movements in 1848 were purely dynastic and feudalist and that the Slav peoples of Austria, 'who lack the very first conditions of national existence', were destined to be absorbed into revolutionary Socialist Germany. The Russian intervention in Hungary 1849 confirmed his association of the Slavs with reaction. In the sixties Bakunin, a Pan-Slav, challenged and finally broke Marx's hold of the First International; this strengthened his hostility to the Slavs still more. Hatred of the Slavs led Marx and Engels into strange paths. Fanatically anti-Russian, they persuaded themselves that the Turkish Empire was an ideal state which might pass straight into Socialism without any period of capitalist transition; they wrote off Gladstone's enthusiasm for the Balkan peoples as English capitalist trickery, and even upheld Disraeli as the champion of freedom and Socialism against Tsardom. Thus, the Socialist Europe to which Marx looked forward was a German Europe, in which Magyars, Turks, and possibly Poles, would be tolerated as partners.

This view was held also by the German liberals and, for that matter, by the Habsburg Empire in its existing Dualistic form: there, too, Magyars, Poles, and in Bosnia Turks, shared the privileges of the 'people of state'. Since industry was most advanced in the German areas, the early Social Democratic leaders in Austria were Germans and hardly acknowledged the national problem: so far as it existed, it appeared as a device by which workers with lower standards, Czechs or Slovenes, were introduced as blacklegs against German trade unionists. Moreover, since Marxism had no Socialist theory of international trade, the Austrian Social Democrats regarded the

1. Even these claims, other than the German, were admitted only with reservations. Italy 'will always be dominated by Germany'. Hungary was supported in hope of the assistance which did not, in fact, reach Vienna in October 1849. Restoration of Poland was demanded in order to provoke the revolutionary war with Russia, which Marx thought necessary for the unification of Germany; if however there was a revolution in Russia, Marx and Engels proposed to partition Poland between Russia and Germany. Engels wrote on 23 May 1851: 'If the Russians can be got to move, form an alliance with them and force the Poles to give way.'

Habsburg Monarchy with innocent Cobdenism and welcomed it as
'a great Free Trade area'. After all, an ambitious trade union
secretary preferred to count his members in Lvov and Trieste, from
the Carpathians to the Alps, rather than be confined to Vienna and
a few neighbouring towns. Besides, since the Habsburg Empire
brought prosperity to the great capitalists of Vienna, it brought
prosperity, too, to the workers of Vienna, who were employed by
these capitalists. Thus Karl Renner, the leading Socialist writer on
national questions, denounced those who sympathized with Hungarian demands for full independence, since 'the Hungarian market
is incomparably more important for Austrian capital than the
Moroccan market is for German'. The German Social Democrats at
least opposed German Imperialist plans in Morocco; the Austrian
Social Democrats supported Viennese economic Imperialism in
Hungary and still more in the Balkans. In exactly the same spirit
a German Socialist supported German Imperialism during the first
German war: 'The ruin of German industry would be the ruin of
the German working class.' So, later, a British trade union secretary,
turned Foreign Secretary, defended British Imperialist possessions
in the eastern Mediterranean and the Persian Gulf on the grounds
that, if these were lost, British workers would feel the loss in their
pay-packets. If the worker seeks to share his master's plunder, he
must also expect to share his master's ruin.

Yet while the Social Democratic politicians supported the unity of
the Habsburg Empire and so denied the national claims of the masses,
they insisted on national freedom for themselves. Marx had supposed
that working-class leaders would remain working-class in outlook;
in fact a Socialist politician or trade union official was an intellectual,
as middle class as a teacher or a bureaucrat. The Socialist leaders
were educated men, with intellectual abilities, as much divorced
from production as Marx himself: they could not escape the nationalist obsessions of their class. Once the non-German workers became
organized, they produced spokesmen of their own, and these were
as nationally conscious as their fellow intellectuals. As a result, the
Austrian Socialists divided the trade unions and even their party into
national sections, united only in name. Thus the jobs in the party and
in the trade unions were distributed, and duplicated, on national lines;
yet the Social Democrats denied this principle to everyone else. The

Socialists of other nationalities certainly took on a German tinge with their Marxism, and, in this sense, Austrian Social Democracy widened the 'Austrian idea'. The party was strongest in Vienna; and Vienna provided the thinkers and writers of the movement. These combined, in true Viennese form, daring arguments and tame conclusions: they used revolutionary phrases to spread throughout the Empire the outlook of the Vienna workers who lived on the custom of the great 'Austrian' landowners and capitalists.

Both Christian Socialism and Social Democracy looked subversive in the nineties. Still, the failure of the coalition ministry in 1895 compelled Francis Joseph to abandon the political system which he had operated, either in liberal or in conservative form, since 1867. The parties could not form a government; and it was useless to bargain with them. The only way out seemed to be a strong man, a saviour who would impose his authority from above. This new saviour – as it turned out, the last saviour of the Monarchy – was Badeni, Governor of Galicia. Badeni, with Polish adaptability, had every qualification. He was a noble and a loyal servant of the Emperor; at the same time, a liberal, even an anti-clerical of a mild sort, and, like all Poles, a centralist; he had been an active, successful governor, yet was supposed to be up to date in his political ideas. His ingenuity tackled the problem of universal suffrage which had baffled the parliamentary politicians: he accepted the principle, yet ensured that it did no harm. In 1896, a fifth layer of constituencies was imposed on the existing 'curial' system, returning seventy-two members by universal suffrage. With aristocratic frivolity, Badeni supposed that the democratic members would be satisfied with a permanent minority.

In any case, this was for Badeni a distraction. Like so many others before and since, he was confident that he could settle the conflict between Czechs and Germans. His immediate attention was focused on the economic compromise with Hungary which had to be passed in 1897; and he hoped to do this with a 'liberal' bloc of Poles, Germans, and reconciled Czechs. Beyond this, he had the idea of restoring Austrian strength and so of imposing new terms of agreement upon Hungary altogether. Foreign events suddenly gave Badeni a free hand. Austria-Hungary ceased to be a European necessity, with all the advantages and disadvantages which that implied. Kálnoky's appeal to German liberal sentiment in 1893 had failed almost as soon as made. By 1894 Caprivi had grown cautious: he would not offer the German backing against France which Kálnoky thought necessary to win England for action in the Near East. Instead, Caprivi, off on another tack, estranged England from the Central Powers by a dispute over the Nile valley. In the autumn of 1894, Caprivi left office, and Hohenlohe, the new German Chancellor, reverted to Bismarck's conservative policy, seeking to renew friendly relations with Russia and no longer favouring the Poles. Both Kálnoky's foreign policy and the Austrian coalition lost German support. Kálnoky supposed that his chance had come again when Salisbury returned to office in England in 1895. The British fleet for the last time, prepared to enter the Straits. This policy was no longer workable. It was technically impossible, since the Franco-Russian alliance; it was sentimentally impossible, since the Armenian massacres. At the end of 1895, England virtually abandoned the defence of the Turkish Empire. Austria-Hungary was left alone and lost her final, feeble ally, when Italy ran into disaster in Abyssinia. Kálnoky, in desperate isolation, was driven to seek the favour of the Vatican; this, he believed, his only hope against the Franco-Russian coalition. To please the Vatican, Kálnoky attempted to interfere in Hungarian politics and to stem the anti-clericalism, which was the latest sounding board for Magyar chauvinism. Instead, Kálnoky was forced from office by Hungarian protest. Isolation, and approaching disaster in the Near East, still faced Goluchowski, his successor. Russia seemed bent on occupying the Bosphorus; and neither Germany nor England would assist Austria-Hungary to oppose her. Suddenly, at the end of 1896, the danger vanished. France vetoed Russia's move; and, in any case, Russia's eyes were turned to the Far East, where she saw prizes easier to come by and of greater size.

Thus, in 1897, Goluchowski achieved, through no merit of his own, the agreement with Russia which had evaded every Austrian statesman since Metternich; and achieved it even without the parade of conservative solidarity which Metternich had found necessary. Goluchowski, as a Pole, remained suspicious of Russia and hostile; only his isolation, and German pressure, compelled him to accept the Russian offer. In May 1897, Austria-Hungary and Russia formally concluded a Near Eastern entente, Russia to free her hands for the Far East, Austria-Hungary *faute de mieux* : it was an agreement in the only form which the Habsburg Monarchy could ever accept, an agreement to postpone the Eastern Question as long as possible. In the contemporary phrase, the Near East was 'put on ice'; and, against expectation, remained in the ice chest for ten years. The Austro-Russian entente brought to Austria-Hungary great relief and yet great danger. She had no longer to fear a war with Russia and needed no longer to seek for allies: she ceased to pander to Italian feeling and did not even trouble about Germany. On the other hand, with the Russian danger removed, she lost her last scrap of 'European mission'. Passions were not restrained by the danger from without; Germans and Magyars especially, the two 'peoples of state' who most feared a Russian advance, could now turn against the Habsburg Monarchy almost as destructively as in 1848. The Austro-Russian entente began for the Monarchy a long period of crisis, this time of crisis from within; and since these crises were not overcome, they left the Monarchy weaker than ever to face the new period of external crisis which began in 1908.

Badeni's great stroke coincided with the ending of the Near Eastern danger; and its effects first displayed the consequences of the Austro-Russian entente. This stroke was the ordinance of 5 April 1897, decreeing that Czech and German should be the languages of the 'inner service' throughout Bohemia.[1] Ostensibly equitable, it gave the Czechs victory in the international struggle, that is, in the struggle for jobs within the bureaucracy. All Czechs learnt German as an international language; German schools in Bohemia were forbidden by the Diet degree of 1868 to teach 'a second provincial language', that is, Czech. Once a knowledge of both languages was demanded for admission to provincial employment, the Czechs would gain a monopoly of official positions in Bohemia. Badeni launched his ordinance without any preparation: like the men of the October Diploma, he was incapable of imagining either popular resistance or popular support. The Austrian nobility, who genuinely cared for Austria, and the Emperor himself were in

---

1. German remained the exclusive language for correspondence with other provinces and with the central government, for military administration, for Post and Telegraphs, and for the Exchequer.

an inescapable dilemma: the Empire could survive only if it won the support of the Austrian peoples, yet the peoples, once reconciled, would end aristocratic privilege and Imperial power.

The Badeni ordinance exploded the German resentment against the dwindling of their former monopoly which had been accumulating since 1879, or even since 1866. The Germans of Bohemia appealed to the Germans throughout Austria, and to the Germans in Germany as well. Schönerer had his opportunity at last. The German nationalist party, which he founded in 1885, had remained a violent and noisy minority. Now Schönerer put himself at the head of the German movement which aimed to reassert the unity of the Empire on a German basis. He himself had not this aim: he believed that the violence, which he inspired, would wreck the Empire and prepare the way for Greater Germany. The German nationalities, spokesmen of the 'people of state', behaved as though they were the representatives of an oppressed minority; and they were seconded by the more moderate Germans, even by the German Social Democrats. They modelled their tactics on the Irish obstruction at Westminster. The Irish wished solely to finish the connexion with England; the Germans, at any rate in theory wished to preserve a strong Empire – it was as though the English members of parliament had resorted to obstruction as a demonstration against the Irish. The Germans of the Reichsrat had not even the wit and ingenuity which dignified their Irish example: violent hooligans, they were worthy representatives of the 'people of state'. The nationalist members shouted and stamped for hours on end; banged desks and hurled inkpots at the Speaker, until at last the police were called in and put an end to this parody of representative government.

Schönerer and his friends appealed from the Reichsrat to the streets. In Vienna, Graz, and Salzburg, crowds of rich respectable citizens demonstrated with all the violence of the hungry mobs of 1848. Meetings were held throughout Germany, and messages of sympathy accumulated. Mommsen, famous historian and high-minded liberal, wrote: 'The brain of the Czechs does not understand reason, but it understands blows. This is a struggle of life and death.' In this crisis Badeni showed that he was far from being the pre-destined saviour of the Habsburg Monarchy. Accustomed to the inarticulate grumblings of Little Russian peasants, Badeni was helpless against the crowds of well-dressed, well-fed German rioters. He could not use troops against the capitalists of the Monarchy, and he would not appeal from the middle classes to the mass movements of Christian Socialism and Social Democracy, which were less dominated by nationalist violence. He had assumed always that he was dealing with the dumb peasant peoples of the eighteenth century; popular resistance to his aristocratic will had never entered into his calculations. All Austria was shaken; and in November 1897, Francis Joseph dismissed the man who had been called in to save the Empire.

Mass demonstrations to force the dismissal of a minister had no precedent since 1848. The German nationalists were astonished at their success; the crowds who followed them still more terrified at it. For if Schönerer had attained his full ambition and overthrown 'authority', the German middle classes would have suffered most, and first. Schönerer wished to wreck the Habsburg Monarchy and to incorporate its territories in Hohenzollern Germany. This was not the ambition of the vast majority of German Austrians. The mobs of Vienna wanted Vienna to be the capital of a great German Empire, not to decay into a provincial town. The movement against Badeni was the culminating-point of the German negations, which did more than anything else to destroy the Habsburg Monarchy. The Germans were not strong enough to preserve Austria as a German national state; they would not allow it to be transformed into a non-national state. They could not capture the dynasty, they dared not over-throw it; they could only obstruct the dynasty when it attempted anything constructive.

Certainly the dynasty deserved its defeat. Only defeat could be expected from an attempt at national appeasement by means of a Polish noble without constitutional experience. Francis Joseph sheltered behind the political irresponsibility of the peoples and their leaders; yet it was the tenacious defence of dynastic power which had debarred the peoples from political experience. Francis Joseph was well-meaning, anxious to preserve his Empire and even to guard over his subjects; what he could not do was to give up any part of the power that he had inherited. The great Austrian structure had been built up round the House of Habsburg; it could survive only if it ceased to be the monopoly of the dynasty. This is the explanation of the end of Austria-Hungary. The ordinance of Badeni was the last attempt by the dynasty to break the deadlock of national conflicts in Austria; though there was afterwards no lack of reforming plans, Francis Joseph had ceased to hope for any change for the better and struggled only against change for the worse. The schemes and efforts of the early twentieth century were defensive. After Badeni the dynasty was content to guard its own coffin.

CHAPTER FIFTEEN

HUNGARY AFTER 1867: KOLOMAN TISZA AND THE MAGYAR GENTRY

IN the early twentieth century the political crises in Austria and Hungary came simultaneously to explosion. Both were caused by middle-class nationalism: in Austria this originated from the development of industry, in Hungary from the decay of agriculture. Francis Joseph's surrender to Hungary in 1867 had a paradoxical effect: the Magyar gentry achieved political success at the very moment of their economic ruin. Abolition of the *Robot* in 1848, faithfully enforced by the Bach hussars, began the decline of the petty gentry; railways and the competition of American wheat completed it. Their estates passed to the magnates, who gained from the abolition of the *Robot* and, capitalistically equipped, could weather the storm of world competition. Over one hundred thousand independent landowners vanished between 1867 and the end of the century; over one third of Hungary was in the hands of the magnates, and one fifth of Hungary was owned by three hundred families.

The gentry, divorced from the land, were saved from extinction by the new character of the Hungarian state. Before 1848 the Hungarian state machine had consisted of the Hungarian Chancellor in Vienna and a few clerks in the Lieutenancy in Budapest, who copied out his rescripts and forwarded them to the sixty-three counties, autonomous bodies administered, as a hobby, by the landowning gentry. The state which Francis Joseph handed over in 1867 was a vast bureaucratic organization on the Austrian model, with state railways, state post office, state health services, and state education; and this state, created by the Bach hussars, now employed the landless 'gentry'. Though the counties recovered their historic autonomy, this counted for little; their only independent function was to assess and collect the land-tax, once the sole source of revenue, now, as in other countries, an interesting survival. The gentry-type of the early nineteenth century was an uncultured farmer, learned only in traditional law and never going further than the county town, except, perhaps, once in his life as a deputy to the Diet at Bratislava. The gentry-type of the early twentieth century was a civil servant, living in Budapest, owning at most the historical family house, though without land, unless perhaps his salary and 'pickings' enabled him to subsidize an unprofitable estate. Thus the gentry, historically the opponents of the centralized state, now identified themselves with it; and by the twentieth century the bureaucratic apparatus found employment for a quarter of a million Magyar gentry.

The gentry had a crude administrative experience in the counties; their real qualification for office was their Magyar character. As in Austria, the national question became a struggle for jobs in the bureaucracy; in Hungary, the struggle was won in advance. Faced with the danger of national competition, the Magyar gentry dared not fulfil the provisions of the Nationalities Law of 1868; on the other hand, to make their work easier, they demanded a knowledge of Magyar from all the inhabitants of Hungary. No state school, elementary or secondary, was ever provided for any national minority; the secondary schools which the Slovaks had set up for themselves were closed in 1874; Magyar was made compulsory in all schools in 1883. The highest expression of this policy was the Education Law promoted by Apponyi[1] in 1907, which imposed a special oath of loyalty on all teachers and made them liable to dismissal if their pupils did not know Magyar. Similarly, the Magyar gentry attacked any political display by the nationalities – drove their few members from parliament and condemned their organizations. By these means, the Magyar gentry gained and kept a monopoly

1. Pronounced: Awponee.

of state employment and of the liberal professions. At the beginning of the twentieth century, 95 per cent of the state officials, 92 per cent of the county officials, 89 per cent of the doctors, and 90 per cent of the judges were Magyar. Eighty per cent of the newspapers were in Magyar, and the remainder mostly German: three million Rumanians had 2·5 per cent of the newspapers, two million Slovaks had 0·64 per cent, and three hundred thousand Little Russians 0·06 per cent. The search for state employment drew the Magyar gentry, too, into Croatia; and, since the administration was controlled by the Magyar governor, the Croat Diet was helpless. The railway system, controlled from Budapest, introduced Magyar officials throughout Croatia and was itself used to increase Croat defencelessness: the Hungarian administration prevented any rail link between Zagreb and Vienna and compelled the Croat railway system to find an artificial centre at Budapest. Even the Croat Diet itself was in part packed in 1887 by giving officials temporarily resident in Croatia a vote even though they already possessed a home and a vote in Hungary.

Magyar nationalism was not exclusive: as the winning of Dualism showed, the Hungarian political nation had unrivalled skill. Aware that the Magyars were a minority in Hungary, the Magyar gentry aimed to keep the nationalities helpless by winning over the few 'national' intellectuals. They were far more concerned to prevent the rise of a Slovak or Rumanian middle class than to increase their own Magyar 'nation', and troubled little about the education of the Magyar peasants; after all, an independent peasant party even of Magyars might have challenged the monopoly of the gentry. The Magyar governing class gained recruits from every nation, though principally from the Germans and the Jews. The Germans, abandoned by Vienna and still more by Germany, remained dominant in commerce and industry, though often acquiring Magyar character in the process. The Jews, emerging from the ghetto as the gentry had emerged from the *comitats*, were the foremost advocates of 'assimilation' and supplied, in literature and the arts, a brilliance which the native gentry lacked.

None of the nationalities in Hungary proper was capable of organized resistance. The Rumanians in Transylvania always received some encouragement from Bucharest; the Serbs in the south, though they received little encouragement, still knew of independent Serbia. On the other hand, Rumania lived in fear of Russia for a generation after the Russo-Turkish war of 1877-8; and Serbia was a dependency of Vienna from 1881 to 1903. The Slovaks and Little Russians of northern Hungary were in yet worse case, for they had no national home beyond the frontier to which they could look. The Slovaks were more severed from the Czechs than at any time in their history. The attempt to create a common 'Czecho-slovak' language had been abandoned; and only the minority of Slovak Protestants preserved Czech sympathies. Even so Slovak Lutheranism, though hostile to the Magyars, looked to Germany rather than to Prague for inspiration. The few Slovak spokesmen were Roman Catholic priests; and these, forming an alliance with the Hungarian clerical party, made anti-Semitism the chief plank in Slovak nationalism. Thus, the Slovaks seemed to confirm all the charges which Magyar and German liberalism had made against them: they were reactionary, clerical, anti-Semitic, and pro-Habsburg. The Magyars had robbed them of a secular middle class; and this Magyar success made them, both in Hungary and when they achieved independence, politically the most immature and irresponsible of all the peoples of central Europe.

The Little Russians of sub-Carpathian Russia had even less political existence. Their national life was preserved only by the Uniate priests, and this Uniate religion, as in Galicia, cut them off from all support. It estranged them from the Poles; it estranged them equally from tsarist Russia, and in Hungary the Little Russians were too backward even to dream of an independent Ukraine. One thing inspired both Slovaks and Little Russians; they found a new national home, or a substitute for it, in America. There is no reason why a peasant should stop at the nearest town, once he leaves his own soil; he might just as well cross the ocean, and in the latter part of the nineteenth century Slovaks and Little Russians took with them to America the national culture they were not allowed to develop in Europe. Like all emigrants, these were more devoted to their traditions than those who had remained behind; they became the rich 'American cousins', returning home to conduct the national struggle with American methods or subsidizing it from overseas. Moreover, the Slav immigrants in America transformed even the

American political outlook: to the original idea of preserving democracy they added the new ideal of promoting national self-determination and so paved the way for the American intervention in 1917 which determined the fate of the Habsburg Monarchy. In this way, too, the Magyars may claim to be the principal authors of the Monarchy's ruin.

Croatia presented a special problem both for the Magyars and for the Croats themselves. In 1848 and after, the Croats had fought for the historic rights of Croatia, not for national freedom; the temporary enthusiasm of Jellačić for the 'Illyrian' idea had been one of those extraordinary anticipations which distinguished the great revolutionary year. The Croat gentry had relied on Imperial protection and now, deserted by Francis Joseph, could think of no new policy. The Croat Diet was dominated by the Party of Right, which continued to demand the 'state rights' of Croatia and still lived in the dream world of medieval law from which the Hungarians had escaped. The Party of Right was clerical, conservative, and pro-Habsburg; its only concession to nationalism was hostility to the Serbs, who, since the incorporation of the 'military frontiers' into Croatia in 1868, made up a quarter of the population. The greatest consolation of an oppressed class or nationality is to feel itself superior to one still more oppressed; and the Magyar rulers of Croatia deliberately favoured its Serbs in order to spur on the Croats against them. When some members of the Party of Right hesitated to make conflict with the Serbs their only political activity, the majority of the party reasserted itself as the Party of Pure Right – meaning pure from any trace of reality. As usual, the most fanatical exponents of this rigid patriotism were converts: Frank, the leader of the Party of Pure Right, was a Jew who had become a Croat from clerical enthusiasm.

Croatia, artificially severed from Austria by the harsh Hungarian frontier and denied control even of its own port at Rijeka, remained a backward agrarian land until the twentieth century. Still, a professional middle class developed in Zagreb, a class with a modern outlook and modern education. A university, though not of the standing of Prague, was founded at Zagreb in 1874; and the intellectuals at last provided a national policy less barren than the 'historic rights' demanded by the gentry and retired army officers who had hitherto composed the 'Croat nation'. The leader of this new movement was Štrosmajer,[1] Bishop of Djakova, the son of a peasant who rose high in the Church and even at court before the development of his national loyalty. Štrosmajer was the real creator of the South Slav idea and thus would have been the father of the South Slav nation if it had ever come into true existence. Gaj, the founder of Illyrianism, had stressed only the common language; Štrosmajer looked forward to a common culture and back to a common past. This act of faith was an intellectual *tour de force* of a high order. Serbs, Croats, and Slovenes were sharply divided by history and by political allegiance; they were divided by religion and by culture. In fact, it needed ethnographers and pre-historians to bring out their common Slav character: hence the importance of archaeology and 'folk-museums' in the creating of South Slav feeling. The Serbs were Orthodox, with a great, though distant, Byzantine past; the Croats and Slovenes Roman Catholic. Croatia had its 'historic' state; the Slovenes were part of unitary Austria and were represented in the Reichsrat; the Serbs had been oppressed by both Turks and Hungarians, yet possessed at last an independent, though diminutive, state. The Serbs had fought their way to freedom and intended to fight further against both Turks and Habsburgs; the Croats, though also fighters, had fought for the Habsburgs and hoped to regain their 'rights' by a renewal of Habsburg protection. The Croats despised the barbarous Serbs and their Balkan ways; in reality, the Serb intellectuals took their culture direct from Paris, while the Croats received it distorted and coarsened through German channels.

No two peoples were more separated by their past. The 'South Slav' idea was an intellectual creation, not the outcome of national development. Štrosmajer was a man of the Habsburg world, even in revolt from it; despairing of the barren dynastic idea, he sought an idea more creative. His object was to bring peoples together, not to divide them into national states; and he believed that this could be done by the manufacture of a common culture. When the Croats under his lead founded an academy — that potent weapon in the national struggle — they named it the South Slav Academy; and he bequeathed to it his unique collection of early

1. Pronounced: Shtross-my-er.

Italian pictures. This gave perfect expression to the intellectual basis of the South Slav movement: Štrosmajer appealed to the class which visited art galleries and believed that they could be won for the South Slav idea by looking at Italian primitives. His belief was well founded. The intellectual middle class of Zagreb followed Štrosmajer's lead; and Zagreb became the birthplace of the South Slav movement. Croatia could not dominate a South Slav union, and Croat 'state rights' could not be merged with South Slav nationalism, as Bohemian 'state rights' were merged with Czech nationalism; therefore the Zagreb intellectuals became South Slavs pure and simple. The Serbs, on the other hand, already possessed their own state and were less susceptible to the appeal of Italian primitives; their practical ambition was to extend Serbia, and they regarded the South Slav idea as no more than a secondary weapon to this end. Exponents of a true national state, they expected to provide the dynasty, the history, and the culture in any South Slav union; there would be no room for the traditions of Croatia. This obvious outcome made Croat patriots the bitterest enemies of the South Slav idea, a hostility quite unthinkable at Belgrade. Thus Zagreb became both the home of the South Slav movement and the centre of opposition to it.

There was little practical cooperation between Serbs and Croats. In Serbia there were no Croats; in Croatia there was always conflict and rivalry between the two peoples. They came together only in Dalmatia. This was not the 'national home' of either; and both enjoyed the liberal conditions of Austrian constitutionalism. The Croats of Dalmatia certainly did not desire reunion with Croatia, which would have put them under Hungarian rule; the Serbs of Dalmatia, cut off from Serbia by Bosnia and Hercegovina, could not hope for union with Serbia. Therefore both could combine as 'South Slavs' against the Italians. The Serbo-Croat coalition, so alarming to the last generation of Austrian statesmen, was thus born of Austrian politics and would never have come into existence if there had been only Serbia and Croatia. It was the creation of men freed from the traditions and jealousies of their national home, as 'Czechoslovakia' was the creation of Czechs and Slovaks from Moravia, or more remotely, in the United States. Theoretically the South Slav idea embraced also the Slovenes; in fact, they were severed from it by the rigid Hungarian frontier and found Vienna nearer than Belgrade or even Zagreb. Their allies in the struggle against Germans and Italians were the Czechs, not the Croats or Serbs; and they needed the unitary Austrian state in order to preserve this alliance. The South Slav question thus depended on the relations between Croats and Serbs; and these would never have been brought together by all the noble inspiration of Štrosmajer, except in Dalmatia, had it not been for the blunders and national violence of the Magyars.[1]

The nationalist fervour of the Magyar gentry was not designed solely to preserve their monopoly of state employment against the minorities; it was also a new, and decisive, weapon in the struggle which the gentry had always waged against the magnates. The magnates, cosmopolitan courtiers with great estates at stake, had favoured compromise with the Habsburgs ever since the peace of Szatmár; the gentry, not looking beyond the *comitats*, had always jibbed at the Habsburg connexion. This was the pattern of 1848: the majority of the gentry supported Kossuth, and the magnates, with a few exceptions such as Andrássy, abandoned him. It was the pattern, too, of the period preceding Dualism: the magnates, including Andrássy, and the more enlightened gentry supported Deák; the majority of the gentry seconded the negations of Koloman Tisza. After 1867, the situation was reversed. The magnates, instead of seeking grants of land by sycophancy at court, became independent agricultural capitalists on a great scale; the gentry, instead of sulking in the *comitats*, entered the service of the state and became dependent on it. The gentry now needed the Habsburg connexion in order to maintain Hungary as a great state. At the same time, they wished to be free from Habsburg interference in order to exploit this state and were quite prepared to pay for their freedom by respecting the prerogatives of the Crown in the army and in foreign affairs. Koloman Tisza was the symbol of this change and indeed the maker of this new Hungary. He amalgamated his party with the followers of Deák and became Prime Minister in 1875. Henceforth he was the loyal agent of Francis Joseph; and no Hun-

1. The 'South Slav' idea of Štrosmajer included the Bulgarians. It would depart too far from the Habsburg theme to examine why, in Bulgaria, the cultural idea never achieved political translation

garian was more 'dualist' and docile in foreign affairs than Tisza, the former leader of the opposition to the Compromise. In fact, in the Bulgarian crisis of 1887, Tisza defended Imperial foreign policy from the attacks of Andrássy.

Tisza and his gentry followers could not maintain themselves solely by the appeal to self-interest: the influence of Kossuth had gone too deep, and national feeling had been burnt in by the bitter experiences between 1849 and 1867. The ceaseless campaign against the nationalities was needed as proof that Tisza and his 'mamelukes' remained good Magyars, despite their subservience to Francis Joseph. Even this appeal to Magyar chauvinism was not enough: the constituencies of central Hungary, with their Magyar inhabitants, remained obstinately Kossuthite in sentiment. Against this Tisza used an unexpected 'electoral geometry'. The constituencies inhabited by Magyars were enormous, often with 10,000 voters; the constituencies inhabited by the national minorities were tiny, with as few as 250 electors, and since few of these could understand Magyar the decision rested with half a dozen officials. Thus the system of Magyar monopoly was maintained by means of 'rotten boroughs', inhabited by non-Magyars.

This system of genius defeated the ambitions of the magnates. They had supposed that Dualism would provide them with high places of glory and profit; like the English Whigs, they regarded government appointments as a system of out-relief for the aristocracy. Instead, their places were taken by gentry-paupers, more industrious and less exacting in their demands; and the magnates were altogether excluded from office. No magnate was Prime Minister after Andrássy left office in 1871; and Tisza did not even insist on a Hungarian magnate as Foreign Minister after the fall of Andrássy in 1879. The tables were turned. The magnates had intended to cooperate with the gentry in order to impose themselves on the Emperor; instead the gentry cooperated with the Emperor to impose themselves on the magnates. The magnates were at a loss. They could not use their traditional method of influence at court: through their own doing, Francis Joseph had renounced direct power in Hungary and, in any case, preferred Tisza to the arrogant, irresponsible magnates. Besides, economic policy compelled them to pose as enemies of the Habsburg connexion: they needed high grain

duties to protect the inflated profits of their great estates and therefore had to whip up Hungarian jealousy of Austria every ten years
when the Tariff Compromise was renewed. Agrarian protection
turned the Hungarian magnates into Magyar nationalists, just as it
turned the Prussian Junkers into German nationalists; and Hungarians, to say nothing of Austrians, had to eat dear bread for the
sake of 'the national cause'.

Thus the magnates, cosmopolitan in upbringing, historically the
betrayers of independent Hungary, had to compete in Magyar
nationalism with the Calvinist squire Tisza, a far truer Magyar.
They could not compete in 'internal' chauvinism: nothing could
improve on the campaign of Tisza and the 'mamelukes' against the
nationalities. Tisza's only weakness was his welcome to the Jews;
and this was exploited by Count Aladar Zichy, leader of the clerical,
anti-Semitic People's party. Not however with success; the Jewish
trader and moneylender, coming from Galicia, affected the Slovaks
and Little Russians more than the Magyars, and Zichy's anti-
Semitic zeal actually turned him into a champion of the Slovaks.
This was not the way to Magyar favour. Nor could anything be
achieved by taking a more idealistic line than Tisza and advocating
a policy of national cooperation. The 'Magyar nation' was composed of civil servants, country squires, and rich peasants; none of
them intellectually gifted, they left Magyar cultural advancement to
the Jews, and these, as converts, were equally intolerant. Even
Deák's moderation had been purely tactical; and his tactics had
been underlined by most Magyars with an open leer. Magyar
nationalism was too deeply rooted in history and social circumstance
to be led by an academic middle class; for that very reason it could
not produce a man of noble character, a Štrosmajer or a Masarýk.
When, at the end of the Empire, Michael Károlyi, last of the
magnates, preached the doctrine of national equality, he succeeded
only in making himself hated as the enemy of Great Hungary.

Thus the magnates, in their fight against Tisza, had no alternative
but 'external' chauvinism. Since they could not win the competition
of 'magyarization', they had to display their patriotism in foreign
affairs. Andrássy, for example, in 1887 attacked Kálnoky for not
fighting, in defence of Bulgaria, the war against Russia which he
had refused to fight, in defence of Turkey, in 1878. Still, Russia had

been only Kossuth's second enemy. The dynasty had been the first. The magnates, enemies of Kossuth in 1848, took up his struggle against the dynasty, the only struggle in which Koloman Tisza could not compete. Tisza and the gentry became defenders of Dualism. Andrássy, son of the maker of Dualism; Apponyi, descendant of generations of Habsburg diplomats; and, later, Michael Károlyi, descendant of the maker of the peace of Szatmár, became advocates of 'personal union', demanding a separate Hungarian army and, by implication, a separate Hungarian foreign policy. Kossuth in exile had long abandoned this programme and advocated a Danubian Confederation free of the Habsburgs. This did not deter the magnates. They captured Kossuth on his death in 1894. His body was brought back in triumph to Budapest; and his insignificant son, returning too, was built up as the leader of the Party of Independence. Magnate patriotism was spurred on by the agrarian distress which reached its height towards the end of the century. Faced with peasant rioters and even threatened by a union of agricultural workers, the magnates turned the discontent from the great estates to the Hofburg and found the cause of all Hungary's ills in the use of German as the language of command in the army. Besides, the Austro-Russian entente of May 1897, removed the safety valve of an anti-Russian policy. There was no Russian peril in the Near East; therefore the dynasty received all the blows of magnate patriotism.

The collapse of constitutional government in Austria, with the failure of Badeni, removed the remaining hesitation of the magnates. There was no fear that a united Austria would be mobilized against them. Further, with the Reichsrat out of control, even the Tariff Agreement, due for renewal in 1897, could not be carried; and the old terms had to be prolonged until 1903. This produced new apologies to Hungary and new verbal concessions: Francis Joseph ceased to be Emperor-King, one person, and became Emperor and King, two persons. With Austria in confusion it seemed impossible for Francis Joseph to resist the attack on Dualism; and the campaign against the common army began in earnest. Thus, thirty years after the making of the compromise, constitutional government broke down in Austria, and Dualism was challenged by an unshakable majority in the Hungarian parliament. The Austrian crisis opened the door for a crisis of the Empire. The Germans, hitherto a 'people of state', had caused the first crisis; the Magyars, still a 'people of state', caused the other. Little did these two privileged nations realize that a third crisis was maturing in the minds of a few Croat intellectuals, as the result of the desertion of Croatia by the dynasty and its oppression by the Magyars. Yet within ten years the South Slav question overshadowed the Austrian constitutional confusion and Magyar agitation alike; and within twenty years the South Slav challenge ended Habsburg dynasty, German predominance, and Great Hungary.

CHAPTER SIXTEEN

DEMOCRATIC PRETENCE: THE INDIAN SUMMER OF THE HABSBURG MONARCHY, 1897–1908

THE fall of Badeni in Austria, the agitation against the common army in Hungary, these marked the end of the partnership with the German middle class and the Magyar gentry which the dynasty had made in 1867. With no danger threatening them from abroad, the 'peoples of state' could take up and parody the programmes of 1848. The dynastic reaction was slower than in 1849, in the end more effective: the 'peoples of state' needed the dynasty to maintain them in greatness and could be brought to heel by a real threat to withdraw dynastic support. Francis Joseph hesitated to make this threat: he had never believed in anything except the strength of the armed forces, and now he did not believe even in that. In the days of the imbecile Emperor Ferdinand, men counted the months until Francis Joseph should come of age and Austria be saved by a young, energetic Emperor. Now with the aged Francis Joseph, men looked forward to his death and the saving of Austria by a young energetic heir. The first of these saviours had been Rudolph, the only son of Francis Joseph: critical enough of the conduct of affairs, he intended to save the Empire by a more violent dose of German liberalism, and would have paired well with Frederick III, who had similar projects for Germany. Fortunately for himself and for others, Rudolph committed suicide. The new saviour, beginning to voice his criticisms at the end of the century, was Francis Ferdinand, the Emperor's nephew. Violent, reactionary and autocratic, Francis Ferdinand combined a crazy insistence on dynastic power with a marriage to a woman of non-royal blood, in breach of the dynastic rules. Clericalism dominated his political schemes. Though aggressively despotic, he proposed to work with the Christian Socialists against the German middle class, and with the Slovak and Rumanian peasants against the Magyar gentry. Later on, he claimed to favour federalism : this was no more than an extension of provincial autonomy, a refurbishing of the October Diploma, and not at all a system of national freedom. For, like all his conservative predecessors, Francis Ferdinand hated national movements as soon as they became democratic; and was as hostile to the Czechs, and even to the middle-class Croats, as he was to the Germans. Francis Joseph resented his interference and disregarded his plans; still, the constant criticism finally pushed him, too, into resistance, especially of Magyar demands.

Badeni was followed in Austria by three years of interregnum, when a bewildering succession of ministers attempted, by a variety of conjuring tricks, to piece together the fragments which Badeni had smashed for good and all. Just as Badeni would have been content with a return to Taaffe's 'mild dissatisfaction', so the ministers after Badeni would have been content with a return to the easy days when the national parties fought over the grammar school at Celje. The ministers no longer dreamt of 'solving' the national question; their highest ambition was that the members of the Reichsrat should cease to throw inkpots at the Speaker. No 'solution' was possible: the Germans would riot unless the Badeni ordinance were withdrawn; the Czechs would riot if it were. Early in 1898 the Austrian government tried a compromise: Czech and German were to be used in the 'inner service' only in the mixed districts of Bohemia, and knowledge of both was to be demanded only of officials who were to serve in those districts. This offended both nations: the Czechs insisted on the unity of 'historic' Bohemia; the Germans feared to lose the mixed districts to the Czechs. The compromise had to be abandoned. The Czechs were satisfied so long as the Badeni ordinance remained in existence – it had no practical significance, since knowledge of two languages could be demanded only of new entrants to the service. The Germans were mollified by an assurance that the ordinance would be revised or withdrawn before it came into practical operation.

The great majority of middle-class Germans, though fervently nationalist, had been shocked to find themselves following the lead of Schönerer; and indeed Schönerer never repeated his success of 1897. He and his small group became openly hostile to the Habsburgs and to everything associated with the dynasty; they advocated the dismemberment of the Habsburg Empire and agitated, too, against Roman Catholicism, the dynastic religion. Dislike of Schönerer led the moderate German leaders to draw up the Whitsuntide programme of 1899 – the most important declaration of German aims between the Linz programme in 1882 and the Easter programme of 1915. Unlike the Linz programme, this expressed the outlook of Germans loyal to the Empire, who wished to preserve and strengthen it. These Germans, too, adopted the Linz device and proposed to lop off from Austria the two provinces without large German minorities which could be safely handed over to historic nationalities; Galicia and Dalmatia were to enjoy their own provincial languages, in the one case Polish, in the other Italian.[1] In the rest of Austria the nationalities were to be allowed to use their own languages for local affairs (as they already did); German was to remain the only 'language of convenience'. This was a true display of German *Biederkeit*: the Germans were prepared to favour the Poles and Italians, with considerable injustice to the Little Russians and Croats; apart from this, their only concession was to transform German from 'the language of state' into 'the language of convenience'. Certainly, it would have been difficult, after the German behaviour in 1897, to defend German as the language of a superior culture.

Still, the Whitsuntide programme seemed to mark a German willingness to return to constitutional politics and to cooperate in the search for a 'solution'. To appease them, the Badeni ordinance

1. These 'concessions' were concessions to master-nations, not to national justice. The Poles were a bare majority in Galicia, the Italian three per cent of the population of Dalmatia.

was withdrawn in October 1899, and German restored as the sole language of the 'inner service' (which it had, in practice, always remained). The Czechs regarded the ordinance, not the system before the ordinance, as the *status quo* from which bargaining must proceed; they wished to grant concessions, not to struggle for them. It was therefore the turn of the Czechs to organize obstruction, and they had learnt well from the German example: once more desks banged in the Reichsrat, inkpots flew, and respectable Czech crowds demonstrated in the streets of Prague. The withdrawal of the Badeni ordinance did not merely end the episode of Badeni; it ended the epoch of middle-class constitutional life in Austria. Francis Joseph gave up the search for a ministerial combination which should possess the support of a majority in the Reichsrat; he gave up even the attempt to fulfil the requirements of the constitution and to secure the consent of the Reichsrat to taxation. Ever since the fall of Taaffe, the permanent officials had performed the real duties of ministers. In 1900 Francis Joseph dispensed with parliamentary ministers, and promoted bureaucrats to the heads of their departments; the chief bureaucrat, now called Prime Minister, merely added a certain contact with the Reichsrat to the burden of his other office duties.

The new system was invented and perfected by Koerber, a permanent official who became Prime Minister in 1900. Koerber's weapon was article 14 of the constitutional laws of 1867, which authorized the Emperor to issue 'emergency regulations' in case of need. Everything, from the budget downwards, now became an emergency regulation. In theory, the regulations could be challenged by a majority of the Reichsrat. Koerber did not fear it: the Reichsrat was as incapable of producing a majority for this as for any other purpose. In any case, Koerber kept the parties 'sweet' by local concessions – schools, railways, or roads – a more cynical Austrian version of the policy of 'log-rolling' by which Bülow maintained himself contemporaneously in Germany. The Reichsrat had no significance except as a meeting place where bargains could be struck between Koerber and the party leaders; it had no influence on policy, and its members had no hope of public careers. They had attained the highest ambition of central European politicians: endless, futile opposition. Koerber would have liked to include some politicians in his government as cover for his bureaucratic nakedness, and invited the German leaders to join him. The reply revealed their preference for opposition and barred any revival of constitutional government in Austria: 'The German parties must leave the appointment of a Minister without Portfolio to safeguard German interests to the Prime Minister; but, if one is appointed, they will not treat it as a *casus belli*.'

Koerber, like all his bureaucratic predecessors since the time of Bach, genuinely hoped for a return to constitutional forms at some time in the future. In 1902 he carried the budget and, at last, the Tariff bargain with Hungary in the legal manner. He did not repeat his success. The politicians shrank from the responsibility of voting for the budget, or even against it. The Reichsrat resumed the character of a 'theatre', with which it had begun in the days of Schmerling; the government became 'provisional' as it had been in 1849. In fifty years nothing had been accomplished except to keep the Habsburg Monarchy in existence; Metternich and the men of pre-March would have felt themselves still at home in the Austria of Koerber. The Reichsrat had lost political weight and significance; this, ironically, lessened national tensions and led to the settling of national differences in more than one province. Nothing was to be gained by carrying provincial grievances to the Reichsrat; therefore men of different nationalities made the best of it and lived together.

The great achievement of these years was the compromise in Moravia, accepted by the Moravian Diet in 1905. This divided Moravia into national districts, administered in the language of the majority;[1] its great novelty was the personal vote, by which a Czech would always vote as a Czech and a German as a German in whatever district he lived: the two nationalities could not fight for control of the Diet, where the proportion was permanently fixed at seventy-three Czechs and forty Germans. This ingenious idea ended the national conflicts in Moravia and was held up as an example for the rest of Austria. It lowered nationality from the expression of a people's will to a mere private characteristic, like a blond complexion; a contemptuous valuation, held especially by Renner and

1. There were, however, guarantees for the minorities and provisions by which a minority could appeal from the district to the provincial court.

other Socialists, who regarded nationalism as a tiresome interference with the 'great Free Trade Empire' – except, of course, when it came to the distribution of jobs within the Social Democratic party. The Moravian compromise certainly showed how two peoples of different nationality could live together in the same province; it did not show how two nations could settle their conflicting historical claims. Moravia was not sacred to the Germans, nor even to the Czechs, despite the Kingdom of Moravia a thousand years before; it was merely an administrative unit created by the Habsburgs. Moravia was the national home of neither Czechs nor Germans. The Czechs had their national home in Bohemia, the Germans in the limitless German fatherland: hence each could compromise in regard to Moravia. The Czechs of Moravia were indeed attacked from Prague for deserting the unity of the historic 'lands of St Wenceslaus'; the Germans of Moravia were accused of neglecting their historic mission. Both were thus brought together by a sulky provincial resentment against the rebukes from their Bohemian cousins; yet both would have been indignant if either Czech or German cousins had renounced the claim to Bohemia as the national home, or part of it.

Two nationalities can live side by side only if their national difference is not underlined by a conflict of histories and cultures. This principle, displayed in Moravia, was shown as strikingly in the far-off Bukovina, the forgotten province severed by Galicia from the rest of Austria. The Bukovina could not be claimed by any one nationality as their national home and had no history over which they could fight. The Rumanians and Little Russians were peoples without a past; the Germans, despite a touch of German mission, were made humble by the arrogance of their Polish neighbours in Galicia and of their Magyar neighbours in Hungary. The Bukovina accepted and worked successfully the Moravian principle of personal nationality and a fixed proportion of nationalities in the Diet. A similar system worked, less officially, in Tyrol between Italians and Germans, though for a different reason: the Italians wished only to be left alone until they could join national Italy, and the Germans left them alone so long as they did not try to tamper with the German character of Tyrol.

The Slovenes, wedged between the Italians and the Germans,

had worked in alliance with the Czechs and imitated them, ever since the days of Schmerling. Their real circumstances were different. The Czechs had a past, though it had been obscured, and that past condemned them to the 'historic' provinces; the Slovenes had less past than any people of the Habsburg Monarchy except the Little Russians and could make simple national demands. On the other hand, the Czechs, despite their 'historic' greatness, had no province entirely their own; the Slovenes by accident possessed in Carniola a province as solidly Slovene as Upper and Lower Austria were German. Carniola was a substitute, at any rate, for a Slovene national home, where they enjoyed cultural freedom and a monopoly of government posts. Their culture was not high, through no fault of their own; there was no Slovene university until after the fall of the Habsburg Monarchy, and therefore Slovene demands were on secondary-school level – they were content with petty provincial appointments and did not demand a share of Imperial posts. The freedom of Carniola was, paradoxically, a handicap to the Slovene minorities in Styria and Carinthia, exposed to a conscious and persistent policy of Germanization; for the few Slovene leaders could be bought off with jobs in Carniola. In Styria, almost entirely agrarian, the struggle was less fierce. Carinthia had an advancing iron industry and lay, as well, on the path of the great railway line to Trieste; here the Germans planned an 'all-German' route to the Mediterranean, and here they made their greatest, and most unscrupulous, national gains. On this 'race-frontier' the Germans defended the existing provinces, employing the arguments used against them by the Czechs in Bohemia; the Slovenes desired, without hope, a redrawing of the provincial boundaries on the national line – a programme denied them even after the fall of the Habsburg Monarchy and two world wars.

Slovene grievances in Carinthia and Styria did not make them hostile to Austria: they turned to Vienna for protection, and this, though feebly given, made the Germans 'irredentist', followers of Schönerer, who looked to Germany for liberation from Imperial restraint. The Slovenes were forced yet more on to the Habsburg side by having a second enemy in their rear, the Italians of the coastal provinces; and the conflict between them made this area a miniature classic of every national issue. The three provinces –

Gorica,[1] Istria, and the free city of Trieste – had a geographic, though not a historic unity. The Slovenes composed the peasant foundation; the Italians the urban top layer, and even in Trieste the majority of the population, though Italian-speaking, was of Slovene stock. With the passage of time and the blurring of the distinction between historic and non-historic peoples, Trieste would, no doubt, have become Slovene, as Prague had become Czech and Budapest Magyar; the Slovene misfortune was to have arrived at consciousness too late in the day. The Italians, aware that their majority was fictitious and precarious, used the arguments of wealth and superior culture which the Germans used in Bohemia; the superior culture was shown in a similar violence and intolerance. After all, the Italians were little affected by national justice; they claimed supremacy even in Dalmatia against the Serbo-Croats, although they were only three per cent of the population.

The conflict at Trieste between Italians and Slovenes set an embarrassing problem for the politicians of the dynasty. The Italians were a historic people; as with the other master-races, the dynasty resisted their national claims, yet spoke the same political language.[2] Still, though the Italian national state had made its peace with the Habsburg Monarchy in the Triple Alliance, the Italians remained subversive, and the dynasty could not make an alliance with them as it had done with the Poles: Trieste, though not part of Italy geographically or economically, ranked with the southern part of Tyrol as the object of Italian irredentism. The dynasty had to secure tolerable conditions for the Slovenes in order to hold the balance even, and thus appeared to follow a democratic course; certainly, a subject people was not so fairly sustained against a master-race in any other part of the Empire. Ultimately, the dynasty intended to escape from this unwelcome alliance by bringing Trieste within the German sphere; this was the purpose of the railway to Trieste through Slovene territory which was completed in 1907. Until this truly 'Austrian' solution was achieved, the dynasty patronized the Slovenes with a wry face; and the Slovenes, otherwise helpless, kept

1. Pronounced: Goritsa.

2. This was literally true in regard to Trieste. This port, deliberately created by Imperial authority, owed its Italian character to the fact that Italian was the maritime 'language of state' in the early nineteenth century.

their national movement respectably clerical and conservative, a last echo of the alliance between dynasty and peasants projected in the days of the October Diploma.

One province remained an exception in the general settlement of local differences. Galicia was still a Polish monopoly, despite the awakening nationalism of the Little Russians. So long as the Reichsrat was elected on a limited franchise, the Little Russians had no voice; after the change to universal suffrage in 1907, the Little Russians could carry their grievances to Vienna and rivalled the German and Czech obstruction of the previous decade. Still, though the Little Russians demanded fairer treatment in Galicia, they had no wish to destroy the Habsburg Monarchy: neither inclusion in tsarist Russia nor in a new national Poland had any attractions for them. The vast majority of the inhabitants of Austria were in the same case: though without enthusiasm for the Habsburg Monarchy, they preferred it to the dangers which would follow its collapse. The Czechs feared inclusion in Greater Germany; the Slovenes feared inclusion in Germany or Italy; most Germans feared rule from Berlin and the loss of their Imperial position. Only the Italians wished to secede from Habsburg rule, and even they wished to keep the rest of the Empire in being as a buffer between Germany and Italy. Moreover, the revival of the provinces which had gone on continuously since the October Diploma produced the desired effect; there were enough bureaucratic posts in the provinces to satisfy the claims of the national intellectuals, yet the Imperial administration remained intact.

There was, it is true, no agreed settlement of national differences in Bohemia. Yet the Czechs were very far from being an oppressed nationality: they possessed their own university and cultural life and gained an increasing share in the administration of Bohemia. Local circumstances in Bohemia were not peculiarly difficult; in fact, they were peculiarly easy, and a settlement on the Moravian lines would have been simpler than in Moravia. The conflict in Bohemia was different in character: it was a conflict over the character of the Habsburg Monarchy. It was not a conflict for tolerable living conditions; it was a conflict between two nations, each determined to assert its historical tradition, a conflict between the Kingdom of St Wenceslaus and the Holy Roman Empire of the

German nation. This conflict was impossible of peaceful solution. The Czechs could not be satisfied with the use of their language: besides, they had it already. They claimed, and had to claim, possession of their national home. If this claim were granted, it would make the Germans of Bohemia a tolerated minority and would thus, by implication, end the German position as the 'people of state'. Dethroned in Bohemia, the Germans must be dethroned too in the Monarchy; and Austria would cease to be a German state. Moreover, the overthrow of one 'people of state' must involve the overthrow of the others; therefore the predominance of the Poles, of the Magyars, and even of the Italians, was bound up with the continuance of national conflict in Bohemia. And similarly the Slovenes and Little Russians, to say nothing of the nationalities in Hungary, could only achieve freedom within the Monarchy through a Czech victory in Bohemia. Hence the Germans of the rest of Austria, supported by the Poles, encouraged the Germans of Bohemia;[1] the Czechs of Moravia and the Slovenes, though themselves contented, supported the Czechs. After all, there was a more fundamental question than the settlement of local conditions: the Habsburg Monarchy still existed as an Imperial organization, and had ultimately to declare its character.

Old Austria, the Austria of Metternich, had rested on the dynasty and had evaded national definition. This Austria perished in 1866. Austria-Hungary was the symbol that the dynasty had made its peace with the Magyars and the Germans, the two master-races: it achieved liberty of action in foreign affairs by giving the Magyars internal independence and a similar liberty of action in 'Austrian' affairs by following a foreign policy friendly to Germany. Despite all talk of the 'Austrian mission', the Habsburg Monarchy was an organization for conducting foreign policy and maintaining a great

---

1. A favourite German device, first adopted at the beginning of the twentieth century, was a decree promoted in the Diets of the German provinces forbidding the teaching of Czech throughout the province. In the provinces without any Czech inhabitants, such as Salzburg, the decree was merely offensive; it imposed great hardship on the Czechs on the borders of Lower Austria and on the thousands of Czechs in Vienna. Though vetoed by the Emperor, as conflicting with the principle of national equality as laid down in the constitution, the decree was often put into practice; in Vienna the Czechs (they numbered 130,000) were deprived even of their private schools.

army: power, not welfare, was its basis. This essential point became
obscured in the thirty years of peace which followed the Congress
of Berlin. So long as Germany remained pacific, the equivocal
position of the dynasty had not mattered; once Germany turned to
'world policy', the peoples of the Habsburg Monarchy were being
dragged towards a war for the German mastery of Europe, unless
the dynasty broke with the master-races. Clear warning was given
in the Moroccan crisis of 1905, first of the German attempts to bring
France and Russia under German control by the threat of war. The
year 1905 was the year of crisis for Austria-Hungary, as for Europe;
it marked the last attempt by the dynasty to recover an independent
position. Could Austria-Hungary, the dynastic state of the Habsburgs,
follow a foreign policy independent of Germany? This was the reality
which underlay all discussions of the 'Austrian problem'. All the
fine schemes for a federal Austria were worthless, so long as they
turned on questions of constitutional machinery;[1] the real question
was whether the dynasty could escape from its partners of 1867
and impose federalism on the Germans and, still more, on the
Magyars.

Great Hungary guaranteed Habsburg friendship with Germany,
as Bismarck had grasped from the beginning; for this very reason,
it enabled the dynasty to balance between the nationalities of
Austria without offending the German Reich. Thus the destruction
of Hungary's privileged position could be advocated for opposite
reasons. It was advocated by the pure 'Austrians', loyal Imperialists
who wished the Empire to escape from the control of the master-
races; it was also the programme of many who wished to turn the
entire Habsburg Monarchy into a predominantly German state.
After all, the 'Empire of seventy millions' had been the programme
of Greater Germans since the days of Bruck and Schmerling; and
reduction of Hungary was preached by such a violent German
nationalist as the historian Friedjung. The campaign against Hungary was taken up even by the Socialists: in this way they could
champion the subject peoples without having to abandon their own
German nationalism. Most of all, by emphasizing Hungary, they
could use revolutionary phrases and yet avoid attacking the dynasty,

1. And doubly worthless when, as with the schemes of Francis Ferdinand and
his circle, they proposed federation of the existing, artificial provinces.

in fact they could even enter into alliance with it. Karl Renner, their leading writer on national questions, proved, to his own satisfaction at any rate, the superiority of the Habsburg Monarchy to national states[1] and called on the dynasty to lead the peoples of Austria against Hungary. Professor Seton-Watson, a friendly observer, says of his book: 'It may be described as a Socialist version of the famous lines of Grillparzer, *Wann steigt der Kaiser zu Pferde?* (When will the Emperor mount his horse?).' It did not cross Renner's mind that the first object of Social Democracy should have been to pull the Emperor off his horse nor that the Emperor, mounted on his people's backs, did not occupy this seat for their benefit. Renner demanded a campaign against Hungary simply to strengthen the Empire. Otto Bauer, with more revolutionary conscience, demanded a revolutionary programme from the dynasty; Hungary, he urged, should be put under martial law in order to institute universal suffrage and to establish trade unions for the agricultural labourers. Fear of responsibility, and German *Biederkeit*, had given many strange twists to the Austrian question; of these none was more bizarre than this picture of the Habsburg army, the army of the Counter-Reformation and of anti-Jacobinism, carrying on its shoulders the banners of democracy and of Socialism. Like the liberals of a previous generation, the Social Democrats pretended to find in the dynasty a champion of the doctrines which they lacked the courage and conviction to win on their own.

Francis Joseph did not accept the revolutionary part so generously offered to him by Renner and Bauer. He was the sole survivor of old Austria, and, despite his resentment at defeat, knew that the events of 1866 could not be undone. Bismarck's moderation, not Habsburg strength, had allowed the Habsburg Monarchy to survive; and Little German policy was the basis for the limited national freedom which the peoples of the Habsburg Monarchy enjoyed. Their destinies were determined at Berlin, not at Vienna; and once the German rulers gave up their resistance to Greater Germany, the Habsburg Empire became useless to its peoples. Germany would never allow the restoration of the Habsburg Monarchy as a truly

1. This low estimate of national states did not prevent Karl Renner's welcoming the completion of German national unity by Hitler in 1938.

independent Power; this would be to renounce the fruits of the victory at Sadova. Moreover, the Habsburg Monarchy could not exist without German support, especially since the withdrawal of England from the Near East. This was less obvious between 1898 and 1907 when the Eastern Question was 'on ice'; hence the relative freedom of action which the Habsburg Monarchy had enjoyed. In 1905 Russia was defeated in the Far East and returned, willynilly, to Europe; in this way, too, 1905 was the crisis year of the Habsburg Monarchy. It was the last moment when it might hope to follow an independent policy.

Events, not policy, dragged Francis Joseph into action: though he acted against the Hungarian constitution, it was to preserve Dualism, not to destroy it, Francis Joseph was driven on by the irresponsible agitation of the Hungarian magnates against the common army. In 1903 the Hungarian parliament refused to confirm the grant of contingents for the army, unless Magyar became the 'language of command' of the Hungarian levies; Francis Joseph answered with a public warning (characteristically issued in an army order) that the constitution of Hungary depended on the fulfilment of the promises of 1867. A new strong man was needed to enforce Dualism on Hungary, and Francis Joseph found him in Stephen, son of Koloman Tisza, as convinced as his father that the Magyar gentry needed the Habsburg dynasty for survival. Stephen Tisza played a stroke of the greatest daring: unable to compete with the patriotic claptrap of the magnates, he resolved to destroy them politically by giving them responsibility. He abandoned the system of government influence and corruption which had kept his father in power; and in January 1905 fought the only free election ever known in Dualist Hungary. Tisza and the party loyal to Dualism were defeated; the majority against the common army returned in force. Francis Joseph accepted the challenge. He broke with constitutional practice and appointed a general, Fejerváry,[1] as Prime Minister – offensive assertion of the common army – with a group of unknown bureaucrats under him. The warning was not enough: the parliamentary coalition still insisted on a Magyar army as condition of taking office. In February 1906 the Hungarian parliament was turned out by a company of soldiers, and the constitu-

1. Pronounced: Fé-yer-vāry.

tion suspended. After forty years of constitutional life, Hungary returned to the absolutism of Bach and Schmerling.

This time, there was neither resistance nor resentment. Constitutional Hungary was a centralized, bureaucratic state; and the bureaucrats, even though gentry, could not risk their positions and pensions. County resistance, once the pillar of Hungarian liberty, had lost its force: the counties covered only a small part of the administrative field, and, in any case, the county officials, too, were now full-time bureaucrats, not gentry secure on their estates. These gentry-officials had applauded the agitation of the magnates, so long as this merely echoed the phrases of Kossuth; they jibbed at making the sacrifices which Kossuth had demanded from their grandfathers. The Magyar Press, though violently patriotic and 'liberal', was in the hands of Germans and Jews who had become Magyars so as to be on the winning side and who now supported the royal commissioners for the same reason. Thus it was easy to suspend the constitution; not so easy, however, to find a solution. Francis Joseph had merely gone back to the temporary dictatorship of the 'Bach hussars', as the Austrian government had returned to the 'provisional' absolutism of Schwarzenberg. There followed the question which had defeated Schmerling: whether the dynasty dared make an alliance with the peasant peoples of Hungary against their lords.

This programme was urged by Francis Ferdinand, with his traditional Habsburg jealousy of Hungarian privileges. Fejérváry threatened to apply it: he encouraged trade unions and, in October 1905, announced the intention of his government to introduce universal suffrage. This was a double challenge to the 'Magyar nation' – at once to their national and class privileges. Universal suffrage would place the Magyars in a minority against the other nationalities; still more, it would place the gentry in a minority against the Magyar peasants and town-workers. The threat was too daring for an Imperial general, who was also a Magyar noble: like the previous threats of Francis Joseph's reign, it was a pistol with the safety-catch firmly locked. After all, as Joseph II had himself realized, the programme of alliance between Emperor and peasants was out of date after 14 July 1789. A programme of agrarian reform and of trade unions for agricultural workers was much beyond Fejérváry: trade unions in the towns did little harm so long as they stayed there – and were indeed tolerated on that condition even in the days of Horthy. Again, alliance with Slovaks and Rumanians was too much for a Magyar general, despite the ill-informed promptings of Francis Ferdinand. The only respectable move was with the Croats; and the Croat attitude determined the outcome of the crisis, though by no means in a way favourable to themselves.

If the 'Croat nation' had remained confined to retired army officers of field rank, Fejerváry would have found ideal allies. This alliance had been possible in 1848 and, for the last time, in 1866. The new Croat leaders were middle-class intellectuals, barred by their liberal outlook from following the example of Jellačić and forming an alliance with the dynasty; nor were they attracted to the friendship of an Imperial general and Magyar aristocrat. These Croat liberals knew their history and remembered the double desertion by the dynasty in 1849 and 1867; besides, universal suffrage was no more welcome to middle-class nationalists in Croatia than in Hungary or in Austria. On the other hand, their very liberalism made them easy victims of Magyar plausibility; after all, the Hungarian gentry had foisted the myth of liberal Hungary on all Europe and had deceived, and were to deceive, far more experienced parliamentarians than these Croat novices. The leaders of the Hungarian coalition claimed to be fighting for national freedom from the Habsburgs and promised that victory for Hungary would bring freedom also for the South Slavs. The Croat liberals, in reaction from the sterile dynasticism of the Party of Pure Right, were persuaded that freedom could be won in cooperation with Hungary, not against it. In October 1905 – at the very moment when Fejerváry announced the policy of universal suffrage – Croat liberals met Croat representatives from Istria and Dalmatia at Rijeka (Fiume). The 'Fiume resolutions' demanded the reunion of Dalmatia with Croatia and agreed to support the Magyar opposition in return for fairer treatment for the Croats. Soon afterwards, representatives of the Serbs in Croatia and Hungary met at Zadar[1] and accepted this programme, which thus became the basis for the Serbo-Croat coalition.

The 'Fiume resolutions' did not threaten the existence of the Habsburg Monarchy, even by the most remote implication; they

1. Italian name: Zara.

asked only for national freedoms enjoyed by most peoples of Austria, and even by the Croats in Istria and Dalmatia. The only 'corporate' demand was not for a South Slav state, nor even for South Slav unity within the Empire; it merely asked for a Croatia enlarged by the reunion of Dalmatia, a demand which the Croats had made in 1867 and even before. The Croat leaders knew nothing of Serbia and were almost unaware of its existence; even the Serb leaders were in little better case. The Zadar resolution contained the vague South Slav sentiment, 'Croats and Serbs are one people'; a gentle repudiation, no more, of the traditional Magyar policy of promoting jealousy between Croats and Serbs, and the middle-class intellectuals remained in separate parties. Even their coalition asked too much of the Serb and Croat peoples. National amalgamation is possibly only when nations are still unconscious; as the vague 'Czechoslovak' sentiment of the Prague extremists in 1848 was evidence of the immaturity of both Czechs and Slovaks. Now Serbs and Croats had passed the stage for a similar operation. Serbia had entered a period of national renaissance with the fall of the Obrenović dynasty in 1903; Peter Karagjorgjević,[1] the new King, expressed a national confidence, at last, come to maturity. In Croatia, too, the South Slav idealism of Štrosmajer was on the wane, as the Croat peasant masses began to swamp the intellectuals of Zagreb. Evidence of this was the Croat Peasant party, organized by Stephen Radić[2] – as aggressively and exclusively Croat as the gentry Party of Pure Right, despite its democratic social programme.

The South Slav idea evoked little response among the South Slav peoples and served even their intellectuals only as a peroration. On the other hand, it evoked an altogether disproportionate response both from the dynasty and from the Magyars. To both, the innocent phrase of Zadar sounded like the trumpet of doom. Imperial and Magyar statesmen alike lost their heads; abandoned the policy of compromise and intrigue which had proved so rewarding in past years; and could devise nothing better than repression. Certainly, the Serbo-Croat coalition completed the reconciliation between Francis Joseph and the Hungarian magnates. The Hungarian opposition had been already tamed by the threat to enfranchise the Hungarian masses; for the magnates feared their own peasants even

1. Pronounced: Karageorgevich.   2. Pronounced: Radich.

more than they feared the nationalities – indeed the 'national struggle' was waged in order to conceal the far deeper class antagonism. Besides, the magnates at last realized that they would be ruined by the victory of their programme: if Hungary were 'freed' from Austria, the Austrian consumer would be freed from Hungarian wheat and would buy cheap food abroad.

Francis Joseph, on his side, had a motive for haste. Habsburg foreign policy had aimed to secure independence of Germany, and the conflict with Hungary was designed to make the Monarchy stronger for this purpose, as Schmerling had sought to subdue Hungary in order to prepare for war against Prussia. Instead the conflict made the Monarchy weaker than ever. In February 1906 Austria-Hungary was dragged at Germany's heels to the Conference of Algeçiras and made to quarrel with England and France for the sake of Morocco; even Italy followed a more independent course. Francis Joseph abruptly changed direction. He was again anxious to settle with Hungary, as he had been in 1867, though still with an anti-German motive: since conflict with Hungary had not strengthened the Monarchy against Germany, settlement with Hungary was expected to do so. The calculation was as false as in the days of Beust: the Hungarian magnates saw clearly that their privileges needed German support, and would have resisted any Habsburg attempt at a truly independent foreign policy. In fact, it made compromise easier for them that Austria-Hungary had just acted as 'the brilliant second on the duelling ground'; flamboyant phrase of William II, which humiliated the Habsburg politicians.

In April 1906 Francis Joseph and the Hungarian magnates renewed the compromise on a pattern familiar ever since the Peace of Szatmár. The magnates deserted the 'national' cause; Francis Joseph deserted the Hungarian masses. The Hungarian coalition dropped its opposition to the common army and to the Tariff Union with Austria; Francis Joseph dropped universal suffrage and appointed a constitutional government. Universal suffrage remained on the programme of this government, as indeed of every Hungarian government until 1918; excuses for postponement were always found, and the corrupt, limited franchise remained virtually unchanged when Great Hungary fell in 1918. The promises made to the Serbo-Croat coalition were equally disregarded. In 1905 Francis

Kossuth had replied to the Fiume offer of cooperation: 'We await you in love and hope.' In 1907 Francis Kossuth, now a Habsburg minister, promoted a bill to make Magyar the sole language on the Hungarian railways even in Croatia; and Apponyi, already the 'grand old man' of Hungarian liberalism, devised an Education Act which deprived the nationalities even of their private schools. These Magyar patriots, once in office, had to follow the same course as the Tiszas, father and son: to cloak their surrender to the Habsburg Empire, they displayed their nationalism at the expense of the minorities and won back the favour of the gentry by the prospect of yet more state employment.

Kossuth's Railway Act, not the Fiume resolutions, first brought the Serbo-Croat coalition to real life. It rescued the Serbo-Croat intellectuals from idealism and made them think in terms of power. They had supposed themselves more far-sighted than the Croat gentry who relied on the dynasty; instead, they had been proved even more foolish. They sought a weapon which they could use, or rather threaten to use, against dynasty and Magyars alike; this weapon could only be alliance with independent Serbia. In 1907, for the first time, the insidious phrase was heard that Serbia was the 'Piedmont of the South Slavs'. This phrase caused panic in Vienna: it touched the wound that could never heal and recalled the dreadful events of 1859 which had heralded the fall of old Austria. All the blunders of Habsburg policy between 1907 and 1914 sprang from the mistaken analogy between the Italian and South Slav movements. Italian nationalism had been truly irreconcilable; therefore South Slav nationalism was supposed to be the same. Force had seemed the only remedy against Italian nationalism; now it was increasingly advocated against the South Slavs. Yet the vast majority of the Croats, and even most Serbs within the Monarchy, desired the maintenance of the Monarchy if only they could obtain tolerable conditions for their national life. The real stumbling-block was not South Slav extremism and irreconcilable nationalism; it was the ruthless 'magyarization' of the Hungarian governing classes, with whom Francis Joseph had again compromised in 1906. In 1905 Francis Joseph had had forced on him the chance to undo the surrender of 1867; in 1906, as in 1867, a policy of cooperation with the subject peoples and classes was not a historic possibility for him, and he had failed to take the chance. This was the last milestone on the road to ruin.

The Hungarian crisis had unexpected repercussions in Austria. The dynasty could not advocate universal suffrage for one parliament and oppose it in the other; besides, in November 1905, even Russian tsardom, under the stimulus of revolution, committed itself to the programme of universal suffrage. In Hungary universal suffrage was opposed by the united 'Magyar nation'; in Austria, there was no unity in the Reichsrat, even among the parties who would be ruined by universal suffrage. The only organized opposition came from the Poles, who demanded – and secured – excessive representation at the expense of the Little Russians. Direct, universal suffrage was forced on Austria by the Imperial will. Francis Joseph, his mind working with a curious delayed action, was suddenly converted by the arguments which had been put before him by Steinbach and Taaffe in 1893; and, once converted, would tolerate no delay. In Hungary, universal suffrage had never been more than a tactical threat; in Austria, it seemed a way of escape from the nationalist conflicts of the middle-class politicians. On the other hand, the Austrian masses, both workers and peasants, had reached a certain political maturity. In Hungary Francis Joseph would have had to become a 'peasant Emperor'; in Austria democracy threatened him only with the company of Karl Lueger and Viktor Adler, two respectable, elderly gentlemen, as Austrian and as Viennese as himself. Francis Joseph's deepest hatred was for liberalism. Against liberalism, he had called in nationalism. Now, by this stroke, he played democracy against both liberalism and nationalism, and recovered greater freedom of action than he had ever enjoyed since 1867.

In the parliament of 1907 the Christian Socialists were the largest party, and the Social Democrats the second; this was a triumph for the Imperial idea. Christian Socialists and Social Democrats both desired to preserve the Habsburg Empire, despite their use of democratic phrases; though they fought each other, the game of *rouge et noir* was played on the Imperial table. The democratic parliament actually provided a majority for government measures: the budget was passed in constitutional form, and the decennial compromise with Hungary at last showed some clauses in Austria's favour. Beck, the Prime Minister who had piloted universal suffrage through the Reichsrat, revived the constitutional practice of a forgotten past and, for a few months, included parliamentary leaders in his ministry. Yet, as usual, Francis Joseph turned against his minister at the moment of apparent success. He had demanded quick results, and the results were not unreservedly satisfactory: national parties still existed, and nationalism asserted itself even among the 'Imperial' Christian Socialists and Social Democrats. The Christian Socialists, despite their clericalism, defended the German monopoly of Vienna; the Social Democrats split into distinct national parties, and the Czech Socialists worked with the other Czech groups in all national questions. It had been supposed that workers and peasants would be free from nationalism; this was true in the days of mass illiteracy. Now Austria had had universal elementary education; and every man who can read and write must define his national allegiance.

Francis Joseph lost confidence in Beck and let him go from office in November 1908. Yet to ascribe Beck's fall to domestic failure would be to repeat the mistake of contemporary observers, who discussed only the internal 'Austrian problem', and failed to see that the true problem was the part played by the Habsburg Monarchy as a Great Power. The Austro-Russian entente over the Near East had given the Habsburg Monarchy a breathing space, in which to recover its independence; and in 1907 the breathing space came to an end. It had not been used to good purpose. Austria-Hungary could have become an independent Power only if an 'Austrian' patriotism had been created which would appeal to the masses. Clericalism and dynastic loyalty could not sustain a great Empire in the twentieth century. Yet Francis Joseph would let his Empire perish rather than allow any fragment of his power to pass into the hands of the people. The resignation of Beck was the sign that the 'revolution from above', never sincere, had been openly abandoned. In October 1908 Francis Joseph reached back over sixty years of compromise and concession, and reverted to the reliance on armed force with which his reign had begun. The Habsburg Monarchy lived only in the Austro-Hungarian army; and the only question for the future was whether this army could survive a war, or still more a defeat.

CHAPTER SEVENTEEN

SOLUTION BY VIOLENCE, 1908–14

KARL RENNER had asked: 'When will the Emperor mount his horse?' There was in Vienna a universal appetite for action; an appetite unsatisfied either by the constitutional conflict with Hungary and its tame conclusion or by universal suffrage in Austria and its inconclusive effect on the national parties. Like an elderly man whose powers are failing, the Habsburg Monarchy sought to recover its youth by a display of virility. Action was demanded by the believers in the 'Austrian mission' to promote culture and a high standard of life; it was demanded by Socialists in the name of trade unions and land reform; it was demanded by German nationalists who wished to reassert the German character of the Monarchy; it was demanded with increasing impatience by Francis Ferdinand; it was demanded by Conrad von Hötzendorff, who had become Chief of the General Staff in 1906 and who thought to find in war a cure for the weaknesses of both Empire and army. Internal action, the boasted campaign against Hungary, had come to nothing; action in foreign affairs had to take its place. In personal terms, Aehrenthal[1] took the place of Goluchowski as Foreign Minister in 1906. He was the last of the many conjurers who promised to revive the Monarchy by a stroke of diplomatic magic. Self-confident and arrogant, with the cocky yapping of a terrier, he despised all his predecessors since Andrássy and proposed to recover for Austria-Hungary the proud independence which she had enjoyed at the Congress of Berlin. In fact, if only he – and the Monarchy – had survived longer, the early twentieth century might have been known as the Aehrenthal era.

European circumstances, in any case, forced action upon him. The Habsburg Monarchy had been humiliated by the subservient role which it had had to play at the Conference of Algeçiras. Goluchowski, doubtless, thought no price too high for the security of

1. Pronounced: Air-en-tāl.

Galicia; all others, even the Germans of the Monarchy, were offended by the results of his policy. Aehrenthal, with little knowledge of domestic politics, proposed to take a more independent line. He had been Ambassador at St Petersburg and flattered himself that he could restore the League of the Three Emperors, or rather the Holy Alliance; for he saw, like Metternich, that Germany would be reduced to the position of junior partner, if Russia and Austria-Hungary were reconciled in genuine conservative principle. He was more ambitious and confident than Metternich in regard to Austro-Russian relations. Metternich had postulated a pacific Russian policy in the Near East as condition of friendship. Aehrenthal admitted both the decay of Turkey and Russia's need for an active Balkan policy after her failure in the Far East; yet instead of organizing resistance to Russia, he proposed to go along with her. He went back beyond Metternich and proposed to revive the policy of Joseph II, when the Habsburg Monarchy too had Balkan ambitions. Metternich and all his successors had feared that, if the Ottoman Empire crashed, the fragments would fall upon their heads; Aehrenthal was ready to give Turkey a push. His was a deathbed daring.

In reality, he was not as independent as he made out. Even the form of his action was dictated to him by events. The renewed compromise with Hungary in 1906 inevitably created a 'Serbian problem'. It created a domestic Serbian problem in the shape of the Serbo-Croat coalition, cheated and disappointed; and Serbia had to be blamed for this, as Metternich blamed 'the revolution' for all the palsy of pre-March. It created, still more, an economic conflict with Serbia itself. Prohibitive tariffs against Serb agricultural produce, especially pigs, were part of the price paid to the Hungarian magnates in 1906 in return for their acceptance of the common army. Serbia refused to be an Austrian satellite as she had been in the time of the Obrenović dynasty. In 1906 she asserted her economic independence: denied Austrian loans, Serbia raised money in Paris and provocatively bought arms from France instead of from the Skoda works in Bohemia. She found an outlet for her livestock through Turkish territory to Salonika; and Germany, lacking a Balkan policy of her own and not unwilling to anger Aehrenthal, provided Serbia with a market which more than compensated for her losses in Austria-Hungary. Aehrenthal belatedly tried conciliation and in 1907 offered Serbia a commercial agreement more favourable than the one denounced in 1906. This proved too favourable, for it was rejected both by the Reichsrat and by the Hungarian parliament and Aehrenthal had to conceal his discomfiture by ascribing it to the malignant hostility of the Serbs.

Thus, the great stroke of foreign policy had to be a stroke against Serbia; and the defeat of the 'South Slav conspiracy' became henceforward the solution for all the difficulties of the Habsburg Monarchy. Aehrenthal dreamt of partitioning Serbia with Bulgaria, a grotesque scheme which would have created a South Slav problem in good earnest. His practical aim was to annex Bosnia and Hercegovina, the two Turkish provinces which had been under Habsburg occupation since 1878. Annexation would end Serb hopes of acquiring the two provinces on the collapse of the Turkish Empire; it would solve, too, the legal tangle, created by the Young Turk establishment of a Turkish parliament in July 1908. More than all this, it would at last clear the way for the fulfilment of the 'Austrian mission'. Even the greatest enthusiasts for the 'Free Trade empire' had to admit that thirty years of Austrian rule had not brought much benefit to the inhabitants of the two provinces: there were no health services, no railways of normal gauge, no popular schools, no self-government even in the villages. All failings were ascribed to the anomaly of occupation. If the two provinces became truly part of the Habsburg Empire, they would receive Diets, schools, trade unions, land reform, roads and railways – whatever it was that the 'Austrian idea' represented to the particular writer or professor in Vienna. Aehrenthal himself talked the language of the 'Austrian idea' and even projected a railway through Turkish territory to the sea in the spring of 1908. The railway was impracticable and was never built; it served to establish Aehrenthal as a man of progressive views.

Annexation of Bosnia and Hercegovina involved a revolution in Austria-Hungary's Balkan policy. Andrássy had staked everything on the survival of the Turkish Empire and had therefore insisted on occupation; Aehrenthal was ready to let the Turkish Empire go and would risk a bargain with Russia. This bargain was made in September 1908. Izvolski, the Russian Foreign Minister, was also on the look-out for a quick success in order to redeem the prestige of Russian tsardom. He agreed to acquiesce in the annexation of the two provinces, if Aehrenthal, in return, would support the opening of the Straits to Russian ships of war. This was the bargain of Buchlov,[1] last futile kick of diplomatic independence by two decaying Empires. Aehrenthal thought he had settled the Balkan rivalry with Russia, which had made the Habsburg Monarchy dependent on Germany; Izvolski thought that Constantinople, secular ambition of the tsars, was within his grasp. Secure of Russia's approval, Aehrenthal proclaimed the annexation of the two provinces on 5 October 1908, and exploded 'the Bosnian crisis'.

Events did not work out as Aehrenthal and Izvolski had expected. England and France refused to agree to the opening of the Straits. More serious, Stolypin, the Russian Prime Minister, insisted that Russian public opinion cared not at all for the Straits and much for the Slav peoples of the Balkans. This had not occurred to Izvolski, nor to most Russians; only when Aehrenthal set out to humiliate Serbia did the Russians discover their affection for the Serbs, and Russian backing for Serbia was thus of Aehrenthal's making. Moreover, the Serbs of Serbia had not troubled themselves about the Serbs in Austria-Hungary, nor even given much thought to Bosnia and Hercegovina; Aehrenthal taught the Serbs to be Yugoslavs. Aehrenthal's great stroke, far from settling the South Slav question, created it. The Serbs could not resist championing the Serbs and Croats of Bosnia, particularly when they were egged on by Izvolski to conceal his own blunders. The Bosnian crisis did not humiliate Serbia, though it ended in her defeat; it humiliated Austria-Hungary, for it pulled her down to the Serb level. As in the old struggle with Piedmont, it raised the standing of Serbia and brought Austria-Hungary into contempt to ascribe all the difficulties of the Habsburg Monarchy to the 'Piedmont of the South Slavs'. Nor did the Bosnian crisis free Austria-Hungary from dependence on Germany. Habsburg diplomacy would have muddled on without finding an issue, if Germany, in March 1909, had not compelled Izvolski finally to abandon Serbia. Austrian statesmen might grumble at this

1. Pronounced: Buhlov.

German patronage: in the eyes of the world they stood under German protection.

Aehrenthal could still have had a war with Serbia, despite the German ultimatum to Russia; and destruction of Serbia had been his original aim. As he began to put it into practice, he ran against the unanswerable problem – what would be achieved by war against Serbia, even if successful? Annexation would people the Monarchy with embittered South Slavs; if Serbia were not annexed, she would become in reality the centre of discontent which Habsburg propaganda had imagined her. The more successful Aehrenthal's policy, the more fatal to the Monarchy; the more fully it was applied, the more insoluble the problems that it would create. Thus, late in the day, Aehrenthal arrived at the conclusions which had been commonplace to every Habsburg Foreign Minister from Metternich to Andrássy and Kálnoky: Austria-Hungary could not afford to acquire Balkan territory and must therefore support the *status quo* in the Balkans, even though this involved hostility to Russia. In February 1909, when the Austro-Hungarian army was already mobilized, Aehrenthal decided against war. Francis Joseph, sceptical of the strength of his army, supported him; even Francis Ferdinand opposed war – though willing to humiliate Serbia, he was yet more anxious not to do anything which would please the Magyars. Conrad, the advocate of war, suddenly found himself isolated; and had to content himself with the proof that the army was capable, at any rate, of mobilization.

Thus, the great stroke of action ended in nothing except a trivial legal change in the standing of the two provinces. The conservative alliance with Russia had not been restored; instead Russia's interest in the Balkans had been revived, and Russian policy directed against Austria-Hungary. The Serbs were left convinced that the Austrian attack had only been postponed and therefore began an anti-Austrian policy in earnest. Occasionally Serb statesmen, fearful of their task, made overtures for a reconciliation; they were contemptuously rebuffed by Aehrenthal. The 'Austrian idea' failed to come to life in the two provinces. There was no 'economic amelioration', no new schools, only a larger bureaucracy and army of occupation. The provinces received Diets on the Austrian pattern. Since the provincial Diets now performed large administrative functions, it had been essential to maintain the representation of the great estates; therefore, despite the introduction of universal suffrage for the Reichsrat, the Diets were left with the old restricted suffrage and the system of 'curial' constituencies. Bosnia and Hercegovina were also initiated into these curial mysteries; in addition the three curias (great estates, towns, and country communes) were each divided in fixed proportions among the three religions, Orthodox, Roman Catholic, and Mohammedan. In this roundabout way, the Mohammedan landowners were doubly over-represented; and Habsburg rule maintained the social inferiority of the Serbo-Croat majority. The 'Austrian idea' had promised great things for the two provinces; as so often, the promises remained unfulfilled, and after 1909 the theorists of Vienna averted their gaze from the impoverished, illiterate peasants of Bosnia and Hercegovina.

The Bosnian crisis left an embarrassing legacy: during the crisis, charges of treason had been trumped up against the leaders of the Serbo-Croat coalition in Croatia as an excuse for war, and now these charges had to stand public examination. The first display was a farcical treason trial at Zagreb, before a tame Croat judge; the forged evidence discredited only the Hungarian rulers of Croatia, and the accused, though convicted, were at once pardoned by Francis Joseph. The half-century since the revolutions of 1848 had established the 'rule of law' in all Europe except the Russian and Ottoman Empires; even the Habsburg Monarchy had accepted the standards of western Europe. The Zagreb trial was the first flagrant retreat from the principle of a tolerably civilized, impartial state; it inaugurated the age of dishonest, political trials, which was to conquer the continent of Europe within a generation. The 'Hungarian nation', despite its boasted liberalism, acted as pioneer of this triumph of barbarism.

Still worse, Aehrenthal, in arrogant folly, involved the Monarchy in the same discredit. He, too, encouraged the campaign against the Serbo-Croat leaders and enlisted the journalistic aid of Friedjung, great historian and wild German nationalist, now converted to the worship of Habsburg power. Neither Aehrenthal nor Friedjung scrutinized the evidence: the articles which Friedjung wrote were to justify war against Serbia, and no one would examine the case for war once it had begun.[1] When Aehrenthal decided against war, he gave the Serbo-Croat leaders the opening to bring a libel action against Friedjung in the Vienna courts; and they easily proved that the documents, notoriously supplied by the Austro-Hungarian Foreign Office, were crude forgeries. Moreover, Masaryk, an outstanding Czech professor, took up the 'Friedjung case' and pressed the charge of forgery against Aehrenthal at the meeting of the Delegations. Aehrenthal made no defence; he was discredited as a clumsy forger in the eyes of all Europe and never recovered his reputation. Indeed the Zagreb trial and the Friedjung case were the moral ruin of the Habsburg Monarchy; they destroyed the fabric of civilized behaviour which had given it a respectable appearance and left it with no basis except force.

Absurdly enough, Aehrenthal had a defence, which he was too proud to use. Masaryk accused the Austrian legation in Belgrade of having manufactured the forged documents. In reality, the legation, already convinced of Serbo-Croat treason, had been the easy victim of a clever forger, and the documents with which Masaryk proved its guilt were further products of the same forger. The Austrian Foreign Office knew this: indeed, more expert than Masaryk, they had warned Aehrenthal against the original 'Friedjung' documents. Aehrenthal was too proud to admit his carelessness; still more, he would not admit the incompetence of Forgács, the Minister at Belgrade, whose cocksure blundering would have brought him high place in any diplomatic service. His attitude revealed the true spirit of the Habsburg Monarchy: it was not tyrannical or brutal, it was merely degenerate and moribund. It would tolerate charges of active crimes which it lacked the energy and ability to undertake rather than admit its real failings of feebleness and mistake. Aehrenthal would have been glad to possess the wit to invent the Friedjung documents; and in 1914 Berchtold preferred to see himself as the maker of the war rather than as the foolish puppet of a decaying system.

---

1. The decision against war was taken the day before the first article was due to appear, and its publication could have been stopped, as was that of the later articles. The Foreign Office officials did not fully realize the inflammatory nature of the articles; and some of them still hoped for war. Most of all, the Austrian system was incapable of rapid action.

The Bosnian crisis, with its unsatisfactory close and its dingy sequel, exhausted the last energies of the Habsburg Monarchy. Initiative ceased in foreign and in domestic affairs. The Austrian statesmen no longer even waited for something to turn up; their only hope was that nothing would turn up, that things would always remain in their convenient state of deadlock. Aehrenthal returned to the pacific policy of his predecessors: restored tolerable relations with Russia, and refused to respond to any provocations from Serbia or Italy. His nearest approach to a policy was the attempt to establish good relations with France. During the Moroccan crisis of 1911, he ostentatiously avoided giving Germany the backing which Germany had given him in the Bosnian crisis; and he asked, though in vain, for the opening of the French Bourse to Austrian and Hungarian loans. A conservative partnership between France and Austria had been, perhaps, possible in the days of Metternich and Guizot; it had been given a last airing by Beust and Napoleon III between 1867 and 1870. After the great upheaval of 1870, neither France nor Austria was a truly Great Power, capable of standing on its own feet. France needed Russian support to keep her independent of Germany; Austria-Hungary needed German backing against Russia in the Near East. The chance once lost in the early days of Bismarck could never be recovered. Aehrenthal found no alternative for the aggressive policy which he had abandoned. Conrad, in isolation, still preached his panacea of a preventive war – against Italy, against Serbia, at any rate against someone. Everyone disapproved of his obstinate bellicosity, and his persistence got him dismissed from his post for a year or so; yet he represented the nearest thing to a positive policy and was bound to get his way in the long run. A war against Italy would have given even the Habsburg Monarchy the tonic of victory; for Italy was a ridiculous imitation of a Great Power, impressive only to professional diplomats and literary visitors. Here again, the shade of Bismarck barred the way: independent Italy was part of the Bismarckian system, and its destruction could only hasten complete German domination in the Habsburg Monarchy.

In domestic affairs, too, nothing real remained. The Reichsrat still met and refused to pass the budget, then averted its eyes while the budget was passed by emergency decree; speeches were made and resolutions passed, while, behind the scenes, the Imperial bureaucracy threw up an ever more monstrous mountain of paper. Czech–German relations in Bohemia were still the object of endless negotiation: new plans propounded, discussed, amended, and finally rejected. Bienerth, the bureaucratic hack who succeeded Beck as Prime Minister in 1908, proposed to create Czech and German Ministers without Portfolio to safeguard Czech and German interests, as the Polish Minister without Portfolio safeguarded the interests of Galicia; the Germans scented an admission that Bohemia was Czech and compelled him to abandon the idea. Stürgkh, another bureaucrat who became Prime Minister in 1912, produced further plans for a settlement and declared in 1914 that the Czechs and Germans were separated by a wall 'the thickness only of a piece of paper'. He did not see that this piece of paper was of impenetrable thickness: it was a literary idea, the conflict of two historical claims, which had separated them all along. Now the Germans were made more assertive by the mounting strength of national arrogance in Germany; and the Czechs ever more apprehensive of having to fight on the German side in a war between Germans and Slavs. The greatest exponents of obstruction in the Reichsrat were the Little Russians, resentful of Polish privilege in Galicia; and they were supported by Czechs and Slovenes on the principle of Slav solidarity.

The Germans, on their side, applied the same method of obstruction in the Bohemian Diet: even the committee of the Diet which controlled provincial administration broke down, and in 1913 Stürgkh suspended the Bohemian constitution. Once more inveterate plan makers hoped that the Imperial government would give a positive lead; nothing was done, suspension had exhausted the creative powers of Vienna. The Reichsrat met, for the last time in the reign of Francis Joseph, in March 1914; it was wrecked by the Little Russians within a few days. When war broke out in August 1914, the Reichsrat, too, was suspended and Austria reverted, without disguise, to the 'provisional absolutism' with which the reign of Francis Joseph had begun.

Old tunes were played also in Hungary. The Hungarian magnates had not been sobered by their defeat in 1906. They renewed their attacks on the common army. This policy had lost all appeal for the Magyar gentry, who had seen their bureaucratic positions threatened during the constitutional struggle. The gentry officials used their skill in violence and corruption to destroy the coalition at the general election of 1910; and a 'mameluke' majority was restored. Stephen Tisza, first behind the scenes and then as Prime Minister in June 1913, surpassed even his father's dictatorial position. He forced through the army bill and acted as the loyal supporter of the common monarchy; in return he was free to carry on the campaign against the nationalities in Hungary and to keep the Magyar masses excluded from political life. He declared: 'Our citizens of the non-Magyar tongue must, in the first place, become accustomed to the fact that they belong to the community of a nation-state, of a state which is not a conglomerate of various races.' Suffrage bills were still introduced, and extension of the franchise often promised; excuses were always found, and a bill of 1914, jettisoned on the outbreak of war, remained as fraudulent evidence of the democratic system which Hungary would have enjoyed 'if only' the war had not intervened.

In reality, the Hungarian state was the monopoly of the gentry, a class which had lost its economic foundation and kept itself in power with Habsburg backing. This was a shaky and doubtful support; the gentry needed more and found it in an alliance with the German and Jewish capitalists of Hungary. Hungarian nationalism had favoured Protection since Kossuth first echoed the economic teaching of List; and the Tariff Union with Austria had been as much a defeat for Kossuth as the common army. It was a safer object of attack; and even without the restoration of a tariff barrier between Austria and Hungary, much could be done by government action to promote Hungarian industry. Hungary set the example which was followed by the 'succession states' after the fall of the Monarchy; and, in so far as Austria-Hungary had been an economic unit, this unity had been sapped by Hungary long before 1918. Economic nationalism had a double advantage: it provided a substitute for the attacks on the common army; and it strengthened the enthusiasm of the 'magyarized' Jews and Germans, who might otherwise have relapsed into Habsburg loyalty. The German capitalists represented a potential 'fifth column' in Hungary from the time of Metternich to the time of Hitler; and needed constant economic reward to make them tolerate political subordination to the impoverished gentry, inept in commerce and industry.

Tisza's victory excluded the magnates from political power; the growth of industry threatened to create capitalist millionaires who would challenge even their economic privileges. They could answer Tisza's nationalism only by appealing to the subject peoples; they could answer economic nationalism only by a democratic appeal to the masses. Both courses were too dangerous; and they stood helplessly by, or ventured themselves into capitalist undertakings. As a hereditary 'governing class', they had abdicated. One magnate, the most daring and almost the wealthiest, repudiated this timid course. Michael Károlyi, once the associate of the younger Andrássy, arrived at last at the programme which Kossuth had belatedly preached in exile. He began to advocate national equality, agrarian reform, and – as natural corollary – a breach with Germany; for a democratic Hungary on good terms with her Slav neighbours would no longer need the backing of the Habsburg or of the German army. This programme demanded impossible sacrifice from magnates less high-principled than Károlyi; it could be achieved only after defeat in war and would then be too late.

Magyar extremism prevailed, too, in Croatia. The Magyar gentry lumped all Croats together as Serbo-Croat traitors, in order to lay hold of their jobs. In 1912 the constitution of Croatia was suspended, and the Hungarian governor became dictator, with a host of Magyar followers. Yet South Slav idealism was confined to a few middle-class intellectuals. The Croat gentry and army officers, organized in the Party of Pure Right, though hostile to Hungary, were yet more fanatically anti-Serb and devoted to the Monarchy. Moreover, the Croat peasant party, now developing a mass following, took the same line, though with more democratic phrases. Radić, its leader, preached the 'Austrian idea'; the task of the Monarchy, he said, was to be 'neither German nor Magyar nor Slav, but Christian, European, and democratic'. The South Slav idea, synthetic and intellectual, won only the educated middle class, which looked at Štrosmajer's collection of pictures; mass nationalism, in Croatia as everywhere else, sprang from the soil and hated its nearest neighbours. In Austria universal suffrage weakened national enthusiasm, though it did not kill it; in Croatia universal suffrage would have killed the South Slav movement, though it would have thrown up a Catholic peasant party favourable to the Habsburgs and hostile to

Hungarian rule. In any case, the Magyar gentry, dodging universal suffrage by every expedient in Hungary, could not introduce it in Croatia. Thus, they denied themselves the only decisive weapon and had to perpetuate the imaginary danger of a widespread South Slav movement.

By 1914 the constitutional mission of the Habsburg Monarchy had everywhere ended in barren failure. Yet men were never more confident of the future of the Habsburg Monarchy than in the last few years before its end. Though *rigor mortis* was setting in, there was no lack of schemes to revivify the derelict corpse; books by Socialists, glorifying the Empire 'above nationality'; books by Germans, praising Austria-Hungary as the standard-bearer of German culture; books by Frenchmen, praising Austria-Hungary as the great barrier against German power; books by army officers, by Catholic priests, by English liberals, even a book by a Rumanian. All recognized the feebleness, the dead weight of bureaucracy, the conflict of national claims; yet all, without exception, looked forward to a 'solution'. This solution, universally expected, was Federalism, attractive name for diverse schemes. To German writers federalism meant the reduction of Hungary to the level of the other provinces, all members of a Germanic Empire; for the Czechs federalism meant an Empire predominantly Slav, with the Germans and Magyars as tolerated minorities; for the academic theorists of Vienna federalism implied a general decline of national feeling – nationalism would dwindle into a personal idiosyncrasy, as Renner estimated it; for the foreigners, French and English, federalism was a pious wish, a refusal to face the dreadful alternative of European war, which the failure of the Habsburg mission must involve. This was the essence of federalist dreams: all shrank from the conflict which would follow the crumbling of the Habsburg mummy and hoped instead that the peoples would become, by some miracle, as moderate and enlightened as Karl Renner and Professor Redlich, as M. Eisenmann and Professor Seton-Watson.[1] The history of Francis Joseph's reign showed that a 'solution' was easy; easy, that is, to

1. Professor Seton-Watson dedicated his account of the Zagreb and Friedjung trials to 'the statesman who shall possess the genius and courage necessary to solve the South Slav question'. The worker of miracles was to be Professor Redlich, a Viennese Jew.

devise innumerable schemes by which all the peoples of the Monarchy would enjoy good economic conditions and a tolerable
national existence. The problem was to get a 'solution' accepted:
and behind this lay the real problem – whether the Habsburg
Monarchy could escape becoming an instrument for the German
domination of Europe. For this problem there was no 'solution'.
The fate of the Habsburg Monarchy had been decided by the war
of 1866; it owed its further independence to the grace of Bismarck,
and must lose it as soon as Bismarck's successors abandoned his
moderate course. Men thought to alter the European position of
the Habsburg Monarchy by changing its internal structure; in
reality a change in its internal structure could come only after a
change, or rather catastrophe, in its European position.

Thus, all the schemes of the pre-war era postulated the impossible.
If only the Monarchy had not been defeated in 1866; if only the
Magyars would accept the Slavs as equals; if only the Germans
would not look to the German Empire; if only the peoples of the
Empire would become again illiterate peasants and return to the
unquestioning dynastic loyalty of the days of the Counter-Reforma-
tion; if only the Habsburgs would promote trade unions and agrarian
reform; then the problem would be solved, for, indeed, it would
not exist. So, standing round a deathbed, the mourners might say:
'If only the dead man would breathe, he would be quite all right.'
This medley of wishes turned into a uniform chorus; if only Francis
Joseph would die and be succeeded by Francis Ferdinand, then
all the various 'solutions' would come true. Those who looked to
Francis Ferdinand knew little of his character: he represented
change, and they foolishly supposed that any change would be a
change for the better. Francis Ferdinand was one of the worst products of the Habsburg House; reactionary, clerical, brutal, and over-
bearing, he was also often insane. He lacked even the pessimism and
hesitation which had made Francis Joseph a tolerable ruler. The
only constant element in Francis Ferdinand's political outlook was
hostility to Dualism: without sympathy for the peoples oppressed by
Magyar nationalism, he had a dynastic jealousy of Hungarian
freedom and wish to reduce Hungary to a common subordination.
For he was equally hostile to the Czechs and even to German
liberals, though not to German nationalism. His ideal was the

absolutist militarism created by Schwarzenberg in 1849; this had been the ideal also of Francis Joseph until he had been taught better by events.

Much was written of the constructive plans which Francis Ferdinand would carry out when he came to the throne. He would refuse to be crowned King of Hungary until the settlement of 1867 had been undone; this much was clear, thereafter his plans turned to smoke. He encouraged clerical nationalism among the Slovaks, sympathized with the Rumanians, and welcomed, most of all, the dynastic nationalism of the Croat Party of Pure Right. He, too, was a 'federalist'. This meant no more than the restoration of a Kingdom of Croatia severed from Hungary and directly dependent on the Emperor. He dared not propose even the union of the Serb lands of Hungary with Croatia, for this would admit the South Slav idea; and his 'trialist' scheme was designed to disrupt the South Slav peoples, as Napoleon's Confederation of the Rhine disrupted the Germans. 'Trialism', in fact, would have provoked South Slav discontent more than ever, would have driven the Magyars into opposition to the Monarchy, and yet have done nothing to settle the conflict between Czechs and Germans in Bohemia. Moreover, the schemes of Francis Ferdinand did not envisage the cooperation of the peoples or advance beyond the 'historico-political individualities' of Old Conservative claptrap. Francis Ferdinand might break with the Magyar gentry and the German bureaucracy, on whom the Empire rested; he would still be faced with the question which had baffled every reformer from Joseph II to Badeni – how could a Habsburg become a Bonaparte, Emperor of peasant peoples? The associates of Francis Ferdinand were professional soldiers and sham-feudal nobles, the Old Conservative bloc of Windischgrätz and Belcredi; only a few clericalist politicians had been added, evidence of the political immaturity of the peoples whom they claimed to represent. The October Diploma represented the utmost of Francis Ferdinand's vision, and the Diploma, two hundred years out of date in 1860, had not been made more modern by the passage of fifty years.

To place hope in any Habsburg was to fail to understand the nature of the Habsburg Monarchy. Kossuth atoned for all his shortcomings by recognizing that the overthrow of the Habsburg dynasty was the first condition for a reconstruction of central Europe.

Michael Károlyi was the only Hungarian to see, and to accept, the consequences of this doctrine. In Austria men were too awed by the physical presence of the Emperor to imagine central Europe without the dynasty: even the most advanced Socialists dreamt of a democratic Socialism imposed by dynastic initiative, and those Germans who hated Habsburg rule desired instead the rule of the Hohenzollerns. Only the solitary Czech professor Masaryk had confidence in the peoples and wished them to learn reality by the exercise of responsibility. Masaryk brought to the cause of intellectual integrity the same fanaticism which others brought to nationalism. He had offended Czech enthusiasts by exposing sacred Czech manuscripts of the early Middle Ages as forgeries of the nineteenth century; he had earned the hatred of both Czech and German extremists by his defence of a Jew against the charge of ritual murder. He believed that the Czech nation could achieve freedom only on the foundation of truth, especially the truth that the 'state rights' of Bohemia were an artificial, outworn tradition; he believed even that the Habsburg Monarchy could find a new vitality, if it rested on honesty and popular will, instead of on intrigue and dynastic interest. Where other more romantic Czechs conducted nationalist agitation until a government job was offered them, Masaryk kept his independence of the Habsburgs and yet hoped to transform the Habsburg Monarchy. Masaryk hated, equally, the pretence of Pan-Slavism; he understood the nature of Russian tsardom and recognized the breach with western civilization that Pan-Slavism would involve. He aimed instead to make Prague the centre of a democratic Slav culture; hence his friendship with the Serbo-Croat leaders which had made him the protagonist of justice in the Friedjung case.

Masaryk and Károlyi became, in 1918, the successors of the Habsburgs: enemies of the dynasty, neither had wished to destroy the unity of peoples which the Habsburgs had once created. Each was devoted to his nation, indeed each represented the highest type of his nation; yet neither was exclusively nationalist or thought in terms of a nationalist state. Károlyi hoped to transform Great Hungary into a federation of equal nationalities, though under Hungarian leadership; Masaryk also hoped for national cooperation, under the leadership of the Czechs. Each was truly independent of the Habsburgs, Károlyi from aristocratic self-confidence, Masaryk from intellectual power. Masaryk, though solitary, had strong links with the Czech people: a nation now advanced in culture, yet free from aristocratic politicians, middle class from top to bottom, and with a deeper respect for intellectual leadership than any other in Europe. Károlyi offered Great Hungary its only chance of survival; the price was too high. The 'Hungarian nation' of 1848 had possessed a true, though narrow, idealism; the 'Hungarian nation' of the early twentieth century believed in nothing beyond the great estates of the magnates and the bureaucratic monopoly of the gentry. Hence, Károlyi's rule in Hungary, when it came in 1918, lasted only six months; Masaryk, with Czech support, created a multi-national state which lasted twenty years and where, balancing above the nationalities and the parties, he acted as a nobler, and more skilful, Francis Joseph. Yet, in the years before 1914, Károlyi saw more clearly than Masaryk. Till the last minute, Masaryk hoped for a moral change which would preserve the united Habsburg Monarchy – an impossible thing to hope from Francis Joseph, Aehrenthal, or Conrad. Károlyi grasped that the essential change must be in foreign policy; this, too, was an impossible thing to hope for without European war.

The ossified carcase of the Habsburg Monarchy kept a balance from its own dead weight. The impulse which brought the gigantic structure down had to come from without; though it could never have achieved its tremendous effect had not all been rotten within. The Habsburg Monarchy could survive internal discontent and even foreign rivalry; both flattered its importance and treated it as a European necessity. What the Habsburgs could not survive was a denial of the need for them. To such a denial force seemed the only answer; yet the more it was threatened the more useless it proved. Italian nationalism had been the David which brought down old Austria; Serb nationalism was the David of Austria-Hungary. The mistakes of Metternich and Buol in Italy were repeated now against the Serbs. Driven wild by the challenge to their existence, Habsburg statesmen lost their skill in balancing and manoeuvre: Serbia became an obsession with them, as Italy had been, and every step they took increased their difficulties. The Bosnian crisis created the Serb peril; the campaign against the Serbo-Croat leaders presented

Serbia with a powerful weapon. Independent Serbia, Orthodox in religion and for long a Turkish province, had little interest in the Habsburg lands. The Serbs aspired to liberate their brothers still under Turkish rule and to recover all the territory once historically Serb; this ambition extended to Bosnia and Hercegovina, not beyond. The Serbs had certainly no reason to feel affection for the Croats, Roman Catholic, pro-Habsburg, and 'western' in culture; they had little sympathy even with the Serbs of Hungary, also too 'western' for the taste of Belgrade. The Great Serb programme was adopted by the Serbs only on Habsburg insistence; the South Slav programme was never more than an auxiliary weapon.

Maintenance of the Ottoman Empire in Europe had been the essential element in Habsburg foreign policy from Metternich to Aehrenthal. In 1912 for the last time, Austria-Hungary tried to impose peace on the Balkans by a coalition of the Great Powers; this move was supported by Russia, alarmed at the approach of the Balkan avalanche, which she had herself helped to prepare. Metternich's conservative alliance made a final appearance, ghostly and ineffective. The Balkan states knew that Russia would not use force against them and were confident that they could defeat Turkey without Russian assistance. In October 1912 the Ottoman Empire in Europe, last fragile prop of the old order, was broken in pieces; and the Habsburg Monarchy stood helplessly by, although its own fall was also being prepared. Berchtold, who had become Foreign Minister on the death of Aehrenthal, saved only the fragment of Albania from the wreck of a century-old policy. Albania, denied to Serbia, was evidence that Austria-Hungary could still exert her will as a Great Power. Yet it was degrading that the sham independence of Albanian brigand chiefs should be treated as essential to the existence of a great Monarchy. Even the creation of Albania was achieved only by repeated mobilizations, expensive demonstrations which lost force with every repetition. And, despite Albania, the Turks had vanished. The national principle had triumphed on every frontier of the Habsburg Monarchy, and the prophecy of Gentz, of Albert Sorel, and of Andrássy, proved true: Austria-Hungary now became the sick man of Europe.

The Balkan Wars marked the virtual end of the Habsburg Monarchy as a Great Power. The Balkans had been Austria-Hungary's 'sphere of influence'; yet, in the crisis, her influence achieved nothing – even Albania was saved only with Italian assistance. Berchtold tried to hold Serbia in check by encouraging Bulgaria against her; this, too, was a failure, with Bulgaria defeated in a few days. Even had it been more successful, the Bulgarian alliance was evidence of Habsburg weakness: it placed Austria-Hungary on the level of a Balkan state. In armaments, as in policy, Austria-Hungary had fallen out of the ranks of the Great Powers. Fifty years before, in the days of Schwarzenberg and Radetzky, old Austria had carried an armaments bill of the same size as France or Russia;[1] in 1914, though ranking only after Russia and Germany in population, Austria-Hungary spent less on armaments than any Great Power – a quarter of Russian or German expenditure, a third of British or French, and less even than Italian.[2] The 'military monarchy' of the Habsburgs was, in fact, the least militarized state in Europe. It possessed military tastes and industrial resources; it lacked the national unity and enthusiasm for a great patriotic effort.

The Habsburg Monarchy was kept in being by German support; even this support had its dangers. Germany, a dynamic Great Power, could not be content with the Habsburg policy of resistance, particularly when this proved unsuccessful. The Germans saw dimly the vision of a new Europe, with Berlin as its centre; in this Europe Vienna had no great place. The Austro-German alliance had been a partnership to preserve the old Europe, and in essence an exclusive partnership of Germany with the Habsburg dynasty and the 'Hungarian nation'. Once the Germans abandoned Bismarck's conservative line, this exclusive partnership was inadequate for them. After all, the Balkan Wars, though a disaster for the Habsburg Monarchy, were not necessarily a disaster for Germany: they were a triumph for the national states, and therefore an incentive to Germany, the greatest of national states. After the Balkan Wars,

1. For most of the nineteenth century, Great Britain spent more on armaments than any other Great Power. The British relied on a great navy and a professional army, both more expensive than an army of conscripts, equipped only with muskets.

2. In the thirty years after the Congress of Berlin, German expenditure on armaments increased fivefold; British, Russian, and French threefold; even Italian increased two and a half times. Austro-Hungarian expenditure was not doubled.

the Germans urged a conciliatory policy towards Serbia and Rumania, even if this involved an amputation of Hungary. Such a
policy, carried to its logical conclusion, would have strengthened
Germany: Hungary would have been reduced to its true national
size, and the rest of the Habsburg Monarchy incorporated in the
German Reich. The Germans followed this line consciously in their
second bid for the domination of Europe; before 1914, they were
still restrained by dynastic scruples and even by twinges of Bismarck's caution. In this sense, the Habsburg dynasty represented a
genuine barrier against German domination – though only so long
as it assisted German expansion by peaceful means.

German advocacy of concessions to Serbia could be silenced by
appealing to German feeling against the Slavs: in foreign, as previously in domestic, affairs, the supposed feud between Slavs and
Teutons was a Habsburg device to keep the dynasty afloat and
also, of course, a Magyar device to exploit German power for their
peculiar benefit. The Balkan Wars roused, as well, the national
ambitions of Rumania in Transylvania; here it was more difficult
to counter German sympathy. William II and Francis Ferdinand,
though from different motives, urged concession on Hungary,
Stephen Tisza answered with obstinate resistance. The beginnings of
German interference in Hungarian affairs reunited Hungary and
the Habsburgs; and Tisza, son of the opponent of Dualism, became
the last strong man of the Habsburg Monarchy. Tisza, like Andrássy
a generation before, feared the effect of war on Hungary's privileged
position. On the other hand, a display of strength was needed to prove
that the Habsburgs were still alive; for, though the Habsburg Monarchy had often been a danger to Hungary, its collapse would bring
dangers even greater. In the past, Hungary had been the chief obstacle
within Austria-Hungary to a warlike policy; now Hungary urged
the Monarchy into action. The situation of 1859 was repeated. Then
Austria had pushed over the established system which benefited her
most and from the fall of which she alone could not gain. In 1914
Austria-Hungary was the only Great Power who could not con-
ceivably gain anything from war; yet, of all the Great Powers, she
alone was consciously bent on war.

Still, there was always a great gap between aim and achievement
in all the Habsburg record; and inefficient in everything, the Habs-

burg Monarchy might have failed to provoke a war, until totally
forgotten by the Great Powers. For, in 1914, the centre of world
conflict had moved from the Balkans to Asia Minor. By a strange
irony, Francis Ferdinand, after all his futile efforts, gave the Habsburg Monarchy its last chance to act as a Great Power. On 28 June
1914, he was assassinated by a South Slav enthusiast at Sarajevo.
The murder jolted the dynasty into action: even Francis Joseph
favoured war, though he despaired of the outcome and, for that
matter, was relieved that the death of Francis Ferdinand had vin-
dicated the principles of dynastic purity which had been infringed
by Francis Ferdinand's marriage. On the other hand, the murder
roused the dynastic feelings of William II, and so silenced the doubts
of German policy. As in 1859, Austrian diplomacy provoked war.
The ultimatum to Serbia was designed to make war certain; it was
drafted by Forgács, the dupe or criminal of 1909, whose name was
hardly a guarantee to the chancelleries of Europe. Still, what the
ultimatum contained did not matter: it ended the long deadlock,
provoked the crisis, and so ensured, sooner or later, a decision for
the fortunes of the Habsburgs.

The men who provoked war, Berchtold, Conrad, and the rest,
had no idea what they wished to achieve. All kinds of schemes were
aired: a punitive expedition, followed by an indemnity; annexation
of part of Serbia; partition of Serbia with Bulgaria and Rumania;
incorporation of Serbia as a dependent Kingdom within the Habsburg Monarchy (last relic of Francis Ferdinand's 'trialism'). These
schemes were ruled out by Tisza, the only man of resolution or
clarity of purpose: faithful to Hungary's needs, he agreed to war
only on condition that Austria-Hungary should not acquire any
Serb territory. War without change was the only thing which could
preserve Great Hungary: an impossibility, though not greater than
the survival of Great Hungary until the twentieth century. Tisza's
veto would have made the war pointless, had it had a purpose. In
fact, war was the purpose. It was an end in itself; the countless
problems which had dragged on so long could all be crossed off the
agenda. 'Provisional absolutism' became 'absolutism for the
duration': no more suffrage bills in Hungary, no more bargaining
between Czechs and Germans, no more throwing of inkpots in the
Reichsrat. Tisza and the gentry officials, Stürgkh and his bureaucrats,

the aged Emperor and the general staff – these directed the lives
of fifty million people. There was no opposition to the war, even
a certain enthusiasm. The Germans recognized that it would restore
their waning hegemony in Austria; the Magyars, relieved at the
elimination of Francis Ferdinand, welcomed the recruiting of
German power in an anti-Slav crusade; the Poles of Galicia were
glad of a war against Russia; the Croats, easily shaking off the few
South Slav intellectuals, were the most eager for war against Serbia;
even the Slovenes hoped that the war might turn against Italy; only
the Czechs were sullenly acquiescent. War did not dismay the professors of the 'Austrian idea': they welcomed it, as they had welcomed the annexation of Bosnia, and supposed that, since war
brought action, it would bring reform. War brought some action,
as much as the Habsburg Monarchy was capable of; it could not
bring a change of spirit. War can only accelerate: it makes a dictatorial state more dictatorial, a democratic state more democratic,
an industrial state more industrial, and – as with Austria-Hungary
– a rotten state more rotten. Czernin,[1] one of the last Foreign
Ministers of Austria-Hungary, judged truly: 'We were bound to die.
We were at liberty to choose the manner of our death, and we chose
the most terrible.'

CHAPTER EIGHTEEN

VIOLENCE REWARDED:
THE END OF THE HABSBURGS
1914–18

THE declaration of war against Serbia was intended to reassert the
position of Austria-Hungary as an independent Great Power; instead, it ended both greatness and independence. The strength of
the Habsburgs lay in suppleness and manoeuvre: faced with danger,
from the Ottoman Turks to Napoleon, they could 'give'. What they
could not risk was a life-and-death struggle, with no prospect of a

1. Pronounced: Chair-neen.

compromise at the end; for, in this struggle, the less sophisticated combatant would survive. In 1859 the Habsburgs had set out to destroy Italian nationalism; in 1914 they set out to 'destroy' Serbia – both impossibilities, even if the Habsburg armies had been victorious, still more so when in 1914, as in 1859, the appeal to force was a failure. The Austro-Hungarian army, invading Serbia, was driven out, and instead the Serbs invaded Hungary; for the Serbs, unlike the Italians of 1859, were a real people with a real fighting force. The greater part of the Austrian army was sent to meet the Russian attack; it also failed. The Russians overran most of Galicia and reached the passes of the Carpathians, only deterred from penetrating into Hungary by the great German victory further north at Tannenberg. By every analogy of Habsburg history, this would have been the moment to make peace: there would have been some concessions to Russia, perhaps even to Serbia, but the Habsburg Monarchy would have remained in existence.

Instead Austria-Hungary was 'saved' by Germany; this 'saving' marked the real end of the Habsburgs. They had offered a tolerable alternative to German rule; the alternative ceased to exist when the Germans took over the military and political direction of Austria-Hungary. Early in 1915 German troops and German generals drove the Russians out of Galicia; late in 1915 German generals directed the campaign which destroyed independent Serbia and carried the Central Powers to the gates of Salonica. Germany was now committed to a bid for the mastery of Europe; and the Habsburgs were no more than German auxiliaries. Only the dynastic sentimentalism of William II prevented the Germans from ordering the Habsburgs out of existence: as it was, Francis Joseph had no more independence than the Kings of Saxony or Bavaria. Austria-Hungary was treated as of no account in the negotiations which preceded the entry of Italy into the war in 1915. The Germans sought to buy Italy off with offers of Austrian territory; Vienna was not consulted, nor even informed. The offers were fruitless: as in 1866 Italy hoped to achieve national unity by military success and therefore insisted on going to war for lands which she could have acquired without fighting; as in 1866, she acquired the lands after military failure. Austria-Hungary was given a last opportunity of reasserting her prestige; she could not take it. The campaign against Italy in 1916, grandiosely planned by Conrad, was indecisive except as evidence of the Monarchy's decline – a Great Power which could not defeat even the Italians was certainly far gone. Once more German troops and German direction were needed to stiffen the shaky Austro-Hungarian front.

Protected from Russia, from Serbia, even from Italy, by German power, the dynasty lost all freedom of manoeuvre. The German Austrians became in truth the 'people of state'; German nationalism and support of the Austrian Empire at last indistinguishable. At Easter 1915, all the German parties, except the Social Democrats, united in a manifesto which restated the Linz programme of 1882 – then the demand merely of a few nationalist fanatics, now the agreed wish of all German Austrians. Even now the German Austrians, though practically at war with Italy and certainly not at peace with the Poles, were ready to recognize the claims of the 'master-races', and proposed to cede Galicia to Poland, Dalmatia to Italy: by thus surrendering half a million South Slavs to Italy, they hoped to cheat Italy of the south Tyrol and Trieste. Relieved of these two embarrassing appendages, Austria was to be maintained as a unitary state, with German as the single official language; Serbia was to be brought under the military and economic control of the Monarchy; and the South Slavs were to be cajoled by the prospect of a South Slav unit within the Empire, once they had given proofs of good behaviour. Many German Austrians had professed conversion to the idea of cooperation between the peoples; these fine phrases now vanished. Once assured of German backing, the German Austrians reverted to the German centralism of Schmerling, and even supposed that Germany had conquered Serbia for the benefit of Vienna. As with Schmerling, their vague offers of national autonomy were confined to peoples under Magyar rule. This stroke of German cunning ignored reality; the Magyars were far from acquiescing in the dismemberment of the lands of St Stephen.

Magyar policy and outlook in the first German war was the greatest *tour de force* in Hungary's history. All other peoples of the Habsburg Monarchy worked for *le roi de Prusse*; *le roi de Prusse* worked for the Magyars. Once the partners of Bismarck and Little Germany, the Magyars became, with equal assurance, allies of Greater Germany and of the German army. They supposed that they could maintain their independence, though all others lost theirs. Tisza became virtual ruler of Austria-Hungary with German support: arrogant and independent, he could yet be relied on not to go with the Slavs. Early in 1915 Berchtold was dismissed on Tisza's orders. Burián, his successor, was the first Magyar to become Foreign Minister since Andrássy; and he established a private telephone connexion with Tisza, so as to receive instructions from his real master. The difference between the shadowy position of the fading dynasty and the strength of the unshaken Magyars was shown in 1916, when the Germans attempted to repeat with Rumania the bargaining which had failed with Italy the year before. For Rumania could be bought only by cession of part of Transylvania, an integral part of the lands of St Stephen; and Tisza arrested the negotiations at the outset. The Magyars had been the principal makers of Dualism; now, recognizing the decay of the dynasty, they prepared for an independent Hungary. Despite the theoretical continuation of the Customs Union, the Hungarian government controlled the export of wheat, and doled it out to Austria, and even to Germany, only in return for political concessions. The self-confidence of the Magyars was unbounded. A minority within Hungary, they had dominated the Habsburg Monarchy; now, a people of ten millions, they claimed, and secured, equality with Germany, a Power seventy millions strong.

Thus, at the last, the dynasty fell into the hands of the two 'master-nations', the Germans and the Magyars; and these had virtually jettisoned the dynasty in favour of Greater Germany and Great Hungary. Yet the dynasty still followed its old rules of existence; and the Habsburgs, with their Empire in dissolution, stretched out lifeless hands to Poland. The Polish members of the Reichsrat declared their support for the war, when all other Slavs were silent; and some Poles, led by the military adventurer Pilsudski, formed a Polish Legion under Habsburg authority. Pilsudski hoped to find in the Habsburgs an alternative that was neither Russian nor German; and his dream of a Great Poland, an independent Great Power in eastern Europe, was as antiquated as the Habsburgs themselves. When the Russian armies were driven out of Poland, political manoeuvres followed. The Germans proposed only to recognize Russian 'Congress' Poland, and even that to remain under German military rule until the end of the war. Habsburg statesmen saw a last chance of dynastic aggrandizement and devised the 'Austro-Polish' solution – 'Congress' Poland and Galicia to be united and to form a third partner in the Habsburg Empire. This was opposed by the Magyars, who objected to being one of three, whether the third were Pole or South Slav, and who besides wished Galicia to remain part of the Austrian unitary state, so that the Poles could offset the Germans. Germany, too, rejected the scheme; for a re-united Poland would inevitably demand from Germany Posnania and the so-called 'corridor'. The Austro-Polish plan was aired in a manifesto; it could not be translated into reality against the veto of both Germany and the Magyars. It was the last wraith of the dynastic ambitions which had sustained the Habsburgs for five hundred years, and haunted eastern Europe the more pervasively in these years from its very ghostliness.

The dynasty might still have shadowy attractions for the Poles, or rather for the Polish landowners. It could offer nothing to the other subject peoples, who now discovered the true meaning of 'cultural nationalism' and the reality of Austria as 'a state above the nationalities'. The 'Austrian mission' turned out to be nothing more than compelling Slavs to fight for German hegemony in Europe. Until the outbreak of war, it had been possible to dream of 'federalism', of Magyar supremacy overthrown, and of a union of free peoples. Now these imaginary possibilities vanished, except in the minds of a few obstinate clericals or incorrigible theorists. An independent Habsburg Monarchy had ceased to exist. German victory might preserve its skeleton; the reality would be a German domination of Austria and a Magyar domination of Hungary, the radical programme of 1848. In 1848 the dynasty could still work with the subject peoples and even find true 'Austrians'; now it was a thin disguise for Greater Germany and Great Hungary. The Slavs and Rumanians, who had clung for so long to Habsburg protection, had to become, willynilly, the enemies of the Habsburg Empire.

Destruction of the Habsburg Monarchy was no part of the pro-gramme of the allies. England was concerned solely with the war against Germany, and thought of Austria-Hungary with the same affection as in the days when Kossuth had been a popular hero: in fact both the Habsburgs and the Hungarians were supposed to need 'saving' from Germany. French policy regarded Austria-

Hungary as a useful weight in a future balance against Germany or even as a possible ally in bilking the promise made to Russia in 1915 of Constantinople and the Straits. Tsardom talked vaguely of a Kingdom of Bohemia under a Grand Duke, during the advance into Galicia in 1914; the talk ended when the Russian armies retreated, and, in any case, had no serious purpose, except to strengthen Russian claims elsewhere. The allies were certainly prepared to renew the amputations of territory which the Habsburg Monarchy had often undergone before; these were not a challenge to its existence, indeed a recognition of it – amputations are not performed on the dead. The Serbs hoped to acquire Bosnia and Hercegovina, and perhaps southern Hungary; their ambition was limited to 'Great Serbia', and they were as hostile to a true South Slav state as the Habsburgs themselves. Italy was brought into the war on the allied side by promises of Habsburg territory in the Treaty of London (1915) – south Tyrol, Trieste, and the northern part of Dalmatia. This was a further, disastrous blow to the South Slav idea. The population of Dalmatia was overwhelmingly Serbo-Croat; in the words of a later Italian statesman, Count Ciano, 'Only the stones are Italian.' The Italians demanded all Dalmatia: the division of Dalmatia in the Treaty of London implied a recognition of Serb, and therefore a denial of South Slav, claims. Rijeka was left out of the bargain; it was thus assumed that a Great Hungary, still dominating Croatia, would continue to exist. Moreover, by claiming Trieste, part of the traditional Reich, and the three hundred thousand Germans of south Tyrol, Italy provoked German national feeling. As a result, she needed the Habsburgs, or their substitute, as allies both against the South Slavs and against Germany. In fact, Italy's later alliances with Hungary and with pseudo-independent 'Austria' were implicit in the Treaty of London. Rumania, too, was brought into the war by promise of Transylvania; also an amputation, not a sentence of death. Rumania, more than any other, balanced between east and west; and, remote from the Reich, was not troubled even by German domination of the Habsburg Monarchy. She intended to acquire Habsburg territory and then to jump back on to the anti-Russian side, a policy which she had started almost in her cradle.

Thus the Slav peoples were as much without allies as before the war began: their only ally was the war itself, which wore out the rickety Habsburg machine. The South Slav idea could not stand the strain of reality, and the Serbo-Croat coalition broke up; only a few Dalmatian Slavs sustained the cause in exile. In peacetime, politics are an affair of ideas and discussion; in wartime, they become an affair of deeds. The Croat masses 'voted with their feet' by marching enthusiastically against Serbia. Radić in 1914 said that the Serbs were 'the unscrupulous enemy of the August Dynasty, of our Monarchy, and especially of the Croat way of life'. This was not a passing outburst. Even in 1917 Korošec,[1] leader of the clerical party which represented the majority of Slovenes, said: 'Our Croat-Slovene people is firmly and entirely resolved to be true and loyal to the death, to the Monarchy and the August ruling house of Habsburg.' As late as June 1918, the Diet of Carniola, almost exclusively Slovene, condemned the 'treasonable' activities of Trumbić,[2] chief South Slav spokesman in exile. These declarations sprang, no doubt, from tactics: the Croats were caught between Magyars and Italians, the Slovenes between Germans and Italians, and both clung to the Habsburgs as a way of escape from lamentable alternatives. Still, there was a deeper element: the 'South Slav idea', intellectual and middle-class, was alien to both clerics and peasants. In fact, the so-called 'South Slavs', Croats and Slovenes, looked to the Habsburgs long after the 'peoples of state', Germans and Magyars, had ceased to do so.

The real challenge to the Habsburgs came from the Czechs, the people who in peacetime had recognized most clearly their need for the Habsburg Monarchy. To preserve the Czechs, Palacký would have 'invented' the Habsburg Monarchy, if it had not existed; to preserve themselves, the Czechs had supported the Habsburgs in 1848 and had made their peace with Taaffe in 1879. Before the outbreak of war, they had been the most genuine advocates of federalism; more sincerely than any other people, they had hoped to restore the independence of the Habsburg Monarchy as a Great Power. Habsburg independence was lost beyond recall; hence Masaryk, the realist, who had sought to transform the Habsburg Monarchy, now, with the same singleness of purpose, sought to destroy it. Of all the Slav peoples, the Czechs alone had a single

1. Pronounced: Koroshets.   2. Pronounced: Trumbich.

enemy. The Poles were threatened both by the Germans and by Tsardom; the Croats by the Magyars, the Serbs, and the Italians; the Slovenes by the Italians and the Germans; the Little Russians by the Magyars and the Poles; the Serbs by the Magyars, the Croats, the Bulgarians, and – more remotely – the Turks. The Czechs were threatened only by the Germans:[1] they had everything to fear from a German victory and nothing from a German defeat. They were not even tied to the Habsburgs by clericalism; for their Roman Catholicism had a unique Hussite character, democratic and national. When the Czechs abandoned the Habsburg Monarchy, they condemned it to death. The Monarchy might survive the amputation of Rumanian, Serb, and Italian lands; independent Bohemia would kill it.

In the first winter of the war Masaryk made his historic decision that the Habsburg Monarchy had ceased to exist and that Mitteleuropa, the 'Empire of seventy millions', had come into existence though not under the direction of Vienna. The Czech people reached the same decision, less consciously and Czech soldiers passed over to the Russians in tens of thousands. Masaryk did not 'destroy' the Habsburg Monarchy; this was done by the Germans and Magyars. What Masaryk did was to create an alternative, or to seek to do so. Masaryk had none of the illusions about the strength of national states attributed to him by later admirers. Germany would remain a Great Power, despite defeat, and therefore the six million Czechs could not maintain their independence without assistance. Masaryk did not share the Pan-Slav belief of Kramář[2] that the Czechs could rely on Russia alone: he understood her better than any man outside Russia and knew that a peace settlement dependent solely on her would always be endangered by her profound indifference to European concerns. Masaryk, the heir of Metternich and the Habsburgs, had to prove that his state, too, was a 'European necessity'; where Metternich preached resistance to 'the revolution', Masaryk preached 'democracy' – the rule of law and the Rights of Man. This was the Idea with which Masaryk came to England in 1915; he hoped to win England, France, and ultimately America for his programme.

1. Or so they supposed. In 1919 and again in 1938 they found that in Těšin they were threatened also by the Poles.

2. Pronounced: Kramarsch.

Masaryk's programme could not be limited to national autonomy, or even independence, for the Czechs. Masaryk was as much a realist as Bismarck; for him, too, the fortunes of nations were determined by blood and iron. He had to create a workable state, not to devise a paper scheme which would satisfy the professors of Vienna. Hence, he spoke always of Bohemia, though this contained three million Germans. National division of Bohemia might have been possible within the Habsburg Monarchy; for an independent state, strategy and economics dictated Bohemian unity. Masaryk hoped that the Germans would recognize the necessity of Bohemia, even for themselves, as the Czechs had recognized the necessity of the Habsburg Monarchy; his real illusion was not in the Germans, but in the allies – he supposed that they would remain united at least as long as the allies of 1815. There was a further item in his programme. He saw that the fall of the Habsburgs must involve the ruin of Great Hungary; national freedom could not stop at the Hungarian frontier. Himself a Slovak, though from Moravia, he had to provide a future for the two million Slovaks, who were even less able to stand alone than the Czechs. Masaryk revived the radical idea of 1848 and proposed to create a single 'Czechoslovak' nation by will-power. Masaryk knew little of the Slovaks; others knew even less. That was his strength in dealing with the allied leaders; it could not solve the Slovak problem. The few conscious Slovak politicians aspired only to cultural autonomy within Hungary; living in the shadow of Magyar arrogance, they could not imagine the disappearance of the Hungarian frontier. Besides, without industries or universities, they had neither economic nor cultural solidarity with the Czechs. They wanted an impossibility – a Habsburg Monarchy free from Germans and Magyars.

Masaryk needed time to convince the allies of the value of Czechoslovak democracy. His greatest fear was of a compromise peace which would leave the Germans in control of central Europe. Until the end of 1915, the war had seemed a purely military affair: battles were won and lost, strong places fell or were defended, campaigns succeeded or ended in disaster. Suddenly, the initial impetus exhausted, events behind the front recovered their importance: policy overshadowed strategy, and the decision passed from generals to peoples. In every country new ministries were formed or new courses followed. Since the war had become too serious a matter to be left to the soldiers, every country was faced with the same question – whether to fight on at the risk of destroying the structure of society. Compromise or the knock-out blow was the issue which lay behind the events of the bitter winter of 1916–17 – behind the rise to power of Lloyd George as much as behind the fall of Bethmann Hollweg, behind the first Russian revolution and the French mutinies. So too behind the changes which followed the death of Francis Joseph in November 1916. The old Emperor had sustained the routine of administration to the end. Even the assassination of Stürgkh, the Austrian Prime Minister, by a pacifist Socialist had not broken the deceptive calm; Francis Joseph had merely recalled Koerber, the Prime Minister of fifteen years before, to occupy the empty desk. Now a pebble was removed and an avalanche started. With Francis Joseph there went the last fragment of Habsburg core, long dead, but still hard; there remained at the centre echoes, ghosts, emptiness.

Charles, the new Emperor, was an *émigrés'* king, not the ruler of a real empire. The fantastic loyalties, the repetition of ancient policies, the divorce from reality – these recalled the Young Pretender or the Comte de Chambord; to complete the effect, the Empress Zita, the inspirer of her husband, came from a dynasty, the Bourbon-Parma, which had been dead fifty years. The advisers of Charles, too, were pale reflections of causes long dead and gone: soldiers trying to talk like Radetzky, in the intervals of receiving German orders; light-minded aristocrats, the remnants of the party of Francis Ferdinand, still dreaming of the October Diploma in the age of Bolshevism and the peasant revolutions; Czernin, last dying echo of Metternich, despairing and maladroit; Professors Redlich and Lammasch, still devising academic schemes of conciliation and still deluding themselves, since they could no longer delude others, with Austria's 'cultural mission'. These tiny groups represented all that remained of the dynasty: spiritually in exile, though still resident in Vienna, they tried for the last time to wield the old Habsburg weapons of negotiation and compromise.

The Habsburg Monarchy faced defeat in war and internal revolution: 1809 and 1848 threatened to coincide. Charles and his court were not taken in by the run of German victories. Rumania was conquered in the winter of 1916, Russia knocked out of the war in the summer of 1917, Italy defeated at Caporetto in the autumn; early in 1918 Ludendorff embarked on his last bid for victory in France. None of these successes brought the peace which could alone save Austria-Hungary from economic and political catastrophe. Charles attempted to escape from the war by negotiations, approaching England and France through his Bourbon-Parma brother-in-law. Even now Habsburg diplomacy clung to its senile plans of aggrandizement, still included the 'Austro-Polish' scheme and hegemony over Serbia in its peace terms. It repaid the German trick of offering Austrian territory to Italy by offering Alsace-Lorraine to France: the offer was without substance, for Charles had no means of enforcing it. The entente statesmen, like Charles himself, still held the delusion that Austria-Hungary existed as an independent Power, and negotiations dragged on almost until the fall of the Monarchy. In reality, the Habsburg army was under German command, and Habsburg economic life absorbed into Mitteleuropa: so long as Germany was successful, Austria-Hungary was tied to her side, and when Germany was defeated, the allies would lose interest in a separate peace. The secret negotiations of 1917 could have no international result, instead ruined the Monarchy at home: revealed to the world by Clemenceau in 1918, they infuriated the Germans and Magyars, whose cause was at stake, and so completed the breach between the dynasty and the former 'peoples of state'.

Attempts at internal reconstruction were equally barren. Charles echoed feebly the hostility of Francis Ferdinand to the Magyars. He tried to put off his coronation at Budapest, so as to avoid the oath to the Hungarian constitution and, still more, to the integrity of the 'lands of St Stephen'. Tisza answered by threatening to stop the food supplies of Vienna; and Charles, cowed by reality, played his part in the thousand-year-old performance – the last occupant of a throne already vacant. Charles resurrected, too, the mildewed project of universal suffrage for Hungary; and his insistence actually drove Tisza from office. This was the end of his success. In this crisis gentry and magnates made up their sham quarrel and renewed the union of the eighteen-sixties against the Habsburg attempt to discover an independent policy. After a brief, futile interval, Tisza was succeeded by Wekerle, a 'magyarized' German, once the nominee of the magnates against Tisza, now ruling with Tisza's support. Constitutional reform returned to its dusty drawer. Food shortage in Vienna and in the industrial districts of Austria made the dynasty and its servants helpless suppliants for Magyar grace. Dualism could be shaken only by defeat in war, and then it would be too late to save the Empire of the Habsburgs.

Even within Austria Charles accomplished nothing. Gestures of appeasement were made: Czech leaders, convicted of high treason, were amnestied. The Reichsrat was revived and met on 30 May 1917. The peoples stated their wishes for the last time within the framework of the Habsburg Monarchy; all were conscious that a revolutionary situation was approaching, and they formulated anew, almost without change of phrase, the programme of 1848. The Germans were committed to the Easter manifesto of 1915; they were satisfied with the virtual incorporation of Austria into Greater Germany which had already taken place and complained only of attempts to recover dynastic independence. The Poles, too, combined to the last liberty for themselves and subjection for others; they wished to recover the monopoly of Galicia which had been infringed during the war and the military occupation, yet sought the aid of the Habsburg army in order to tear Ukrainian territory from prostrate Russia. Hence they agreed with the Germans in wishing to preserve Austria, excluding of course Galicia, as a unitary state. These Polish ambitions were challenged by the Little Russians, now somewhat more vocal than in 1848: they demanded the national partition of Galicia or even, more vaguely, a great Ukrainian state under Habsburg suzerainty.

As in 1848, the alternative to the programme of the 'master-nations' was presented by the Czechs, with some support from the Slovenes. They had not challenged the sacred Hungarian frontier except at the height of the revolutionary year; now they dared to challenge it once more. The Czechs demanded the union of all Czechs and Slovaks 'in a single democratic Bohemian state'. The South Slavs – principally Slovenes with a few Croats from Dalmatia – demanded 'the unification of all territories of the Monarchy inhabited by Slovenes, Croats, and Serbs in one independent body, free from all foreign domination'; this demand was sustained by invoking the rights of the Crown of Croatia. Thus both Czechs and South Slavs would dismember historic Hungary and the unitary state of Austria for the sake of nationalism, yet claimed historic Bohemia and historic Croatia for themselves. This programme made sense in 1848 when the dynasty still possessed an independent strength and could play off Bohemia and Croatia against Greater Germany and Great Hungary. To suppose that the dynasty could impose concessions on the 'master-nations' had been the great blunder of those who had placed their faith in Francis Ferdinand; it was an even greater blunder in 1917. A 'federal' reconstruction of the Habsburg Monarchy could have taken place only as a voluntary concession from the Germans and Magyars. Michael Károlyi preached national conciliation to a handful of followers in Hungary; he had no counterpart among the Germans. The Germans and Magyars had won and held their dominant position by their strength; hence the weaker the dynasty became, the more it had to go with them. From start to finish there was no other historic possibility for the Habsburgs than partnership with the Magyars and the Germans, even though this partnership destroyed the Habsburg Monarchy. For the hold of the two 'master-nations' could be shaken only by defeat in war; and this defeat would destroy, even more certainly, the hold of the dynasty.

Charles could offer the Czechs and the South Slavs only what he offered the allies: negotiations without substance. He proposed a 'ministry of the nationalities' under Professor Redlich, profound exponent of the 'Austrian problem'; in this way the nationalities would be brought to 'recognize' the continued existence of the dynasty. Czechs and South Slavs still hoped to turn the dynasty to their own purpose and would therefore recognize it; they would not, however, recognize the Hungarian frontier. Besides, they would not enter a ministry in order to continue the war; Germany would not tolerate a ministry formed to make peace. The German veto was supported by a Hungarian threat to cut off the supply of food; together the two were decisive. Professor Redlich returned to the academic contemplation of the 'Austrian mission'. Charles fell back on Seidler, another dim bureaucrat, who hawked around offers of 'cultural autonomy' – the stale Socialist device for keeping the peoples without say in Imperial affairs. Cultural autonomy had its attractions in peacetime; now the only 'autonomy' that mattered was escape from fighting for the German mastery of Europe.

The efforts of Charles to break away from the German alliance and to overthrow the hegemony of Germans and Magyars within the Habsburg Monarchy seemed to be the last convulsive twitchings of the dynasty; in reality rather the jerk which preludes the ending of *rigor mortis*. By the summer of 1917 the attempts were over. Nothing had changed, for nothing could be changed without bringing down the empty shell of the Monarchy; there was nothing to do except to wait for decomposition. The Habsburg Monarchy made a last appearance on the stage of world history at Brest-Litovsk, negotiating with Russia as a German satellite. Czernin cut a big figure in debate, solemnly disputing with Trotsky whether the principles of self-determination were applied in Austria-Hungary. He had no more freedom of action than the Bulgarian delegates and less than the Turkish. He broke off negotiations when the Germans broke off, resumed when they resumed, signed when they signed. His sole concern was to lay hands on Russian wheat for the starving peoples of Vienna; and he eagerly welcomed the invention of a fictitious 'Ukrainian' republic which would make peace apart from the Bolsheviks. Even this involved Czernin in new difficulties: to curry favour with the Ukrainians, he agreed to cede to them the district of Cholm, although its western part was Polish. The Poles, already indignant at the existence of a Ukrainian republic where they had hoped to extend the dominion of a future Great Poland, broke at last with the Habsburgs. This was disastrous for the Austrian government, which could not maintain even a semblance of control over the Reichsrat without Polish support. Attempts were therefore made to undo the Cholm bargain – new offers made to the Ukraine, new withdrawals to please the Poles, everything finally left in confusion, the Poles estranged, the Ukrainians not won.

The Treaty of Brest-Litovsk brought only the briefest alleviation for the economic chaos of central Europe. The Imperial system was manifestly breaking down. Thousands of deserters, organized in 'green bands', roamed the countryside; the currency slid downwards at an ever-increasing rate; production was coming to a standstill; no coal, no food, no direction, no control. Prisoners of war returning from Russia brought with them Bolshevik ideas, or at any rate the contempt for 'authority' which had inaugurated the Russian Revolution. Under the impulse of Otto Bauer, himself back from

Russia, the Social Democrats abandoned 'cultural autonomy' and advocated national self-determination; the dynasty was thus abandoned by its most loyal supporters. The national self-determination which the Social Democrats demanded was self-determination for the Germans in Bohemia, a device to save them from Czech rule; it occurred to the Social Democrats to advocate self-determination for others only in October 1918, and even then they remained fanatical defenders of the provincial 'integrity' of Carinthia against the national claims of the Slovenes.[1]

In 1848 the threat of social revolution had rallied the possessing classes to the Habsburgs; now it had the opposite effect. Dynastic authority was obviously incapable of mastering the storm; new national states might do so. National revolutions were supported as the substitute for social revolution, particularly as even the most extreme Socialist leaders were, by the very fact of being educated, themselves nationally conscious. In January 1918, the Czech members of the Reichsrat and of the three 'Bohemian' Diets combined to demand a sovereign state of their own 'within the historic boundaries of the Bohemian Lands and of Slovakia' – at this revolutionary moment it did not matter that 'Slovakia' had never existed at any time in history. This programme marked the real breach of the Czech capitalist and intellectual classes with the dynasty. In the allied countries, too, the threatening collapse of central Europe finally brought success to the *émigré* leaders; they convinced the allies that they alone had the 'authority' to stave off Bolshevism. Masaryk was the first to accomplish this. Early in 1917, the allies had included the 'liberation' of the Czechoslovaks 'from foreign rule' among their war aims, though only by accident;[2] yet a year later, they still supposed this to be compatible with the preservation of Austria-Hungary. The decisive stroke was the organization of a Czechoslovak Legion in Russia. When the legion kept itself untainted with Bolshevism, finally indeed fought against the Bolsheviks, the enthusiasm

1. So, too, in 1945, the Social Democrats accepted power from the National Socialist authorities in the name of 'a free, indivisible Carinthia'.

2. The allies had meant to specify 'Italians, South Slavs, and Rumanians'. The Italians objected to 'South Slavs' and would swallow only the vague 'Slavs'; the French therefore added 'Czechoslovaks' to give the programme a more concrete look.

of the allied statesmen – at last shown a non-Bolshevik alternative to the Habsburgs – was unbounded. In the summer of 1918 Masaryk and his National Council were recognized by England and France 'as trustee of the future Czechoslovak government'.

Events in Russia had another fortunate sequel for Masaryk. Visiting the Czechoslovak Legion there after the first Russian revolution, he was caught by the second; and had to return to Europe by way of Vladivostok and America. President Wilson, a professor in politics, might easily have been taken in by the professors of the 'Austrian mission'; instead, Masaryk, a professor greater than they, won Wilson for the cause of national self-determination according to his own interpretation – an interpretation that transformed historic Bohemia into the national state of the Czechoslovaks. Moreover Masaryk found in America Slovak and Little Russian communities – settlers from northern Hungary who had retained their national consciousness while growing rich in America. It had been a weakness of Masaryk's position that the Slovaks and Little Russians in Hungary, being without political voice, could not give evidence of support for him; perhaps also fortunate, since they would not have supported him, if they had been free to do so. As it was, he could use the Slovak and Little Russian emigrants in America as a substitute. These, having left Hungary for the New World, were ready to repudiate it for the sake of Czechoslovakia. Slav islands in an Anglo-Saxon world, they had a community of feeling with the Czechs which they had never felt at home, especially when Masaryk was able to offer them, prosperous American citizens, a Czechoslovakia saved from Bolshevism. Certainly they bargained with Masaryk: the Slovaks, imitating their former masters, hoped to play the part of Hungary in a new Dualist state and demanded federal equality; the Little Russians, with no real interest in either Czechs or Slovaks, demanded autonomy, such as Galicia had possessed in Austria.[1] Masaryk explained, though not perhaps insistently enough,

1. The acquisition of the Little Russian districts of north Hungary was a late addition to Masaryk's programme. He had supposed that, on the dissolution of the Habsburg Monarchy, they would be included in Russia; and he held them only as trustee for Russia until she should recover. This trust was discharged in 1945. There was also a strategical consideration: since he could not have the common frontier with Russia, which he regarded as essential, he had to secure a common frontier with Rumania as a substitute.

that he could not commit the future Czechoslovak state; for him the demands were only proposals, and the essential need was to create a united Czechoslovak movement with which to impress the allies. The Slovaks and Little Russians were later to complain that they had been outwitted: since Masaryk was a philosopher, they had expected him to be also a simpleton – a most unreasonable assumption. As it was, Masaryk achieved his aim: on 3 September 1918, he and his National Council were recognized by the United States as the *de facto* government of Czechoslovakia. The alternative to the Habsburgs was thus in existence before the formal dissolution of the Habsburg Monarchy. Though Masaryk could not make events, he anticipated them and moulded their course.

The South Slav movement was without such conscious direction; indeed Masaryk's prestige had to be great enough to carry both Slav ideas, and he was almost as much the founder of Yugoslavia as of Czechoslovakia. Oddly enough, Yugoslavia, the 'South Slav' state, owed its existence to German success: if Serbia and Italy had been victorious in 1915, both would have opposed it. When Serbia was overrun by the Germans in 1916, the Serbian government, too, became exiled; and high-flown schemes are always more welcome in exile than at home. In July 1917 Pašić,[1] Prime Minister of Serbia, and Trumbić, South Slav leader from Dalmatia, met in Corfu and at last agreed on a kingdom of the Serbs, Croats, and Slovenes under the Karagjorgjević dynasty. Italy was reconciled to the South Slavs by Caporetto, last victory of the Austro-Hungarian army; brought to the edge of disaster, she could not neglect any weapon against the enemy. In April 1918 a Congress of Oppressed Nationalities met in Rome; and the Italians, soon to establish over the Germans in Tyrol and the Slovenes in Istria an oppression besides which Magyar rule at its worst would appear liberal, here presented themselves as the leaders of the oppressed. Henceforth the South Slav movement, though not formally recognized, was tolerated and encouraged by the allies.

Czechoslovakia was in legal existence, Yugoslavia next-door to it. This sealed the fate of the Habsburgs: there was no way open for negotiations and nothing to negotiate about. In August 1918, Germany was defeated on the western front; in September Bulgaria

1. Pronounced: Pashich.

collapsed and fell out of the war. Habsburg diplomacy sought peace on any terms or on no terms at all: recognition of the dynasty was all that mattered. Negotiations were opened with Wilson, offers made to the Czechs and South Slavs, solely in the hope of an answer; for any answer would imply that the dynasty still existed. On 4 October, Austria-Hungary accepted Wilson's fourteen points and left it to Wilson to determine the future form of the Monarchy. Henceforth, as a Vienna newspaper wrote: 'Austria has a Prime Minister who resides at Washington. His name is Woodrow Wilson'; perhaps Wilson would accept the appointment and so recognize the dynasty. The national leaders were once more offered a 'ministry of the nationalities', this time under Lammasch, another professor learned in the 'Austrian mission'; no national leaders responded, they had no interest in any Habsburg ministry. On 16 October, the dynasty took the plunge into federalism, after seventy years of discussion: Austria was to be a federal state, with national councils cooperating with, and therefore recognizing, the Imperial government. Fittingly enough this posthumous scheme contained a clause which made it worthless: 'The reconstruction [into federal states] in no way infringes the integrity of the lands belonging to the Holy Crown of Hungary.' Even at this last extremity the Habsburgs surrendered to Magyar threats.

Only outcome of these vain manoeuvres was a change of ministers: the worthy Lammasch and Redlich at last in office. Even stranger, Andrássy, son of the founder of Dualism, became Foreign Minister to undo his father's work. On 21 October Wilson replied: having recognized the Czechoslovak government and the justice of South Slav claims, he could not accept 'autonomy' as the basis of peace; 'They, and not he, shall be the judges of what action on the part of the Austro-Hungarian Government will satisfy their aspiration.' On the same day the Czechoslovak government in Paris formally issued its declaration of independence. One final effort was made by the Habsburg dynasty to prevent its corpse being carted from the international stage. On 27 October Andrássy, replying to Wilson's note, accepted the independence of the new states and offered to negotiate with them – perhaps at last someone would recognize Habsburg 'authority', over whom or what did not matter. It was too late; the Andrássy note never received a reply.

Instead the national leaders carried disintegration to its conclusion. On 28 October, the Czechoslovak republic was proclaimed in Prague and took over the government from the Imperial authorities. The Slovaks had only reached the point of demanding 'autonomy' within Hungary; they were swept off their feet by the news that Czechoslovakia already existed and, though still negotiating with Budapest, accepted the new state, somewhat breathlessly, on 29 October. The Slovenes and Croats, no longer protected by the dead hand of the Habsburgs, found themselves defenceless against the danger from Italy and became South Slavs as the lesser evil; even the Croat Diet, with its 'Pure Right' majority, accepted partnership with the Serbs. The Yugoslav state was proclaimed in Zagreb on 29 October; and an improvised National Council took over government there the following day. The Imperial authorities surrendered without resistance; national consciousness seemed to have reached maturity. The collapse of the dynasty and of the master-nations gave the subject peoples sudden self-confidence – though only temporary, long enough to make their national states.

The dynasty was not rejected only by the subject peoples; the master nations, too, lost interest in it once their supremacy over the 'lower races' was destroyed. Besides, by abandoning the dynasty, the master nations, imitating their former subjects, hoped to pass themselves off as oppressed peoples forced to fight against their wills and so to slip over into the ranks of the allies. The Italians had shown the way in 1915, when they deserted the Triple Alliance; they were to receive Trieste and mastery over half a million South Slavs as a reward. The Poles did even better: having had a foot in each camp throughout the war, they now transformed themselves into allies, yet kept all the benefits of working with the Habsburgs. The common Finance Minister of Austria-Hungary became Finance Minister of the Polish Republic with hardly a day's interval. Galicia, after some delay, remained Polish, despite its three million Little Russians, as in the 'Austro-Polish solution'; and the Poles made their domination more respectable by conquering more Ukranian territory from Russia two years later. In fact, the Poles were the residuary legatees of Brest-Litovsk; yet, at the same time, they acquired Posnania and the 'corridor', fruits of German defeat.

The Magyars were still resolved to preserve Great Hungary.

With the Habsburgs gone, or, still worse, recognizing the new national states, the only alternative was the way of Kossuth, the revolutionary republic of 1849. The Magyar governing class was equipped for every extremity: they could provide evidence even of their change of heart. Michael Károlyi, once the most unpopular man in Hungary and soon to be so again, became for a moment the leader of the 'Hungarian nation'; after all, no one could challenge his record – a genuine friend of the Slavs and an enemy of the Germans. On 31 October, Károlyi was appointed Prime Minister by Charles over the telephone; three days later he was able to announce that the work of Kossuth was accomplished with Habsburg approval – Hungary was a separate state with her own army, though this army was in dissolution. It only remained to convince the nationalities that Hungary would be henceforth a commonwealth of equal peoples and to persuade the allies that the Magyars had been an oppressed nationality; in other words, that Károlyi truly represented the 'Hungarian nation'. Unfortunately for Hungary and for central Europe, Károlyi was not Masaryk; he had not carried his peoples with him.

The German Austrians followed the example of the others. Their concern was to save the German areas of Bohemia from being included in Czechoslovakia. They had opposed the Socialist programme of self-determination so long as it had implied the surrender of their domination over others; now self-determination suddenly became their salvation, and clericals, Imperial generals and ministers, and Christian Socialists all crowded behind the Socialist leaders. The German members of the Reichsrat turned themselves into a German National Assembly and on 30 October proclaimed the state of 'German-Austria'[1] – a state without boundaries or definition, which should embrace all German subjects of the Habsburgs. Unworkable in itself, a meaningless collection of fragments, it could exist only as part of Germany. Hence the government of 'German-Austria' was composed of Socialists, representatives of the 'oppressed'. The German-Austrians took part in the transformation scene which Imperial Germany staged for the benefit of the allies:

1. This was the official name of the new state, and the only one which represents its character. The Allies insisted on the meaningless name 'Austria'; they hoped to prevent the German-Austrians being German by forbidding them to call themselves so, truly an 'invention' of Austria which would have surprised Palacký.

free German-Austria placed the responsibility on the Habsburgs, free Germany on the Hohenzollerns – two vanished dynasties – in the hope of being admitted to the comity of free nations. Both Hungary and German-Austria failed to foresee that, with the defeat of Germany, the allies would become more concerned to stem Bolshevism than to promote democracy; would approve of President Masaryk, of the King of Serbia, and even of ,the King of Rumania (who belatedly re-entered the war on 9 November, two days before its close) as guardians of order, not as rulers of free states, and would not distinguish clearly between Károlyi and Otto Bauer on one side, Lenin and Trotsky on the other.

By the end of October every people of the Empire had abandoned the Habsburgs and had established its own national state; there remained the Austro-Hungarian army, still defending itself on Italian territory. This was not the army of Radetzky, dumb peasants without national feeling; the army too succumbed to the national torrents which had swept away the Imperial organizations at home. Croat regiments were taking the oath of loyalty to the South Slav state, Czech regiments to the Czechoslovak republic; the fleet hoisted South Slav colours and anxiously sought some Yugoslav authority, so as to avoid surrendering to the Italians; on 1 November Károlyi ordered all Hungarian troops to return home. Finally, on 3 November, the Austro-Hungarian high command, negotiating in the name of an Empire which no longer existed, concluded an armistice of surrender with the Italians. After the armistice had been signed, but before it came into force, the Italians emerged from behind the British and French troops, where they had been hiding, and captured hundreds of thousands of unarmed, unresisting Austro-Hungarian soldiers in the great 'victory' of Vittorio Veneto – rare triumph of Italian arms. The bulk of the Austro-Hungarian army fell to pieces, each man finding his way back to his national home as best he could amidst confusion and chaos.

Last relics of the Habsburg Monarchy were the Emperor and the Lammasch government, 'a cabinet posthumous to the state'. The great Habsburg Monarchy had shrunk to a single room where elderly bureaucrats and professors gloomily surveyed each other – all that remained of the 'Austrian idea', so fine on paper, so catastrophic in reality. They had no task left except to negotiate for the Emperor's personal safety; mere ghosts, they faded from the page of history, even this unaccomplished. Charles was alone with his empty rights. On 11 November he renounced all share in the governmen of German-Austria, on 13 November of Hungary. He would not abdicate. Withdrawing first from Vienna and soon from Austria, he carried with him into exile the last threads of the Habsburg shroud.

EPILOGUE: THE PEOPLES WITHOUT
THE DYNASTY

THE disappearance of the Emperor Charles ended the Habsburg Monarchy; it did not end the problems of central Europe, rather made them more acute. The Monarchy had not been a 'solution'; it had rested on scepticism in the possibility of a 'solution' and had therefore sought to conserve, though without faith, institutions which had long lost moral sanction. The dynastic Empire sustained central Europe, as a plaster cast sustains a broken limb; though it had to be destroyed before movement was possible, its removal did not make movement successful or even easy. The Habsburgs left two problems as their legacy to the peoples whom they had protected, exploited, and finally lost; an internal problem of authority, an external problem of security. States had to find a new moral basis for obedience at home; they had, more urgently, to find a means of protection against the weight of Germany, the only Great Power on the European continent. This was the problem which had destroyed the Habsburgs: they had been lost when, in 1914, Austria-Hungary became a German protectorate. Within twenty years the same problem destroyed the settlement of 1919.

The peace-makers of 1919 fulfilled, with some reserves, the bargains made with Italy and Rumania in order to bring them into the war. In addition, the Poles carried off Galicia as they had always intended to do. These ostensible works of national liberation were so embroidered with historical and strategical arguments that the 'liberated' nation was not much more than half the transferred population – and in the case of Italy much less.[1] For that matter,

1. Galicia was almost equally divided between Poles and Little Russians; the Poles claimed it on historical grounds and promised the Little Russians an autonomy which they never received. The Rumanians insisted on the historical unity of Transylvania and added claims to Hungarian territory on ethnic grounds: about a third of the population they acquired was Magyar, a fifth German. The Italians demanded the line of the Alps, a strategic claim, and the historical inheritance of the Republic of Venice; two fifths of the population they acquired was South Slav, one fifth German.

despite the invocation of 'self-determination', neither Poland nor Rumania was a true national state: the Poles were rather less than two thirds of Poland, the Rumanians rather more than two thirds of Rumania. The Poles and Rumanians were the 'people of state' on the Hungarian model; the other nationalities, as in old Hungary, possessed only minority rights, which, as in Hungary, they were unable to exercise. As a new refinement, the minorities of Poland and Rumania, though not of Italy, were put under the protection of the League of Nations; this was no more effective than the protection of the Habsburgs had been in Hungary.

These were amputations from the old Habsburg centre. 'Self-determination' was supposed to operate with full force in the Habsburg territories that remained. The former 'master nations' certainly received the blessings of 'self-determination', much against their will. The Magyars at last achieved their ambition of a national state, though in a way they had not expected: Hungary was deprived of her subject peoples, and of a good many Magyars as well. The seven provinces[1] which inherited the name of 'Austria' composed a German national state, and, if they had had real self-determination, would have merged into Germany. Czechoslovakia and Yugoslavia, the two new states, both claimed to be based on nationalism and to have found in it the uniting principles which the Habsburg Monarchy had lacked. The Czechs and Slovaks would become one people, as the Piedmontese and Neapolitans had become Italian; Serbs, Croats, and Slovenes would merge into Yugoslavia, as Prussians, Saxons, and Bavarians had merged into Germany. The analogy was near; not near enough to prove true.

Italy and Germany had certainly brought together people from different states, with various cultural backgrounds and even, in the case of Germany, with various religions. Still, both had possessed for centuries a common culture; there had always been an 'ideal' Italy and Germany existing in the consciousness of men. Czechoslovakia and Yugoslavia had no such background. They had been 'invented', the one by Masaryk, the other by Štrosmajer, in the spirit of Palacký's saying: they were necessary and therefore had to exist. The bishop dismissed the obstacle of conflicting religions; the professor dismissed a

1. In republican Austria, Vienna was also marked as a province; a new province, Burgenland, was created of the territory acquired from Hungary.

thousand years of history. Štrosmajer and Masaryk created states; failed to create nations. Perhaps Masaryk could have beaten together Czechs and Slovaks if he had applied to them the 'blood and iron' methods with which Cavour and all his successors treated the inhabitants of southern Italy; this method was not within Masaryk's philosophy. Bismarck, or even Hitler, could not have united the German states if they had fought on opposite sides so fiercely and so long as the Serbs and Croats. Besides, the German states, despite their high-sounding names, were all the creations of yesterday; even Prussia had a trivial history compared to that of Serbia. Where was Prussia in the days of Stephen Dušan? Moreover, nationalism could bridge the gap between Protestant and Roman Catholic; it could not bridge the wider gap between Roman Catholic and Orthodox. Perhaps, in any case, the temper of the times had changed; the age of national amalgamations was over. All, even the Slovaks, had schools, distinct literature, and intellectuals who fought for jobs in the bureaucracy.

As a result, Czechoslovakia and Yugoslavia, despite their national theory, reproduced the national complications of Austria-Hungary. Constitutional Austria had contained eight nationalities;[1] Czechoslovakia contained seven;[2] Great Hungary had contained seven nationalities;[3] Yugoslavia contained nine.[4] Czechoslovakia became a unitary state, in which the Czechs were the 'people of state', as the Germans had been in constitutional Austria. Yugoslavia had a period of sham federalism; then it too became a unitary state, which the Serbs claimed as their national state, after the model of the Magyars in Hungary. The Czechs had fifty years' experience of bargaining and manoeuvre. With tireless ingenuity, they offered endless paper schemes to the Germans of Bohemia; and these often acquiesced in the position of a well-treated minority, as the Czechs had acquiesced in their position in old Austria. At bottom, the Germans no more renounced the inclusion of Bohemia in Germany

1. Germans, Czechs, Poles, Little Russians, Slovenes, Serbo-Croats (a real amalgamation in Dalmatia), Italians, Rumanians.

2. Czechs, Slovaks, Germans, Magyars, Little Russians, Poles, Jews.

3. Magyars, Germans, Slovaks, Rumanians, Little Russians, Croats, Serbs.

4. Serbs, Croats, Slovenes, Bosnian Moslems, Magyars, Germans, Albanians, Rumanians, Macedonians (though these were not allowed an official existence).

than the Czechs had renounced the claim to all the 'Lands of St Wenceslaus'. The Presidency of Masaryk served to answer the great 'if only' of Habsburg history: if only the Habsburgs had been more far-sighted and democratic. Czechs and Germans were not reconciled; instead it became finally clear that the two could not live within the boundaries of the same state.

The Czechs could outplay the Slovaks; they could not satisfy them. Masaryk had hoped that the Czechs and the Slovaks would come together as the English and the Scotch had done; the Slovaks turned out to be the Irish. In the same way, the Serbs could master the Croats; they could not satisfy nor even, being less skilful politicians, outplay them. They, too, had their Irish problem and found no advance on the methods of Balfour. Slovaks and Croats, the two discontented nations, both dreamt of the resurrection of Francis Ferdinand; both desired the return of a Habsburg Monarchy, Roman Catholic, non-national, and sympathetic to the richer peasants. Since this Habsburg Monarchy had perished and could never be restored, the two peoples, in reality, played the game of Greater Germany which had inherited from the Habsburgs; and both were active agents in disrupting the settlement of 1919 in Germany's favour.

Thus, the Czechoslovak and Yugoslav principles, which had been put forward as expressions of nationalism, turned out to be new versions of the 'Austrian idea' – devices for holding together peoples of different nationalities. Both ideas had some reality. Land reform, with its break-up of the great estates, killed off the 'Austrian' class of territorial nobility, which had sustained the old Empire; and the 'Austrian' great capitalists, when not ruined, were concentrated in Vienna. Industrialized Bohemia provided an alternative: an educated class of liberal outlook, ready to undertake the responsibilities of state. This governing class was unique in Europe: held together by a humanistic philosophy, they sustained an authority 'above the nationalities', as the Habsburg aristocracy had once done. The parallel was complete when Masaryk resorted to Francis Joseph's device of a cabinet of officials, independent of parliament. Yugoslavia lacked an educated middle class or the wealth to create it; equally without a territorial aristocracy, its governing class was the army officers, too narrow a basis for any state. Some 'South Slavs' remained among the Croat intellectuals; since this made them opponents of Greater Serbia, they too were enemies of the regime and often, indeed, drifted on to the side of their old enemies, the Croat patriots.

The political problem in every central European state sprang from the Habsburgs' greatest work: the preserving of the peasantry. Before 1918, nobles and peasants, the two 'Austrian' classes, balanced each other, though they often formed a united front against the urban capitalists and intellectuals. After the great land reforms, the balance was overthrown. Aristocracy survived only in Hungary; as a result, the most reactionary state in central Europe was the only one, twenty years after, which had preserved constitutional forms and even something like the rule of law. The 'peasant democracies' proved to have no respect for democracy or for law; the peasants could not, of themselves, produce an élite. The agrarian parties soon outdid the French Radical party, their prototype, in corruption; the peasant politicians, lacking any basis of principle, whipped up national hatreds to conceal their own illicit gains. Czechoslovakia was spared the full impact of 'agrarianism' by Bohemian industry and the University of Prague. All other central European states, except Hungary, became 'police states'; Metternich had foreseen long ago that this must be the inevitable outcome of peasant rule.

Still, the settlement of 1919 did not fall simply from inner corruption and the failure to find a 'solution' to insoluble problems. Czechs and Germans might have bargained interminably in Prague, as they had once bargained interminably in Vienna; and perhaps all South Slavs would one day have accepted Serb history, if King Alexander had managed to erect the 'Chinese wall' which Metternich had demanded in the early nineteenth century and the Magyars after 1867. Even the corruption and tyranny of peasant politicians would have found a term, as industry developed and a leisured middle class came into existence. The 'succession states' certainly suffered from poverty; this was not new, nor was it caused by the fall of the Habsburg Empire. Indeed, the fall of the Habsburgs, though it did not of itself solve the problem, made its solution possible for the first time. The poverty of central Europe was due to the great estates, which survived under Habsburg protection, and to the concentration of industry in German hands. Both these could be undone after the liberation from Habsburg rule; and the level of agricultural and industrial production rose in all the succession states during the decade after the first German war. These states were then devastated by the great economic crisis. The crisis did not originate with them; it originated in the United States, the greatest economic unit in the world. Indeed, if the succession states had been independent longer, they would have been more able to defend themselves. As it was, they had relied on the markets of western Europe; and the closing of these put them economically at the mercy of Germany.

Failure against Germany ruined the settlement of 1919, as it had ruined the Habsburgs. The true 'Austrian mission' had been to preserve the peoples of central Europe from Mitteleuropa; this mission ended when the Habsburgs became German satellites in 1914. Czechoslovakia and Yugoslavia, the two creations of 1919, were not strong enough of themselves to withstand German power. A defensive union of central Europe was impossible from the same cause which had destroyed the Habsburg Monarchy: the conflict between master and subject peoples. Paradoxically, the Habsburgs remained the only unifying principle even after their fall: the Little Entente of Czechoslovakia, Rumania, and Yugoslavia, existed for the sole purpose of resisting a Habsburg restoration – it never agreed on the more serious question of resisting Germany.

Yet restoration of the Habsburgs was desired by no one, except the Slovaks and Croats. The Hungarians had put up with the Habsburg connexion only so long as it gave them domination over their subject peoples and an inflated position in the world; after 1919 they preferred the advantages of a 'Kingdom without a King', in which the Regent was an Admiral without a navy. Hungary remained irreconcilable. Ostensibly desiring frontier adjustments, the Magyars really aspired to restore 'thousand-year-old Hungrary' and clamoured for it the more in order to divert peasant attention from the survival of the great estates. Not strong enough to challenge alone the settlement of 1919, the Magyars sought the 'revisionist' alliance first of Italy and then of Germany; this repeated the pattern of 1848. Indeed, on the triumph of Germany, the Magyars claimed a principal share in their success; Bethlen, their most skilful politician, wrote in 1938: 'Although Hungary was free to choose, she refused to join the Little Entente, thus rendering invaluable service to Germany and making it impossible for a strong bloc antagonistic to Germany to be created.' The Hungarian calculation did not prove successful; they failed to monopolize Hitler, as they had once monopolized Francis Joseph. Hitler took the opening which Schmerling had missed and played off Rumania and the Slovaks against the Magyars. Paul Teleki, last exponent of Tisza's school, confessed the bankruptcy of Great Hungary when he committed suicide in April 1941.

The German 'Austrians' had seemed at first sight less irreconcilable. The republic established in 1918 was genuinely democratic; and belief in democratic cooperation between Vienna and Prague was Masaryk's greatest delusion. The Austrian Social Democrats never forgot their German Nationalism: they regarded the German republic with exaggerated sympathy and Czechoslovakia with exaggerated suspicion. Separation from Germany was always a grievance for them, never a principle. The pure 'Austrians' were the debris of the old Empire – bureaucrats, army officers, and priests – and Hungary was the only neighbour whom they regarded with any sympathy. The 'Austria' to which they were loyal was a historical memory, not a territorial state; and even the memory was smudged and confused. By an absurd misunderstanding, every inhabitant of these seven German provinces was supposed to possess the 'Austrian' qualities, which had been in reality class characteristics of state officials and territorial nobility; every 'Austrian' had to be easy-going and flirtatious, to love music, and to wear Tyrolese costume. It would have been as sensible to dress English factory-workers in pink hunting-coats. Democratic 'Austria' lacked reality. The democrats were not 'Austrian'; the 'Austrians' were not democrats. The two fought each other and exhausted themselves in the process. In February 1934, the clerical 'Austrians' overthrew the democratic republic; in July 1934, threatened by German nationalism, they put themselves under Italian protection – an humiliating outcome for the heirs of Metternich. This expedient was also futile: there was no room for a 'revisionist' league of Italy, Hungary, and Austria, which should yet resist Germany. Italy and

Hungary became Germany's jackals; 'Austria' Germany's first victim.

Yet Hitler's occupation of Vienna in March 1938 was an act of national liberation for the inhabitants of 'Austria'; it freed them from the last relics of the Habsburgs and united them with their national state. Hitler was not merely Austria's greatest gift to the German people: he was the triumph of Austrian policy and Austria's revenge for the defeat of 1866. Prussia became the prisoner of Vienna; and the best elements in Prussian society died at the hands of Hitler's hangmen after 20 July 1944. Hitler had learnt everything he knew in Austria – his nationalism from Schönerer, his anti-Semitism and appeal to the 'little man' from Lueger. He brought into German politics a demagogy peculiarly Viennese. The Reich which he created to last for a thousand years was nothing more than the 'Empire of seventy millions' projected by Bruck in 1850, and warded off by Bismarck in 1866. It would have been unreasonable, indeed, to expect to find in 'Austria' a barrier against domestic and foreign policies which were entirely 'Austrian' in origin and in spirit.[1]

Thus, the settlement of 1919 failed to discover within itself the strength which the Habsburgs had also lacked, and was equally dependent on the policy of the Great Powers. Like Metternich, Beneš,[2] the spokesman of the new settlement, had to convince the victors of 1919 that the 'succession states' were a European necessity. Monarchical solidarity had a real existence after 1815; democratic solidarity did not survive 1919. The politicians of central Europe thought that they had performed a miracle and escaped from German hegemony without becoming dependent on Russia. The basis of this miracle was alliance with France: the expedient attempted by Metternich and Talleyrand in 1815, by Metternich and Guizot in 1846, by Beust and Napoleon III in 1867, and even dreamt of by Aehrenthal in 1911, seemed at last achieved. This was the greatest delusion of the inter-war system and proved its destruction.

1. Thus Srbik, biographer of Metternich, and Glaise-Horstenau, historian of Austria-Hungary's military defeat, both began as 'Great Austrians' and ended as National Socialists. Hitler offered the rule of force which they had demanded, in vain, from the Habsburgs.

2. Pronounced: Benesh.

The succession states relied on French strength; France expected them to provide the strength which she lacked. After 1870, France owed her position as a Great Power to the survival of the Habsburg Monarchy; this had concealed the fact that Germany was the only Great Power on the European continent. France, too, was ruined by the fall of the Habsburgs: she, once the enemy of the Vienna settlement, was now the last remnant of Metternich's Europe and could not succeed where he had failed.

Hitler's war brought European politics back to reality. The Habsburgs had attempted to provide a third way between Germany and Russia; they had failed, and none other existed. President Beneš had once preached the view that Czechoslovakia lay between east and west; at the end of the second German war, he declared instead that Czechoslovakia lay between Germany and Russia. The 'succession states' no longer balanced; they chose Russian protection against German domination. The moral was drawn most clearly in Germany's nearest neighbours and lost its force where German power seemed more remote. The Czechs tried to combine democracy and a Russian alliance; it took a Communist dictatorship to guarantee this alliance in Bulgaria or Rumania. Still, the western Powers, England and America, had nothing to offer in eastern Europe except protests; quite apart from military aid, they were not even prepared to assist the shifting of industrial power to eastern Europe, which is the only solution of the 'German question'. If Anglo-American policy were successful and Russia compelled to withdraw behind her frontiers, the result would not be national liberation; it would be the restoration of German hegemony, at first economic and later military. Or rather, it would be national liberation of a sort, for the unchecked working of the national principle was itself an instrument of German hegemony. Slovakia and Croatia could be 'independent nations' only in a German system.

After the second German war, 'Austria' was once more called into existence by decree of the victors. Though its record of resistance against Hitler was inferior to that of Prussia, it was treated as a 'liberated' country; and the Vienna Opera once more worked overtime in order to establish the existence of an 'Austrian' culture. Hungary had land reform at last imposed upon her. This eliminated the great aristocracy who had sustained in Hungary a certain element of civilization; it no more created a democratic peasantry than it had done in the 'succession states' after the first German war. The gentry officials adapted themselves to Communist partnership as they had once adapted themselves to partnership with the Habsburgs; they were no more likely to be reliable partners in the one case than in the other. Even now, they did not abate their nationalist policy within Hungary: the Slovak and South Serb minorities remained without schools or legal equality.

The two multi-national states, Czechoslovakia and Yugoslavia, were still in search of an idea. The Czechs settled, if not solved, the problem of Bohemia by returning the Germans to their 'national home', for which they had so long clamoured. They were no nearer reconciliation with the Slovaks. War had driven them further apart. The Czechs had undergone a harsh German tyranny; the Slovaks were the pampered favourite of Hitler's Europe, and the Slovak Communists alone welcomed reunion with Prague. In fact, only a Communist Slovakia would preserve the unity of Czechoslovakia; the price would be the ruin of Czechoslovak democracy. Faced with unwelcome alternatives, the Czechs used once more the method of delay which they learnt from the Habsburgs; and hoped that industry and education might in time create in Slovakia a humanistic middle class, which would make Masaryk's Idea a reality.

In the first German war, Czechs and Slovaks fought side by side in the Czechoslovak Legion; Serbs and Croats fought against each other. Few Slovaks fought in the second German war, none side by side with the Czechs. Serbs and Croats at last fought together in the great partisan war; this made Yugoslavia, as the Franco-German War of 1870 made Germany. 'Democratic, federal Yugoslavia' translated into practice the great might-have-been of Habsburg history. Marshal Tito was the last of the Habsburgs: ruling over eight different nations, he offered them 'cultural autonomy' and reined in their nationalist hostility. Old Yugoslavia had attempted to be a Serb national state; in new Yugoslavia the Serbs received only national equality and tended to think themselves oppressed. There was no longer a 'people of state'; the new rulers were men of any nationality who accepted the Communist idea. The Habsburgs had been urged for more than a century to follow this course: Metternich had been accused of Communism in Galicia in 1846 and Bach of

'worse than Communism' in 1850. No Habsburg since Joseph II
had taken the risk; dynastic loyalty was too weak a force to enter
such a partnership. More fortunate than the Habsburgs, Marshal
Tito found an 'idea'. Only time will show whether social revolution
and economic betterment can appease national conflicts and
whether Marxism can do better than Counter-Revolution dynasticism in supplying central Europe with a common loyalty.

THE POLITICAL AND ETHNOGRAPHICAL STRUCTURE OF THE HABSBURG MONARCHY

1. *Territorial Structure and Changes*

IT would need a long essay to explain the casual forces of marriage, diplomacy, and luck which brought together the 'lands of the House of Austria'. These lands acquired the title of the Empire of Austria in 1804. The Empire lost territory in 1805 and again in 1809; it regained territory and acquired new at the Congress of Vienna, and the Treaty of Vienna (1815) gave the Habsburg Monarchy the definition which it kept to the end with certain modifications. Cracow was annexed in 1846. Lombardy (except for the four fortress towns which composed the Quadrilateral) was surrendered in 1859; Venetia and the rest of Lombardy in 1866. At the Congress of Berlin in 1878 Austria-Hungary was given the administration of Bosnia and Hercegovina (which remained theoretically part of the Turkish Empire) and also the military occupation of the Sanjak of Novi-Bazar. In 1908 Bosnia and Hercegovina were annexed and the military rights in the Sanjak abandoned.

It is sometimes said that the Austrian Empire was a 'natural unit'; this catch-phrase only means that it was large and had existed for a long time. Many economic ties had grown up with the centuries; these were certainly not 'natural'. There was no geographic unity. Vorarlberg is geographically part of Switzerland, Tyrol of southern Germany; many districts of Tyrol are inaccessible except from Germany. Carinthia and most of Styria are separated from the Danube valley by a great mountain barrier and belong to the Adriatic hinterland, as do Carniola and the coastal provinces; in fact 'Solvenia' has a natural unity, though it has never existed in history. Dalmatia had no geographic connexion with Austria, nor any economic connexion, except as a Riviera for Imperial bureaucrats. Bohemia is severed from Moravia by a line of hills; the Elbe, not the Danube, is its great river, and its economic outlet is Hamburg, not Trieste – a geographic fact with unwelcome political implications. Galicia was severed from Austria, except through a narrow corridor at Tešin; it was divided even from Hungary by the barrier of the Carpathians. As for the Bukovina, it was cut off from everywhere, a meaningless fragment of territory for which there could be no rational explanation.

Hungary had a geographic unity, in so far as it was made up of the great plain of the middle Danube; this unity did not cover Croatia, which had much more 'natural' unity with Carniola or Bosnia. The Austrian Empire looked an impressive unit on the map; its reality, as Austria-Hungary, often prevented unity in the interests of Hungary. Thus, there was no railway connexion between Moravia and the Slovak districts of northern Hungary; and no important railway between Zagreb and Vienna. The forty-odd miles between Zagreb and the junction with the Vienna–Ljubljana line took almost three hours with the fastest train; and all freight had to go by Budapest. There was no railway communication between Dalmatia and Croatia, and virtually none between Dalmatia and Bosnia; in fact Dalmatia had better communications with its hinterland in Roman times. All these defects, and many more, were made up after the fall of the Habsburg Monarchy. Far from being a 'natural unit', the Habsburg Monarchy was a geographic nonsense, explicable only by dynastic graspings and the accidents of centuries of history.

2. *National Composition*

National statistics were a constant weapon of political struggle; in 1919 they became a deciding factor in the drawing of the frontiers, though they were not designed for that purpose nor suited to it. They had many limitations. The census of 1846 was taken by Imperial officials without national allegiance, though no doubt with unconscious German prejudices: having no propaganda purpose, it took the test of 'mother tongue', and therefore gave something like a historical picture. The later censuses were made by the local administrations and were conducted as political battles; the test was the 'language usually used', a test which always injures a minority and usually favours a dominant people. For instance, *The Times* correspondent in Vienna in 1910 was recorded as German, since this was the language which he used when shopping. On all the 'language frontiers' astonishing variations occurred, according to the whim of the local officials; thus, entire Slovak villages disappeared at one census and reappeared at the next. In other words, population figures are least reliable in the disputed areas, although they were used to determine the fate of these areas in 1919 and on many later occasions.

Still, except in Hungary, the census gives a generally fair picture of the national balance in the countryside, where the figures represent the nationality of unawakened peasants. National statistics have much less meaning in the towns, where they represent only the dominant culture; thus both Prague and Budapest had misleading German majorities in the early nineteenth century, majorities composed largely of Czechs and Magyars who returned to their own nation in the days of cultural revival. Trieste is the most striking example of an artificial national majority prolonged until the twentieth century: the census of 1910 recorded only a third of the population as Slovene,[1] although more than half the population was of Slovene origin and would, no doubt, have returned to its native loyalty with the full awakening of Slovene culture.[2] The 'artificial' nationality of the towns is of great interest to the historian; it cannot be decisive in the drawing of frontiers, and everywhere in Europe the rule has been accepted that the towns go along with the surrounding countryside. Trieste has been the only exception to this rule, to my mind a crying case of national injustice.

Further, national statistics only count heads: they cannot record national consciousness or economic weight. A Little Russian peasant who has never heard of the Ukraine cannot be counted as the equal of a Pan-German enthusiast. A true national picture would have to

1. The first count in 1910 was made by the local, Italian, officials; this recorded only 36,000 Slovenes. Imperial officials revised the inquiry and discovered 20,000 Slovenes who had been 'overlooked.'

2. A distinguished Italian disputed this statement to me with the argument: 'Men are of monkey origin; but they do not return to their native loyalty.' This is another curious example of the cultural arrogance of the 'master nations'. It is of course true that Slovene culture has never been high enough to produce a Mussolini.

show the number of elementary schools, secondary schools, universities, newspapers, and publishing houses possessed by each nationality. It would have to divide the Empire according to the nationality of the landowners, of the employers of labour, of the shopkeepers, of the intellectuals – schoolteachers, lawyers, trade union secretaries – and so finally down to the peasants. It would be particularly important to record the nationality of the voters under the limited franchise which always existed in Hungary and until 1907 in Austria.

The crude figures which follow are therefore included only for purposes of illustration. The population of Austria-Hungary in 1910 was roughly:

Germans	12 million	23 per cent
Magyars	10 million	19 per cent
Rumanians	3 million	6 per cent
Slavs	23½ million	45 per cent
Others	2½ million	5 per cent

If the Slavs and Rumanians held together as 'subject peoples', they were a majority. On the other hand, if the Poles (five million) went over to the Germans and Magyars, this gave the majority to the 'master nations'. Hence the political importance of the Poles and the privileges which they enjoyed. However the massed figures for Austria-Hungary have no serious political importance; it is more useful to break them up into figures for the Austrian provinces and for Hungary, as in the next two sections.

3. The National Balance in the Austrian Provinces

Population of constitutional Austria in 1910:

Germans	9·950 million	35 per cent
Czechs	6·436 million	23 per cent
Poles	4·968 million	17 per cent
Little Russians	3·519 million	12 per cent
Slovenes	1·253 million	4 per cent
Serbo-Croats	·788 million	2·8 per cent
Italians	·768 million	2·75 per cent
Rumanians	·275 million	·98 per cent

These figures draw even more striking attention to the decisive position of the Poles: the Germans could maintain a majority only with their support.

The 'Germanic-Alpine' lands had been the starting point of the dynasty, with the exception of Salzburg, an acquisition during the Napoleonic Wars. Of these provinces, *Vorarlberg, Salzburg, Upper Austria* and *Lower Austria* were exclusively German. There were a few Italians in Vorarlberg, and Czechs filtered over the frontier of Lower Austria. Vienna, which was included in Lower Austria, had, of course, peoples of all nationalities, especially a Czech minority, which increased from 2 per cent in 1850 to 5 per cent in 1890 and 7 per cent in 1900. *Tyrol* was exclusively German north of the Alps; the more southerly half of 'south Tyrol' was Italian, and the Italians were advancing steadily until 1914. Given another fifty years, the Italians would have accomplished peacefully and without disturbance that transformation of all 'south Tyrol' into an Italian area which they afterwards failed to carry out by brutality and violence. *Styria* and *Carinthia* were German, with compact Slovene minorities on their southern border; in both this minority was declining, both absolutely and relatively. In Styria in 1910 the Slovenes were 29 per cent of the population (409,000 Slovenes to 983,000 Germans); they had been 31 per cent in 1900. In Carinthia the Slovenes numbered 101,000 (29 per cent) in 1890; 92,000 (25 per cent) in 1900; 82,000 (20 per cent) in 1910. Carinthia, lying on the route to Trieste and with a developing iron industry, was the scene of strenuous 'Germanization' and the worst blot on the record of constitutional Austria. The Austrian republic outdid this record and claimed to have reduced the Slovenes to 23,000.

Carniola was, and always had been, overwhelmingly Slovene. In 1846 there were 428,000 Slovenes and 38,000 Germans; in 1910 520,000 Slovenes and 28,000 Germans. Thus many Germans had 'converted' themselves into Slovenes.

The three 'provinces of the coast' were Gorica, Istria, and the free city of Trieste. In *Trieste* the Italians were in a majority; the Slovenes were making up on them, by 'conversion' and by immigration from the surrounding countryside. There was also a rising German minority, which usually sided with the Italians. In 1880 there were 89,000 Italians, in 1910, 119,000; in 1880, 26,000 Slovenes, in 1910, 59,000 (an increase from 22 per cent to 29 per cent); in 1880, 5,000 Germans, in 1910, 12,000. In *Gorica* the Slovene majority was outpacing the Italians; 129,000 Slovenes in 1880, 154,000 in 1910; 73,000 Italians in 1880, 90,000 in 1910. In *Istria* the South Slav majority was mainly composed of Croats, who increased their lead by immigration from Croatia. There were 122,000 Croats in 1880, 168,000 in 1910; 114,000 Italians in 1880, 147,000 in 1910; 43,000 Slovenes in 1880, 55,000 in 1910. The three provinces, which for many purposes composed an administrative unit and which certainly possessed a 'natural' unity, had a clear South Slav majority, despite the fact that the figures were distorted in favour of the Italians.

Dalmatia was always exclusively Serbo-Croat, except for the thin layer of an Italian upper class. In 1880 there were 440,000 Serbo-Croats, in 1910, 501,000; in 1880, 27,000 Italians, in 1910, 16,000. Many of the Italians were thus disguised Serbo-Croats who gradually returned to their own people. The Serbs were mainly in the northern part of Dalmatia; however a separate record is unnecessary, as the Serbo-Croat coalition was a reality in Dalmatia – and nowhere else.

The 'lands of the Bohemian Crown' were Bohemia, Moravia, and Silesia. *Bohemia* had 62 per cent Czechs to 38 per cent Germans – three and a half millions to two millions; *Moravia* had 70 per cent Czechs to 30 per cent Germans – one and a half millions to six hundred thousand. In Moravia the two nationalities were mingled; in Bohemia the Germans were mainly on the fringes – the Sudetenlands, as they were later (erroneously) named – though there were German pockets throughout Czech territory and vice versa. The proportions of Czechs and Germans had changed little in the course of a century. This formal statement conceals the fact of the Czech renaissance: in 1815 Bohemia and Moravia had been to all appearance German, in 1910 the Germans were struggling to resist the position of a tolerated minority. *Silesia* was predominantly German, with a large Polish population in its eastern part: 281,000 Germans, 178,000 Poles, 129,000 Czechs. The Poles, who supplied the industrial working class, were increasing more rapidly than the other two peoples, partly from a higher rate of natural increase, mainly by immigration from Prussian Silesia, where conditions were less attractive to them.

Galicia presented a deceptive geographical division – the west

Polish, the east Little Russian. The landowners and officials through-out Galicia, however, were Polish; and the economic and political advantage actually carried the Poles to a fictitious majority. In 1846 there had been under two million Poles to two and a half million Little Russians; in 1910 there were four and three-quarter million Poles and just over three million Little Russians. Since the natural rate of increase of the Little Russians was higher than that of the Poles, very many who were returned as Poles must have been in reality Little Russians. In addition the Poles counted most Jews as Poles in 1910.

The Bukovina was the most nondescript of Austrian provinces, the peoples not even geographically distinct. Roughly there were Little Russians in the north and Rumanians in the south; add to this a large German population, some Poles, and some Magyars. In 1910: 305,000 Little Russians, 273,000 Rumanians, 168,000 Germans, 36,000 Poles, 10,000 Magyars. The three master peoples were static. The Rumanians had increased since 1846 from 209,000, the Little Russians from 108,000. The Rumanian increase is at the natural rate; the Little Russian increase was largely by immigration from Galicia.

Bosnia and *Hercegovina* were the last fragment of the 'common' monarchy, not provinces of Austria. One million eight hundred thousand Serbo-Croats made up 96 per cent of the population; of these a quarter were Moslems.

4. *The National Composition of Hungary*

The 'lands of the Crown of St Stephen' were Hungary, Croatia, and Transylvania. *Transylvania* lost its identity and was absorbed into unitary Hungary first in 1848 and again in 1867. The Magyars pushed up their position there from 24 per cent in 1846 to 34 per cent in 1910 (368,000 to 918,000); this gain was principally at the expense of the Germans who fell from 14 per cent in 1846 to 8·8 per cent in 1910 (222,000 to 234,000). The Rumanians almost held their own; 916,000 (60 per cent) in 1846; 1,500,000 (55 per cent) in 1910. This Rumanian predominance was, however, concealed by the incorporation of Transylvania into Hungary. Unitary Hungary had counties, not provinces; these were merely electoral and administrative divisions, all, of course, controlled by Magyar officials.

Hungary (excluding Croatia-Slavonia but including Transylvania) had in 1910:

Magyars	9,944,000	54 per cent
Rumanians	2,948,000	16 per cent
Slovaks	1,946,000	10·7 per cent
Germans	1,903,000	10·4 per cent
Little Russians	464,000	2·5 per cent
Serbs	462,000	2·5 per cent
Croats	195,000	1·1 per cent

The Jews (5 per cent) were counted as Magyars; if these are deducted, the Magyars become a minority even in the 'lesser Hungary'. As it was, they seemed to have increased from 46 per cent in 1880 (and less than a quarter of the population in the eighteenth century) to 54 per cent in 1910. The Magyars gained from the Slovaks and the Little Russians and, in the towns, from the Germans; they lost ground to the Rumanians and Serbs and to the German peasants on the western border. The census of 1910 was taken after half a century of magyarization and with every device of Magyar pressure; it showed remarkable discrepancies with the census taken by the various succession states after 1919.

The Magyar population lay in the centre of Hungary with the other people grouped round the edges – Slovaks in the north, Little Russians in the north-east, Rumanians in the east, and Serbs in the south. These generalizations are rough and misleading: there was, for instance, a compact block of Magyars in the very east of Transylvania. The extreme south was an inextricable tangle, with almost as many Magyars and Germans as Serbs. This area had once been a separate Serb Voivodina and was claimed by them again in 1848.

The Magyars excluded Croatia-Slavonia from their statistics when they wished to show that they were a majority of the population; they included it when they wished to show the greatness of Hungary, and, in this 'Great Hungary' of twenty millions, the Magyars remained a minority – in 1910 48 per cent. *Croatia* had always been a separate unit. After 1867 the military frontiers, which had been administered directly from Vienna since the expulsion of the Turks, were surrendered to Hungary. The larger part was united with Croatia, to form Croatia-Slavonia. This surprising act of generosity had a simple explanation: 'Slavonia' was mainly inhabited by Serbs, whom the Magyars hoped to play off against the Croats, as they did with great success. This Serb territory became the focus of Croat ambitions and was the scene of the worst Croat atrocities during the Second World War. In 1910 there were 1,600,000 Croats and 650,000 Serbs – together 87 per cent of the population. There were also 100,000 Magyars – mostly officials, railway administrators, and business men. In Croatia the smaller landowners were actually Croats; the great estates were owned by Magyars.

The Croats claimed that Dalmatia belonged to the Croatian Crown and seats were reserved for the Dalmatian representatives in the Croat Diet; in reality Dalmatia was part of constitutional Austria and was represented in the Reichsrat. The Croats also claimed *Rijeka*, which the Magyars maintained as a free city. Rijeka was originally purely Croat: in 1851 12,000 Croats and 651 Italians. Since the Magyars were too far from Rijeka to conquer it themselves (though there were 6,500 Magyars in 1910), they deliberately encouraged Italian immigration and gave Rijeka an exclusively Italian character. The Magyars had ten secondary schools and four elementary schools; the Italians had five secondary schools and twenty-one elementary schools; the Croats had no schools at all. As a result in 1910 there were 24,000 Italians and only 13,000 Croats. The Italians repaid this Magyar backing by not claiming Rijeka in the Treaty of London; this did not prevent their seizing it illegally when Hungary proved unable to keep it.

BIBLIOGRAPHY

A DETAILED bibliography may be found in the following: Charmatz, *Wegweiser durch die Literatur der österreichischen Geschichte* (1912); *Bibliographie zur Geschichte Österreich-Ungarns in Weltkriege 1914–18*; and *Bibliographie zur Geschichte Österreich-Ungarns, 1848-1914* (Hefte 2/3 and 4 of the *Bibliographische Vierteljahrshefte der Weltkriegsbücherei*). All three are weak on books in Slav languages.

The history of the Austrian Empire from its creation in 1804 to its fall in 1918 is not covered by any single book. The indispensable introduction is Wickham Steed, *The Hapsburg Monarchy* (1913); this work by a contemporary observer has great penetration. Springer, *Geschichte Oesterreichs seit dem Wiener Frieden 1809* (volume I, 1863; volume II, 1865) is still of capital value for the period which it covers. Thereafter Charmatz, *Oesterreichs innere Geschichte von 1848 bis 1907* (volume I, 1911; volume II, 1912) provides a chronological summary. *Die Nationalitätenrecht des alten Oesterreichs*, edited by K. G. Hugelmann (1934), is an encyclopedic work with much useful information. Louis Eisenmann, *Le Compromis austro-hongrois de 1867* (1904), though ostensibly dealing only with part of the period, is a work of superlative genius which illuminates the whole; no greater work of history has been written in this century.

The period before 1848 is exhaustively covered in Srbik, *Metternich, der Staatsmann und der Mensch* (1925); not unduly laudatory, it is shapeless, weighed down with undigested material. The best short account of Metternich is C. de Grünwald, *Vie de Metternich* (1939). There is a good life of *Friedrich von Gentz* by Paul R. Sweet (1941). The spiteful memoirs of Kübeck (*Tagebücher*, 1909) are useful. The vast collection of Metternich's papers is mainly concerned with foreign affairs; his view of the pre-March era is better displayed in Hartig, *Genesis of the Austrian Revolution* (1850).

Heinrich Friedjung, *Österreich von 1848 bis 1860* (volume I, 1908; volume II, 1912) gives the best account of the revolutions of 1848 and serves as a substitute for a life of Bach, whose papers Friedjung used; it can be supplemented by Friedjung's *Historische Aufsätze* (1919). *Rückblicke und Erinnerungen* by Hans Kudlich, 'the peasant's son', though long-winded, is invaluable for the peasant movement in 1848 and the Act of 7 September. The chief authority for the period 1848–67 is now Redlich, *Das österreichische Staats- und Reichsproblem* (volume I, 1920; volume II, 1926). This enormous work is summarized in the earlier chapters of Redlich, *Francis Joseph* (1928); this latter has little value for the period after 1867 until the last years of the Monarchy when Redlich drew on his personal experiences. There is a useful biography of *Prince Felix zu Schwarzenberg* by Adolf Schwarzenberg (1946). Foreign policy in this period is described in A. J. P. Taylor, *The Italian Problem in European Diplomacy* (1934); H. Friedjung, *Der Krimkrieg und die österreichische Politik* (1907); C. W. Clark, *Francis Joseph und Bismarck* (1934); and H. Friedjung, *The Struggle for Supremacy in Germany, 1859–1866* (abridged English translation, 1934), a masterly work. A different, *gesamtdeutsch* version of the same period is given by Srbik, *Deutsche Einheit* (four volumes, 1936–42).

The first period of Austria-Hungary has to be studied mainly in biographies, such as Wertheimer, *Graf Julius Andrássy* (1910–13), a devastatingly long and unreadable work; Beust, *Aus drei Viertel-Jahrhunderten* (1887); Charmatz, *Adolf Fischhof* (1910); Ernst von Plener, *Erinnerungen* (1911–12); Schäffle, *Aus Meinem Leben* (1905); Taaffe, *Der Politische Nachlass* (1922). The first decade of the twentieth century is well described by a supporter of Koerber in R. Sieghart, *Die letzten Jahrzehnte einer Grossmacht* (1931). Baernreither, a believer in the 'Austrian mission' of economic amelioration, left papers of value: *Fragments of a Political Diary* (1928) is concerned mainly with Bosnia; *Der Verfall des Habsburgerreiches* (1938) with the episode of Badeni.

Works on international relations, which are especially concerned with Austria-Hungary, are G. H. Rupp, *A Wavering Friendship: Russia and Austria 1876–1878* (1941); A. F. Přibram, *The Secret Treaties of Austria-Hungary* (1920–21); A. F. Přibram, *Austrian Foreign Policy 1908–1918* (1923); Bernadotte Schmitt, *The Annexation of Bosnia* (1937); E. C. Helmreich, *The Diplomacy of the Balkan Wars* (1939).

There are many useful books on particular nationalities. On the Germans, P. Molisch, *Geschichte der deutschnationalen Bewegung in*

Oesterreich (1926) and *Briefe zur Deutschen Politik in Oesterreich* (1934)
On Hungary, L. Eisenmann, *La Hongrie contemporaire, 1867–1918*, does
not, despite its title, go beyond 1848. The best conservative history
is G. Szekfü, *Der Staat Ungarn* (1918); the best statement of the
opposite view is J. Diner-Denes, *La Hongrie; Oligarchie-Nation-Peuple*
(1927). R. W. Seton-Watson *Racial Problems in Hungary* (1908) is a
work of great historical importance: it first exploded the myth of
'liberal' Hungary.

There are two general histories of the Czechs, which also contain
all that there is to say about the Slovaks. R. W. Seton-Watson,
A History of the Czechs and Slovaks (1943) covers also much of the
general history of the Habsburg Monarchy in the nineteenth century;
S. Harrison Thomson, *Czechoslovakia in European History* (1944) is
rather a series of independent essays. An older book, E. Denis, *La
Bohême depuis la Montagne Blanche* (1903) is mainly useful for its
account of the Czech literary renaissance; in political history after
1848 it gives an idealistic version too favourable to the Czechs. The
prolonged attempts at compromise in Bohemia are described in
the opening of E. Wiskemann, *Czechs and Germans* (1938).

On the Rumanians, R. W. Seton-Watson, *A History of the
Roumanians* (1934). For the South Slavs, R. W. Seton-Watson, *The
Southern Slav Question and the Habsburg Monarchy* (1911). H. Wendel,
Der Kampf der Sudslawen um Freiheit und Einheit (1925) is somewhat
rhapsodical. The profound conflict between the Habsburg principle
and Serb nationalism is illuminated in a work of genius by Rebecca
West, *Black Lamb and Grey Falcon* (1941); no greater and no more
deserved tribute has ever been paid to a people.

General discussions of the 'Austrian question', though out of
date, possess a historical value. Crude historic federalism is advocated in Popovici, *Die Vereinigten Staaten von Gross-Oesterreich* (1906);
barefaced Social Democratic Imperialism in Renner, *Grundlagen und
Entwicklungsziele der Oesterreichisch-ungarischen Monarchie* (1906); and
a more sophisticated 'revolutionary' version in Otto Bauer, *Die
Nationalitätenfrage und die Sozialdemokratie* (1907). One of the few
Hungarian liberals diagnoses the ills of the Monarchy in O. Jászi,
The Dissolution of the Habsburg Monarchy (1929); this book would be
most valuable if it were not unreadable.

The reign of Charles is excellently, though heavily, recorded in

Glaise-Horstenau, *The Collapse of the Austro-Hungarian Monarchy* (1931); the work of Masaryk during the first German war in R. W. Seton-Watson, *Masaryk in England* (1943). There is a brilliant short account of 'The Downfall of the Habsburg Monarchy' by L. B. Namier in volume IV of the *History of the Peace Conference of Paris* (1921). The inter-war years, into which my epilogue has briefly trespassed, are discussed with great ability and knowledge in Hugh Seton-Watson, *Eastern Europe between the Wars 1918–1941* (1945).

This list does not exhaust the books that I have consulted, some with profit, most without.

INDEX